Schirmer Scores

A Repertory of Western Music

THE CELESTIAL ORCHESTRA AT THE CREATION

Engraving by Adrian Collaert after design by Jaen van der Straet in *Encomium Musices,* Antwerp, ca. 1590. Instruments in upper row: bass shawm or pommer, cornett, tenor cornett or lysard, imaginary shawm-dulcian, trombone, harp, fretted cello, lute, cornett; lower row: shawm or bladder-pipe, tambourine, cornett, cornett or shawm, panpipes, cymbals, shawm, cornett or shawm.

Schirmer Scores

A Repertory of Western Music

By **Joscelyn Godwin**

COLGATE UNIVERSITY

SCHIRMER BOOKS

A Division of MACMILLAN PUBLISHING CO., INC.
New York

Collier Macmillan Publishers
London

SCHIRMER BOOKS
A Division of Macmillan Publishing Co., Inc.
866 Third Avenue, New York, N.Y. 10022

Collier Macmillan Canada, Ltd.

Library of Congress Catalog Card Number: 75-557

Printed in the United States of America

printing number

   3 4 5 6 7 8 9 10

Dedicated
to **Anthony Damiani**
who taught me what to
listen for in music

PREFACE

University teachers of introductory music courses are fast discovering that the visual aid of a score is a great help even to the musically "illiterate." Irrespective of previous experience, any student can learn to associate sight with sound, and to follow a simple score with interest and pleasure. This increases immensely his or her powers of concentration and understanding of musical forms, which are often so hard to grasp through the ear alone.

This anthology is intended to satisfy the teachers and students of such introductory and appreciation courses, and it is primarily to them that the annotations are addressed. But it may also find a place in more specialized courses on music history, theory, and analysis in which it is desirable for the students to own a comprehensive body of material between two covers. They, too, may find stimulus as well as documentation in the annotations.

The topical arrangement of the book reflects today's unique viewpoint, from which we can see history as a whole, rather than as a straight line "progressing" from the primitive to the present. Chapters II–VIII trace the approaches of various historical epochs to some of the basic functions of music, each one equally valid and, in its way, equally sophisticated. Chapter I illustrates the debt of Medieval and Renaissance music to plainsong, and Chapter IX asks the question "Where do we go from here?" since we seem nowadays to be at the most crucial point in musical history since polyphony was developed in the early Middle Ages.

The material can, naturally, be used in any order whatsoever. The historical chart on page 1090 is designed to facilitate a chronological approach, in which the anthology may be used alongside any general history book. Introductory courses, on the other hand, may do well to start with popular and familiar pieces such as *St. Louis Blues* (**29**), *My Old Kentucky Home* (**26**), *The Entertainer* (**16**), and the tune of *The Star-Spangled Banner* (**23**), which I have included specifically to help the beginner in score reading. They might then proceed to some of the other songs (including the Medieval ones) before following the simple instrumental pieces in Chapters II and VII. Through chamber music and vocal scores they could gradually approach the complexities of full orchestral music. But some may prefer to start with something more imposing, perhaps a piece from Chapter VI or VIII, and thence to move on to styles less easily appreciated.

The highlighting system provides guidance through the more labyrinthine scores, although the routes I suggest should never be regarded as the only possible ones. These, like the annotations, can serve merely as a starting point for further explorations by the student. The teacher, too, may use the commentaries as a fund of ideas to be amplified, discussed, and in some cases perhaps demolished.

The inventive teacher can use this book alone, though it may also be amplified by any of the better introductory texts, or by specially selected readings. With this in mind, I have favored in my annotations ideas, rather than the facts which every instructor knows and every textbook repeats. There is, however, ample factual content in the discographies and suggestions for further listening and reading; the glossary, which contains all unfamiliar terms found both in the commentaries and in the scores themselves; the index, which shows the incidence of many important features throughout the collection; the chronological chart; and the dates of works and composers, the latter given to the day for the sake of those who enjoy anniversaries or amateur horoscopes.

Everyone will have his or her own complaints about the selection of contents. I have tried above all to do justice to the central composers of our tradition, from Bach through Wagner, and secondarily to provide a brief but efficient survey of early music. Some painful exclusions have been dictated by space and by the copyright restrictions which prevent a comprehensive coverage of modern music: hence the absence of Hindemith, Copland, Messiaen, and Stockhausen, to name but a few. But there remain many familiar and some unfamiliar masterpieces, which I hope will give others as much delight, at first or at fiftieth meeting, as they continue to give me.

I am most grateful to the Colgate University Research Council for a generous grant towards my expenses; to Sidney Solomon and Ken Stuart of Macmillan Publishing Co., Schirmer Books Division, for their professional guidance and cooperation; to Mel Wildberger for his careful preparation of many of the scores; to my cousins Alastair, Duncan, and Guy Boyd, and above all to my wife Sharyn, for doing all the things which this book caused me to leave undone.

Contents

I Plainsong and its Progeny

II Dances, Useful and Ornamental

III Music and Poetry

IV Music and Drama

V The Virtuoso

VI The Grand Manner

VII The Music of Friends

VIII   The Sonata Idea

IX   Looking Forward?

Schirmer Scores

A Repertory of Western Music

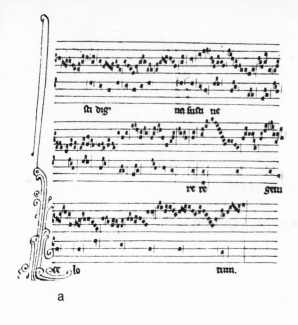

a

b

c

d

FOUR MANUSCRIPTS

a   Wolfenbüttel, Helmst. 1099 ("W2"), showing part of 1b.

b   Montpellier, Fac. des Méd. H 196 ("Mo"), showing opening of 1c.

c   Paris, Bibliothèque Nationale, fr. 1584, showing the *Deo gratias* of 6b.

d   Paris, Bibliothèque Nationale, fr. 9346 (Le Manuscrit de Bayeux), showing part of 49.

Plainsong

and its progeny

Western civilization, regarded in the context of the human race and its history, is something quite unique and, in a way, anomalous. Since the Renaissance, it has gone against all the norms of traditional societies in philosophy, social structure, and the arts. In painting, for example, only Europeans—and, of course, Americans—have explored the dimension of depth or perspective; in music, we are alone in exploiting the "vertical" dimension of harmony* or polyphony*—the use of chords,* and the simultaneous sounding of different melodies.

This chapter focuses on the divergence of Western music from the roots which it has in common with world music. In order to find music comparable to that of other civilizations, we have to go back to the early Middle Ages, when music was monophonic* and there was nothing but melody* and rhythm.* We can tell from pictorial evidence that there was plenty of secular singing, playing of instruments, and dancing, but no actual musical notation has survived for these activities before the thirteenth century. In the "Dark" and Middle Ages, literacy—and especially musical literacy—was largely limited to churchmen. As a result, the only sources of music surviving from the pre-polyphonic period are collections of music for the liturgy of the Church.

This body of liturgical music, composed and written down anonymously at various times, is known as *chant* (from Latin *cantus*=song) or, more specifically, as *plainchant* or *plainsong.* * As the examples show, it is totally without harmony, and even without any rhythm beyond that which the words give it. (Hence it is best written in tail-less black notes, which have no metrical connotations.) One could say the same of Jewish Synagogue music, or of the *alap* (prelude) to an Indian raga. In all three cases there is simply melody: but melody of great beauty and immense subtlety and variety.

Thousands of plainsong melodies have survived. This is not surprising when we remember that for a millenium and a half it was the official music of the Roman Catholic Church—and that for most of that time this was the only Church in the Western world. The authorities in the Vatican were always careful, until recently, to preserve the plainsong repertory unchanged and with the Latin words from which it is inseparable. Therefore, in order to comprehend plainsong, and for that matter any sacred music of the Medieval or Renaissance eras, it is essential to have some idea of the purpose for which it was used: the adornment of the Church's liturgy, of which the central pillar is the Mass.

The primary purpose of the Mass (represented in Protestant churches by the Eucharist or Holy Communion) is the consecration by the priest of bread and wine, symbolic of Christ's Body and Blood, which are sometimes consumed by those present. (In earlier days it was usual for lay people simply to attend the service without participating—hence the old term, to "hear Mass.") The remainder of the service prepares for this climactic event through prayers, readings, and ritual actions, which include portions that may be set to music and sung by the congregation or choir. The most important of these are named from their opening words: *Kyrie eleison, Gloria in excelsis, Credo, Sanctus,* and *Agnus Dei.* They are said or sung unchanged at almost every celebration of the Mass, and are hence known as "The Ordinary of the Mass." It is these sections that later composers have preferred to set to original music. I have selected plainsong settings of the Kyrie, Sanctus, and Agnus Dei, and polyphonic settings of all five Ordinary sections.

As each year goes round, the Church celebrates an annual cycle of feast days, fast days, and commemorations. Some of these have found a place even in the secular world: Christmas, Mardi Gras (the day before the forty-day fast of Lent), and Hallowe'en (the evening before All Hallows' or All Saints' Day). In the Church's calendar, however, scarcely a day in the year is without its celebration, be it an important feast such as Easter or Corpus Christi Day (see **4**), one of medium status such as St. Mark's Day or The Finding of the Cross (see **1**), or some minor celebration commemorating a saint or martyr. This affects the Mass, for while most of it is invariable, there are parts that vary according to the occasion: these are called "The Proper of the Mass," being "ap-propriate" to a certain day or season. The Proper sections which may be sung were rarely set by later composers, since they could only be used for a day, or a few days, each year, but all of them have plainsong tunes, and these constitute the greater part of the chant repertory.

A typical ceremonial or High Mass, then, would have included the following items sung in plainsong (separated by spoken prayers and readings, not listed here):

ORDINARY	PROPER
	Introit
Kyrie eleison	
Gloria in excelsis	
	Gradual
	Alleluia
	Tract or Sequence
Credo	
	Offertory
Sanctus	
Agnus Dei	
	Communion
Ite missa est	

The Church's day contains, in addition to the Mass, no fewer than eight other services: the Offices, or Hours. These were consistently performed only in monasteries, cathedrals, and similar institutions, and only two of them, Matins and Vespers, received much attention from later composers (see **44**). But they, too, could largely be sung in plainsong. They consist primarily of the Old Testament Psalms, with certain other Ordinary and Proper sections. Among the latter are the hymns *Pange lingua* (**4b**), sung at Vespers on Corpus Christi Day, and *Aeterna Christi munera* (**3a**) for Matins on the feasts of Martyrs.

The liturgical background of plainsong is, admittedly, an involved affair. But the Church's liturgy is in a way its grandest artistic achievement, surpassing the Romanesque and Gothic cathedrals in logical complexity, splendor, and religious meaning. The Mass in particular is surely the ultimate "happening," in which all the arts—architecture, wood and stonecarving, stained glass, painting, embroidery, goldsmithery, perfumery, declamation, music, and disciplined movement—reach the height of their powers in honor of the Christian mystery.

When the time became ripe for the development of polyphony, the best minds of Europe were in the service of the Church. No wonder, then, that they turned for their inspiration to plainsong. At first they would compose or improvise a line that harmonized the plainsong melody, note for note. Later, apparently in the early twelfth century, they would sing two or more notes against each one of the plainsong (see **1b**). In the thirteenth century portions of chants elaborated in this way were sometimes taken out of context, and new poems were added to the long melismata* of the upper part. The added words gave the name to this new form: the *motet** (French, *mot*=word). Certain portions of plainsong became particularly favored for this treatment (see **1c**), and many alternative upper parts were composed over them with Latin or French words, some of them religious, but most of them secular. Three- and even four-part motets were written in which, strangely enough, all the parts have different texts. It is this characteristic that distinguishes the Medieval from the Renaissance motet: in the latter, all the parts sing the same text, even though a plainsong melody may still be present (see **4c**).

One line of descent from plainsong, which has been traced briefly here (**1a, b, c**), gave birth to a popular form of polyphonic secular music which had no literary connection with the chant. It is a measure of the degree to which all activity, to the Medieval man, was permeated with the thought of his Maker, that in a motet such as **1c** a couple of love songs should find themselves in company with a chant commemorating the Cross. This kind of consciousness was to be reversed in the Renaissance, when Masses would be based upon secular songs.

This brings us to another line of descent, in which chant melodies were incorporated into polyphonic settings of liturgical texts (**3, 4, 5, 6**). At first the texts were the same (see the Mass movements by Machaut and Dunstable), then later other, "irrelevant" plainchant themes were used (see those of Josquin and Palestrina), and Masses were composed on secular songs and even musical jokes and puzzles.

The third offshoot of plainsong dispenses altogether with words, and illustrates a curious little corner of liturgical history. It was customary in many countries from the fourteenth to the eighteenth centuries to allow the Ordinary of the Mass to be performed by the organ, alternating verses or phrases with either the choir, if present, or the spoken voice of the priest. The organist would usually improvise on the plainsong melody of his verses, but some composers supplied ready-made "improvisations" for the less inspired, or as models. I give settings of the Kyrie from two Organ Masses of this kind (**2b, c**).

Suggestions for further reading The definitive work on the principal school of plainsong is Willi Apel, *Gregorian Chant* (Bloomington, 1958). On its use in the Renaissance, see Edgar H. Sparks, *Cantus Firmus in Mass and Motet, 1420–1520* (Berkeley, 1963). The encyclopedic works of Gustave Reese, *Music in the Middle Ages* (New York, 1940) and *Music in the Renaissance* (New York, 1954) are unsurpassed. Albert Seay, *Music in the Medieval World* (Englewood Cliffs, 1965) is more readable. On the period in general, see the contrasting ideas of J. Huizinga, *The Waning of the Middle Ages* (New York, 1949) and C. S. Lewis, *The Discarded Image* (Cambridge, 1964): they treat respectively the era of Dufay and the Medieval world picture. J. A. Jungman, *The Mass of the Roman Rite* (New York, 1951) explains the liturgy. On individual composers, see Gilbert Reaney, *Machaut* (Oxford, 1971), Manfred F. Bukofzer, "John Dunstable, a Quincentenary Report," in *The Musical Quarterly* 40 (1954) 29–49, Charles Hamm, *A Chronology of the Works of Guillaume Dufay* (Princeton, 1964), Jerome Roche, *Palestrina* (Oxford, 1971). The definitive work on Josquin, Helmut Osthoff, *Josquin Desprez* (Tutzing, 1962–65) is unfortunately untranslated. Robert Wangermée, *Flemish Music* (New York, 1968) gives a sumptuously illustrated account of the period from Dufay to Lasso.

GREGORIAN CHANT
Alleluia dulce lignum
Words from the Roman Rite.

In the Gregorian chant repertory, the word "Alleluia" (Hebrew, *Hallelujah* = praise ye the Lord) is usually set with a long melisma on the last syllable (known as a *jubilus*), and the same melody returns during the verse that follows. Here the melisma is repeated five times in the course of the piece, giving it a real sense of unity.

1a.

This Alleluia is part of the Mass Proper for The Finding of the Cross, an event celebrated on May 3. Its melisma was a favorite of early polyphonists, who identified it by the word "sustinere" or by the synonymous "portare."

SCHOOL OF NOTRE DAME DE PARIS
Organum duplum: *Alleluia dulce lignum*
(Second half of 12th century).

1b.

Two extracts from a setting of No. **1a** are given here. They serve to illustrate the first unified and organized repertory of polyphony. The manuscripts in which this repertory was preserved date from as late as the fourteenth century and come from places as far apart as Scotland and Spain, thus showing how long and widespread was the influence of this Parisian school. Two distinct styles are visible here: *organum*, in which the lower voice or *tenor* (Latin, *tenere*=hold) sings the original plainsong in long notes of varying duration, and *discantus*, in which the parts move together in regular meter. In order to extend the setting of the word "sustinere," the composer repeats the plainsong melisma on the italicized syllable.

There is much dispute among scholars as to the rhythmic interpretation of this music, and my version is only one among several possibilities. The facsimile given at the head of this chapter shows the section containing "sustinere" from the manuscript known as "W2,"* the source for this version.

(Central portion omitted)

dig - - - - - - - - - - -
-na sus - ti ne - - - - - -
- - - - - - - - - - - -
- - - - - - - -re
re - - - - - - - - - - gem

(Ending omitted)

ANONYMOUS
Motet: *Mout me fu grief/Robin m'aime/Portare* (Late 13th century).

1c.

The most important musical form of the thirteenth century was the motet. These pieces, amazing in their variety, have one thing in common: they use a pre-existing melody, usually a plainsong, as their basis. Here we meet again the melisma of Nos. **1a** and **1b**, taken entirely out of its liturgical and even its musical context and set to a repetitive rhythm. "Mout me fu grief" is a song in its own right, found in many other sources. "Robin m'aime" is also found elsewhere, in a little "musical" by the trouvère* Adam de La Halle (ca. 1240–1287) entitled *Le Jeu de Robin et Marion*. This is a play about Robin Hood and Maid Marion, written for the French court at Naples and first performed in 1285. It contains several songs which may have been Adam's own, or else existing folk songs. With considerable ingenuity, the anonymous composer of this motet has combined two pre-existing monophonic songs with the "sustinere" melisma.

The facsimile at the head of this chapter shows the beginning of this motet in the great Montpellier manuscript.* Whereas in the preceding piece the parts were written out above one another in score,* here the scribe has saved space by writing them separately. Thus the tenor ("Portare") is compressed at the bottom of the page, while the other parts proceed in parallel columns above it.

Recordings: of **1c**: Everest 3270 (*Medieval Music and Songs of the Troubadours,* Musica Reservata); SOL-R 332 (*French Court Music of the Thirteenth Century,* Musica Reservata); Tel. S-9504 (*Weltliche Musik um 1300,* Studio der frühen Musik).

Compare: 1b, 2b, 6b, 19, 20; other motets and conductus of the period.

lis, Quant vous ver _ rai? Da _ me de va _ lour, Ver _ mel _

[m'ai _ me, Ro _ bin m'a; Ro _ bin

le comme rose en mai, Pour vous sui en grant do _ lour.

m'a de _ man _ dé _ e, si m'a _ vra.]

GREGORIAN CHANT
Kyrie eleison ("Cunctipotens") from Mass Ordinary IV
(10th century).
Words from the Roman Rite.

The *Kyrie eleison* is one of the two survivals of the Greek language in the Roman Catholic liturgy. Each sentence is sung three times, and the last of the resulting nine sections is set to a slightly extended melody. In the tenth and eleventh centuries the text was often expanded ("troped")* thus:

| Kyrie, | Cunctipotens | Genitor | Deus, | eleison. |
| *Lord,* | *All-powerful* | *Father* | *God,* | *have mercy.* |

2a.

The name "Cunctipotens" remained after troping was abolished (1543) as a convenient way of specifying this particular Kyrie tune, which was the most popular one for later adaptations.

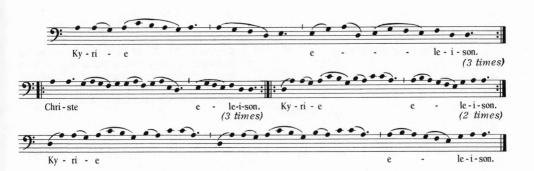

ANONYMOUS
Organ setting of part of Kyrie "Cunctipotens" from Faenza   MS.* 117   (14th Century).

2b.

The *Faenza Codex* is the largest surviving source of Medieval instrumental music. It contains mainly arrangements of songs (including some by Machaut and Landini), and a few sacred pieces which suggest that the collection as a whole is intended as organ music. Here the plainsong is in the lower voice, with a freely composed upper part. The rhythmic interest and complexity of the latter is remarkable, and gives one an idea of how virtuosi such as Landini may have earned their reputations. In some places the original manuscript is illegible, and I have resorted to conjecture.

The performance of this piece in a liturgical setting would proceed as follows (the Christe and second Kyrie settings are not given here):

Plainsong	Kyrie	Kyrie	Christe	Kyrie	Kyrie
Organ		Kyrie	Christe	Christe	Kyrie

Recordings: none.

Compare: 2c, 7, 19, 20; the figurations of fourteenth century Italian vocal music; early keyboard music, e.g. *Robertsbridge Codex* (ca. 1325), *Ileborgh tablature* (1448), Paumann, *Fundamentum organisandi* (1452).

GIROLAMO FRESCOBALDI

(baptized September 9, 1583–March 1, 1643)

Setting of part of Kyrie "Cunctipotens" from *Fiori Musicali* (1626).

2c. This is a setting of the *Christe eleison* from No. **2a**. Here the plainsong is in the third or tenor part (in whole notes), treated somewhat freely. The piece is of interest for its chromatic* subject, a favorite device of Frescobaldi though by no means a novelty by this time.

Recordings: Allegro al III (Frescobaldi: *Fiori Musicali*. Noehren, organist);

Compare: 2b, 3b, 50, 51, 52; Frescobaldi's toccatas and other keyboard works; the anonymous Organ Mass published by Attaingnant in 1531; chromatic madrigals of Willaert, de Rore, Gesualdo, and Monteverdi.

PLAINSONG HYMN

Aeterna Christi munera

Words 5th century, possibly by St. Ambrose.

The melody for this hymn, originally used for Matins on feasts of Martyrs, was frequently set to other words, and the words to other music. The tune is found in the *Liber usualis*, the standard plainsong collection, with the text *Jam lucis orto sidere* (p. 224). Modern hymnbooks usually give it in a later, simplified version with several other verses.

3a.

Ae - ter - na Chri - sti mu - ne - ra A - po - sto - lo - rum glo - ri - am,

Lau - des fe - ren - tes de - bi - tas, Lae - tis ca - na - mus men - ti - bus.

GIOVANNI PIERLUIGI DA PALESTRINA

(ca. 1525–February 2, 1594)

Gloria from Missa Aeterna Christi munera (published 1590).

Words from the Roman Rite.

3b.

Palestrina's reputation as the supreme composer of religious music and the paragon of the polyphonic style made him until recently the most famous composer of the pre-Bach period. His music had a certain clarity of sound and a unity and purity of style that seemed to later generations an ideal worthy of imitation. So, for over three hundred years music students have been taught the "Palestrina style" as an obligatory part of their basic skills in handling counterpoint.*

This style is based, first, on the principle of imitation.* The archetypical Palestrina motet or Mass movement consists of a series of "points of imitation": short motives* that come in each voice in turn, e.g.:

```
       motives
voice 1        a              b          c
voice 2     a        b             c           d   etc.
voice 3         a    b        c          d
voice 4      a            b         c
```

Of course it is rarely so simple as this scheme suggests. In this Gloria there are many words to be set, and Palestrina cannot afford the time to let every phrase of the text be used in this way. So he economizes, compressing and omitting entries thus:

```
        motives (x denotes motives which only occur once)
bar no.  1   2   3   4   5   6   7   8   9  10  11  12
voice 1  a              b      }          c        c
voice 2      a                   c
voice 3                  b       }                      x
voice 4  x               b          c       c
```

The principle of double imitation—two parts against two, as in motive "c"—is very common in sixteenth-century music. Although the higher and lower voices are generally contrasted, other pairings will sometimes be made to vary the tone color,* as in bars 27–30. And as a complete contrast to the imitative texture, the whole choir will sometimes sing together in the same rhythm (bars 31–32, 36–37, 53–54).

The beginning of the hymn tune appears, somewhat altered, in the first two motives of the Gloria. This technique of freely adapting all or part of the plainsong (or other theme) is known as "paraphrase." The presence of B♯'s is due to the notation of the original: at this period there was no natural (♮) sign, so composers used a sharp to cancel a flat, and vice versa.

Recording: Argo 5186 (Renaissance Singers, Howard, cond.).

Compare: 2c, 4d, 8, 49, 50, 51, 52; Palestrina s other Masses and motets, especially the more sensuous *Missa Papae Marcelli*; the Masses of Victoria and Byrd.

GREGORIAN CHANT
Credo I (9th century).
Words from the Roman Rite.

4a.

The Creed is the central statement of the Catholic faith. The first three sections deal with the three persons of the Trinity: God the Father, the Son (whose life is summarized here), and the Holy Ghost. The last section describes in brief the work of God on earth, through the Church and through its baptized members. Since the text is quite long, it is set almost entirely with one note to a syllable. This is the simplest style of Gregorian chant. The other styles are called "neumatic" and "melismatic:" in the first, each syllable will have a "neum," i.e. a single symbol in early Medieval notation, which may indicate one, two, three, or four notes. The two hymns (**3a, 4b**) and the Agnus Dei (**6a**) are in this style. A melisma is a larger group of notes—up to forty, in some cases—which are sung to one syllable. The melismatic style is appropriate to short texts, such as those of the Kyrie (**2a**) and Sanctus (**5a**).

PLAINSONG HYMN

Pange lingua gloriosi corporis mysterium
Words by St. Thomas Aquinas (1263).

This noble hymn was written for the establishment of the Feast of
Corpus Christi, and is sung at second Vespers on that day (the second
Thursday after Whitsunday or Pentecost). This became one of the principal feast days of the Middle Ages, on which the celebrations would
include magnificent processions of townsfolk, dignitaries, and priests
bearing the Host: the consecrated bread that represents the Body
(*Corpus*) of Christ. There are six further verses set to the same tune.

4b.

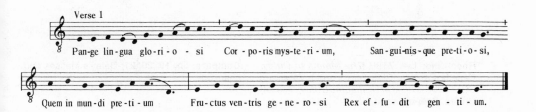

Verse 1

Pan-ge lin-gua glo-ri-o-si   Cor-po-ris mys-te-ri-um,   San-gui-nis-que pre-ti-o-si,

Quem in mun-di pre-ti-um   Fru-ctus ven-tris ge-ne-ro-si   Rex ef-fu-dit   gen-ti-um.

GUILLAUME DUFAY

(ca. 1400–November 27, 1474)

Pange lingua gloriosi (ca. 1430).

4c.

Dufay was the greatest composer of his generation. Like Josquin, Lassus, Byrd, and Monteverdi, he excelled in all the current styles and forms. His settings of twenty-two hymns for the Church year are intended to be sung in alternate verses with the plainsong, which the upper voice paraphrases. The words here are those of the second verse of the hymn: the odd-numbered verses would have been sung in plainsong, as above.

In his younger days Dufay was strongly influenced by the suave, consonant style of the English school, as the closeness of this piece to Dunstable's (**5b**) demonstrates.

Recording: Lyr. 7190 (*The Motets of Dufay*, Capella Cordina, Planchart, cond.). Vanguard BGS-5008 (*Music of Guillaume Dufay*, Dessoff Choirs, Boepple cond.)

Compare: 5b, 19, 20, 21; Dufay's Masses and chansons.

JOSQUIN DES PREZ
(ca. 1465–August 27, 1521)

Credo from Missa Pange lingua (ca. 1514–21).

4d.

Although he was recognized in his own time as the greatest among musicians, the superiority of Josquin's music was long afterwards concealed by idolization of Palestrina's style (see **3b**). Now he is again given his due as the Renaissance composer whose achievement compares best to that of his contemporaries Michelangelo and Leonardo da Vinci. Just as they brought painting and sculpture to a new degree of realism, so Josquin made music depict human emotions with a new precision and force.

The Credo from this, his last Mass, is, like Palestrina's Gloria (**3b**), written in the free paraphrase technique. Josquin, however, uses not only the hymn tune *Pange lingua* (**4b**), but also one of the traditional plainsong tunes for the Credo (**4a**). The movement is divided into five sections, as follows:

bars	based on
1-42	Pange lingua
43-90	Credo
91-134	Pange lingua
135-174	Credo
175-end	Pange lingua

Josquin is far more leisurely than Palestrina in his approach to this even longer text. He begins with a lengthy duet—a favorite device of early Renaissance composers—repeats it note for note in the upper parts, and often afterwards repeats words and phrases. Compared to his style, Palestrina's seems monotonous and even effeminate: the emotional range here is enormous, from the hushed enunciation of the central mystery at *Et incarnatus* (bar 91) to the boisterous swing of *Confiteor* (bar 183), where all the voices join in the first subjective statement of the Creed. But this is music by a very individualistic composer, who would never have served, as Palestrina did, as a model for students.

Recordings: Turn. 34431 (Spandauer Kantorei, Behrmann, cond.); Dec. 79410 (New York Pro Musica, Greenberg, cond.); Tel. S-9595 (Prague Madrigal Singers, Venhoda, cond.).

Compare: 3b, 8, 49, 50, 51; the remainder of the Mass; Josquin's motets; the Masses of Obrecht and Ockeghem; Gustav Holst, *The Hymn of Jesus,* which uses the same hymn.

GREGORIAN CHANT

Sanctus from Mass Ordinary VIII (11th or 12th century). Words from the Roman Rite.

The Sanctus, sometimes called the *Trisagion* (*Greek*, "thrice holy"), is an invocation used also in the Jewish Synagogue and in the Greek Orthodox Church. The text is of Old Testament origin (see introduction to Chapter VI), and it is accompanied at High Mass with the ringing of bells and the swinging of censers.

5a.

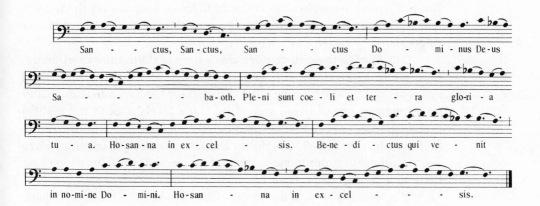

San - - ctus, San - ctus, San - - ctus Do - mi - nus De - us
Sa - - - - - ba - oth. Ple - ni sunt coe - li et ter - ra glo - ri - a
tu - a. Ho - san - na in ex - cel - sis. Be - ne - di - ctus qui ve - nit
in no - mi - ne Do - mi - ni. Ho - san - na in ex - cel - - - sis.

JOHN DUNSTABLE

(ca. 1370–December 24, 1453)

Sanctus (No. 13 in Collected Works).

5b.

In the early fifteenth century it was common, especially in England, for composers to write isolated movements rather than to set the complete Mass Ordinary as a whole. This is one such movement by the foremost composer of Europe at this period. Dunstable's music was widely known throughout the Continent, and through his influence some features of the English school became part of the common language of early Renaissance composers. The most noticeable of these stylistic traits is the frequent use of consecutive sixths, thirds, and $\frac{6}{3}$ chords (e.g. bar 115f.), and the general ascendancy of these sounds over the fourths and fifths which had previously been considered the only consonant intervals.

The later fourteenth century was a time of rhythmic experimentation. In this piece we can see all manner of cross-rhythms* and syncopations* (which prove quite difficult for modern musicians), and an interesting use of triple meter* on three levels: that of the eighth-note (e.g. bars 13–14), that of the quarter-note (*passim*), and that of the half-note (e.g. bars 5–6, 24–25). In the latter cases, the bar-lines have been dropped in order to make the pattern clear. The subjugation of all parts to a single beat was at this time unknown.

The plainsong is to be found, little changed, in the lowest part. This type of setting, in which the pre-existing melody is held by the tenor part while the other parts move freely around it, is called *cantus firmus* (Latin, "fixed song"). This contrasts with the later and freer paraphrase settings illustrated by **3b** and **4c**. The principle of the *cantus firmus* persisted through the Baroque era, where we find it, for instance, in many of J. S. Bach's cantatas and organ chorale settings.

Recordings: none.

Compare: 1c, 2b, 3b, 4c and d, 6b, 19, 20, 21, 45; Dunstable, *O Rosa bella*; music of the *Old Hall Manuscript.**

GREGORIAN CHANT

Agnus Dei from Mass Ordinary XVII (13th century) Words from the Roman Rite.

6a.

This Agnus Dei has an unusually wide range for a plainsong tune. Although the structure of the text is A A B, composers have often set it in the musical form A B A. Such is the case both with this plainsong and with Machaut's setting.

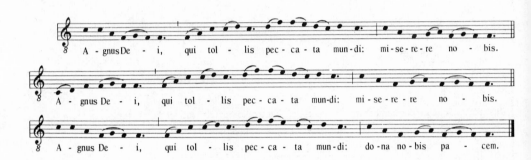

A - gnus De - i,   qui tol - lis pec - ca - ta mun-di: mi-se-re-re   no - bis.

A - gnus De - i,   qui tol - lis pec - ca - ta mun-di: mi-se-re-re   no - bis.

A - gnus De - i,   qui tol - lis pec - ca - ta mun-di: do-na no-bis   pa - cem.

GUILLAUME DE MACHAUT

(between 1300 and 1305–April, 1377)

Agnus Dei and Ite missa est from Messe de Nôtre Dame (1340?).

Machaut's Mass is the earliest surviving setting of the Ordinary by one composer. It has naturally attracted much attention from musicologists and performers, but no one has yet been able to give it a firm date. The music of the short-texted movements (i.e. all but Gloria and Credo) are in motet style: the tenor has the plainsong melody, and the upper voices have independent and more active parts. The tenor is supplemented here by another low part, the *contratenor*, which saves the composer from being bound exclusively to the plainsong for his bass line: when he does not want the tenor note as the root* of a chord (e.g. at the beginning), he places the contratenor beneath it. This practice marks the beginnings of purely harmonic thought.

This is another *cantus firmus* setting (see commentary to **5b**). The tenor of the Agnus Dei is taken from the above plainsong tune, with a few ornamental notes inserted. The tenor of the *Ite missa est*, a short response sung at the end of Mass, is taken, curiously enough, from the same Sanctus as Dunstable used. Both tenors are isorhythmic (Greek, *isos*="same"), meaning that they use repeated rhythmic patterns that do not necessarily coincide with the phrasing of the melody. The repetitions are marked here by Roman numerals.

The facsimile at the head of this chapter shows an original manuscript of the *Ite missa est*. (The words are those of the response "Deo gratias.") This manuscript is in "choirbook" format: all the parts are shown on a single page from which the whole choir reads. There is no reason to believe that instruments would have been used at a performance of this Mass.

6b.

Recordings: many.

Compare: 1c, 2b, 5b, 19, 20; the remainder of the Mass; the *Messe de Tournai,* the only other complete Ordinary setting of the fourteenth century, and a probable influence on this Mass.

pec - ca - ta mun - di:
ca - ta mun - di:
- ca - ta mun - II -
- ca - ta mun -

mi - se -
mi - se - re -
di: mi - se - re - re
- di: mi - se -

re - re no - bis.
re no - bis.
no - bis.
- re - re no - bis.

Agnus tertium super primum

Moresca (see 8), engraving by Israel van Meckenem, ca. 1480.
The music is supplied by a pipe-and-tabor player.

Dancers (representing Diana and Apollo), from Carlo Blasis,
Traité élémentáire, théorique et pratique de L'art de la danse,
1820: the first practical treatise on classic ballet.

2

Dances,
useful and ornamental

Just as the music derived from plainsong is subsidiary to other things occurring in religious services, music written for dancing usually takes second place to the activity it accompanies. There is nothing so trivial as the worst dance music: here alone a bad composer can get away with nothing but a beat and a certain amount of appropriate background noise. None of this, needless to say, is included here; but it is only fair to say that several of these pieces are not first-rate. The *saltarello* (**7**) is not as inspired as the roughly contemporary piece by Landini (**20**), nor does the *mourisque* (**8**) compare with Lassus's or Palestrina's works (**50,3b**). Schubert's waltzes (**13**) are charming, but trivial in comparison to his songs and quartets (**24,56**). Scott Joplin wrote catchy tunes, but in *The Entertainer* (**16**) he seems to be running out of inspiration on the last two pages. On the other hand, dance music has always had a tendency to burst its bounds and assert itself as music to be listened to or played for its own sake, and examples of this kind are naturally of greater musical interest to us.

Take the case of the *allemande,** a sober dance in two eight-bar phrases* whose steps could be described as "one-two-three-kick." The basic version of a popular allemande tune (**9a**) could well be used for dancing, but Daniel Batchelor's difficult and ingenious variations on it (**9b**) would soon call attention away from the dancers to the lutenist. By Purcell's time, the allemande had become obsolete as a dance, yet as a musical form was still going strong. His simple example (**10**) is in six-bar phrases, which would disqualify it in any case for ballroom use: dancers must be able to count on regular periods, especially in Renaissance and Baroque dances where the interest lies not so much in the individual steps as in the patterns which the dancers make on the ballroom floor. The allemande from Bach's *French Suite* (**11**) is still more ornamental, in every sense. All that is left of the original dance is the quadruple meter* and binary form.*

Something similar happened to the *polonaise.** Originally a Polish ceremonial dance, it was taken up by composers in the eighteenth century and idealized into an instrumental piece by Johann Sebastian Bach (**11**), his son Wilhelm Friedemann Bach, and others. By 1800 it was still occasionally used as a dance, even outside Poland, and Schubert and Beethoven wrote simple polonaises that would serve for accompaniment. Chopin's polonaises, on the other hand, like Bach's allemandes, are purest fantasy, and undanceable (**14**).

The most successful of all ballroom dances is surely the waltz, which has held the floor since it first appeared around 1800. It was immediately popular, for the very understandable reason that it was the first dance in which the partners could embrace each other. This was a symptom of the new, relatively comfortable bourgeois culture that followed the French Revolution, and made possible the survival of composers independently of royal or noble patronage. Schubert (who, it must be said, only just survived) supplied the voracious demand for waltzes by writing enormous numbers (see **13**) and by playing the piano for dancing parties. One suspects that he could improvise gems like this for hours on end. The more aristocratic Chopin would not have needed to stoop to this. His waltzes, like his polonaises, are emphatically for listening and playing: in them it is not the feet that dance, but the heart (**14,15**).

Two dances from opposite ends of the historical spectrum, the fourteenth-century Italian saltarello (**7**) and Scott Joplin's Rag (**16**), have more in common than meets the eye. Both are popular in feeling, and invite the performer to add something of his own to the written notes. One can imagine a Medieval fiddler or piper going on to play further tunes of his own invention, each ending the same way as the model; and one can certainly regard a ragtime piece such as *The Entertainer* as a mere beginning for virtuoso performers. The dedication "to James Brown and his Mandolin Club" suggests that it is not simply a piece for piano, to be played in this way and no other (as are the Chopin dances). Most music of the pre-1800 era, in fact, requires some addition on the performer's part (see especially **54**), and no non-Western musical culture excludes improvisation as ours has come to do (see Chapter IX, however, for some new developments in the other direction). But popular musicians have always been ready to improvise—not least because many of them, from jongleurs to jazzmen, have been musically illiterate, hence free from the dependence on the printed or written page that can become slavery. Performers who want to get closer to the spirit of early pieces such as this saltarello will learn more from jazz or Indian musicians than from books.

There are dances to be danced, and dances to be listened to, but also dances to be looked at. The latter are known as *ballet*. Beginning in the fifteenth century as part of the paraphernalia of court ceremonial, ballets were given throughout the Renaissance era for the entertainment of royalty (especially visiting royalty), at marriages, and whenever a major celebration was called for at court. These entertainments would include music, poems written in honor of those present, dances of all sorts, and also such jollities as clowns, performing bears, and fireworks. The aristocracy might themselves take part in the events: on one famous and tragic occasion in 1393, at the court of Charles VI of France, the king and five noblemen dressed up as Wild Men (part of a Medieval tradition of semi-human forest dwellers) and performed a dance incognito, during which their costumes of pitch and hair caught fire in a candle. Only the king and one other man survived the horror that ensued.

The *mourisque* and "Battle" pavane from Susato's collection (**8a & b**), though not specifically attributed to a particular ballet, refer to such diversions. The morisca was a comic dance in which the performers imitated Moors, or Arabs, blackening their faces and dressing in outlandish costumes with bells on their feet. Sometimes they would mime a battle with other dancers dressed as Christian knights. The present-day Morris (="moorish") dancers of England (and America) are continuing this tradition.

During the sixteenth and seventeenth centuries it was customary for the king and his courtiers to take part in the ballets (or, in pre-Commonwealth England, in "masques"), and the dances would generally be unified by a plot or pervasive theme. In the French court of Louis XIV (1643–1715) the ballet became the main form of entertainment, and even in operas composed for public performance by Lully and, later, Rameau there was always much dancing. Hence, when Gluck's opera *Orpheus and Eurydice* was to be performed in Paris in 1774, he had to add ballets to satisfy French taste and custom (see **12**). Even as late as 1860, when Wagner's *Tannhaüser* was accepted for the Paris Opéra, the composer had to rework much of the music to accommodate sufficient dancing.

The histories of ballet and opera are closely intertwined until the end of the nineteenth century, when the famous ballets of Tchaikovsky (*Swan Lake* 1876, *Sleeping Beauty* 1889, *The Nutcracker* 1892) inaugurate a new era, inspired by the virtuosity of Russian dancers. The Russian Ballet, directed by Sergei Diaghilev, with its star dancer Vaslav Nijinsky, dazzled the capitals of Europe from 1909 until well after the Russian Revolution. They did not perform the already "classic" works of Tchaikovsky, but ballets by a new generation of young composers, foremost of whom was Igor Stravinsky. With the three great early works he wrote for Diaghilev's company, *The Firebird* (1910), *Petrouchka* (1912), and *The Rite of Spring* (1913), ballet took the lead in musical developments as a whole (**17**). But by the time of Diaghilev's death in 1929 the excitement over the form had died down, while the music remained as a less ephemeral monument to Stravinsky's creativity. Nowadays, balletic performances of these works are rare in comparison to concert performances, and at least in the case of *The Rite of Spring* many feel that the dancing is an undesirable distraction from the music.

We live in a society and an era that seems to be forgetting how to dance, either through inertia or through an affected casualness incompatible with the precise movement (and the courtly behavior) that makes dancing a pleasure. Ballet suffers in English-speaking countries (though not elsewhere) from erroneous assumptions about male dancers, with the result that boys are unwilling to learn the art for fear of being thought effeminate or queer. These are things that will change, but it will take time. And in the United States, for better or worse, we will surely never have a President, however autocratic, who commissions ballets and, like Louis XIV, dances in them with his advisors and their wives!

Suggestions for further reading On the dance in general, see Louis Horst, *Pre-Classic Dance Forms* (New York, 1969); Frances Rust, *Dance in Society* (New York, 1969); Mary Clarke and Clement Crisp, *Ballet: An Illustrated History* (New York, 1973). On the music of the period from Susato to Gluck, Friedrich Blume, *Renaissance and Baroque Music* (New York, 1967) is succinct, Manfred Bukofzer, *Music in the Baroque Era* (New York, 1947) more analytical. Interesting books on composers are: F. B. Zimmerman, *Henry Purcell, His Life and Times* (London, 1967), Hans David and Arthur Mendel, *The Bach Reader* (New York, 1966), Martin Cooper, *Gluck* (New York, 1935), Alan Walker, ed., *The Chopin Companion* (New York, 1973), and Stravinsky's books of conversations and collaborations with Robert Craft, 1959–69. Scott Joplin's life is described in his *Collected Piano Works* (New York, 1971). The world of the early music printer is described in a book on a contemporary of Susato, Daniel Heartz, *Pierre Attaingnant, Royal Printer of Music* (Berkeley, 1969).

ANONYMOUS
Saltarello (14th century).

7.

The British Museum manuscript (Add. Ms. 29987) from which this "jumping dance" comes is an Italian source of the fourteenth century, and contains the largest surviving collection of such monophonic dances. The favorite accompaniments for Medieval dancing were the pipe and tabor (see Plate 2), and an ensemble of shawms* with slide-trumpet.* But these pieces would fit best on a solo stringed instrument such as the rebec* or the vielle.* The style differs from contemporary vocal music in its many repeated leaps of fourths and fifths (e.g. at the beginning). The form is that of an *estampie*,* the most usual instrumental form of the time, derived from the plainsong *sequence*:* the melody of each small section is repeated (with first and second endings). In this case, the endings are all uniform, giving the impression of a refrain.

Recordings: DL79438 (*Medieval Roots*, N.Y. Pro Musica). Tel. S-9466 (*Frühe Musik in Italien, Frankreich und Burgund,* Studio der frühen Musik).

Compare: plainsong melodies; **2b**, **18**, **20**; other estampies.

repeat from % to ✛,
then continue

repeat from % to ✛,
then continue

repeat third line, then % to ✛ (end)

TIELMAN SUSATO

(d. ca. 1561)

a. *La Mourisque*
b. *Pavane "La Bataille"* (published 1551).

8.

Susato led a varied life as flutist, town trumpeter, music copyist, composer, and publisher in Antwerp. He issued many books of chansons, and a single set of instrumental part-books (the usual way of publishing music in his time). The latter collection, called *Danserye*, contained a wealth of dance pieces for all occasions: allemandes, pavanes, galliards,* basses danses, etc., all set for four-part ensemble. In his introduction he says that they are "suitable to be played on all musical instruments," which means, for the Renaissance, that the four fundamental types of ensemble can be used: "whole" or "broken" consorts,* of loud or soft instruments (see Glossary and commentary to **52** for further explanation). The "Battle" pavane is a piece of program music* which combines the stately tread of the pavane* with trumpet calls and the imitation of kettledrums. Naturally loud instruments would be most appropriate here. The mourisque or morisca, a basse danse,* would sound equally well on a consort of viols,* recorders, or plucked instruments.

Recordings: Ang. S-36851 (*Pleasures of the Court*; Early Music Consort, Munrow, cond.) Dec. 79419 (*Renaissance Festival Music*, N.Y. Pro Musica, Greenberg, cond.)

Compare: 9, 22 (a pavane), **44, 50;** Clément Jannequin's chanson *La Guerre,* a vivid vocal battle-piece and the ancestor of this pavane.

a.

b.

ANONYMOUS

Monsiers Almaine (16th century).

This is the basic version of a very popular dance tune of the period around 1600—or so one assumes, from the number of arrangements that have survived. "Almaine" is an English corruption of *allemande*, the French word for "German." Presumably it refers either to the provenance or to the supposed character of the dance: grave and fairly slow. By 1600 allemandes were going out of fashion for dancing, but had only just begun their long career as instrumental pieces of increasing complexity. These are the parts for viols and flute from the simple setting in Thomas Morley's *Consort Lessons* of 1599.

9a.

Recordings: Ang. S-36851 (*Pleasures of the Court*; Early Music Consort, Munrow, cond.), with additional parts for lute, cittern, and pandora.

DANIEL BATCHELOR

(fl. before 1610)

Monsiers Almaine, from Varietie of Lute Lessons, published 1610.

9b. Daniel Batchelor, or Bachelar, is represented in manuscript collections by many Pavanes, Galliards,* and other pieces for lute. This fine set of variations on the preceding Allemande tune was published in a combined tutor and anthology for the lute by Robert Dowland, son of the famous John (see **22**) and himself a professional lutenist.

The lute was to the sixteenth and early seventeenth centuries what the harpsichord* was to the eighteenth and the piano to the nineteenth: the universal instrument on which anything, if suitably arranged, could be played. It was an essential part of the furnishings of a well-stocked house, and of the accomplishments of a cultured person. The English lute school, which must be ranked as the finest of its time, produced original fantasias* of immense complexity, and arranged madrigals and dances, equipping the latter with extravagant variations such as these. This arrangement is a real showpiece, displaying the full range of the instrument and retaining only the harmonies of the original piece.

Recordings: RCA LSC-3196 (*The Golden Age of English Lute Music,* Bream); DG 2530079 (*English Guitar Music,* Behrend)

Compare: variation technique in **37, 39**; three keyboard settings by Byrd in *The Fitzwilliam Virginal Book,* Vol. I, pp. 234, 238, 245.

HENRY PURCELL

(1659–November 21, 1695)

Suite No. 1 in G major (published 1696).

Purcell was one of the few great English composers born after 1600. There was little competition between 1650 and 1900, during which time English composers imitated in turn Purcell, Handel, Haydn, Mendelssohn, and Brahms. Purcell, the last great original, was in a unique position to assimilate both the Italian style of Corelli and the French style of Lully, supposedly irreconcilable. Had he lived longer, it might have been he, rather than Johann Sebastian Bach, who first fused these styles with his native one. As it was, his music covered a vast range of expression, from the early fantasias for viols (the genre is illustrated by 52) to French-type overtures and suites and Italian-type trio sonatas. But most of all he was a composer of vocal music, both solo and choral. It was this that influenced Handel when the latter emigrated to England in 1712.

A Choice Collection of Lessons for the Harpsichord or Spinet was the title of a posthumous publication in which Purcell's widow issued suites* and other compositions which he had written at various times. The suites are sets of from three to ten different dance-like movements. Each includes an "Almand" (=allemande) and a courante* (both "obligatory" movements of the standard Baroque suite).

The technique required by these pieces is so simple that they have often been used—and may well have been written—for teaching children and beginners. They illustrate the French style of ornamentation,* in which single notes are decorated and emphasized with trills* and mordents.* Originally these would have been written as shorthand symbols, not as the small notes which appear in this edition. Those in the fourth bar of the almand should be played as full eighth notes.

10.

Recordings: Oiseau OLS 149 (Purcell's Complete Harpsichord Suites, Nef); Dec. 710149 (Sylvia Marlowe, Harpsichord: Henry Purcell)

Compare: 9, 11; notice that the prelude begins with a chord progression found elsewhere in interesting elaborations, e.g. Mozart, "Drei Knäbchen" quintet from The Magic Flute; Beethoven, Piano Sonatas Ops. 79, iii, and 109, i; Chopin, Butterfly Étude, Op. 25, No. 9, etc.

JOHANN SEBASTIAN BACH

(March 21, 1685–July 28, 1750)

French Suite No. 6 in E major, BWV 817 (between 1717 and 1722).

11. Bach's nineteen principal keyboard suites (six "French," six "English," six Partitas, and the *French Overture*) show the late Baroque suite raised to its highest development as a set of idealized dances. The *French Suites* are his shortest and simplest, and seem to have been used by Bach as teaching pieces. They were not published in his lifetime, but numerous copies exist, most of them made by his pupils. The designation "French" is a later addition, apparently prompted by the similarity of some movements to compositions of the French school which remained simple, short, and fairly close to their actual dance models. Actually this suite is eminently international, as shown by the provenance of its dances:

Allemande* —	Germany
Courante* —	France
Sarabande* —	Spain
Gavotte* —	France
Polonaise* —	Poland
Minuet* —	France
Bourée* —	France
Gigue* —	England

The titles printed in boldface are the invariable members of the classic suite as established by Froberger in the previous century. It is questionable whether suites were meant to be played from beginning to end, or whether they were to be regarded as collections from which one could pick and choose movements as one pleased. A long suite such as this one can certainly be monotonous if heard as a whole, because every movement is in the same key.

In some sources, this suite is prefaced by the E major Prelude from the first book of Bach's *Well-Tempered Clavier.** It is rich in examples of two-part invertible counterpoint, and every movement, as one would expect, is in binary form.

Recordings: many, but hear especially Thurston Dart's performance on the clavichord* (unfortunately without the ornamented repeats which he could so beautifully have added): Oiseau 60039.

Compare: 9, 10 (allemandes), **14** (polonaise), **53, 54:** Bach's other suites for keyboard, violin, cello, orchestra; suites of Froberger, Pachelbel, Handel, and Rameau; consider differences of interpretation on harpsichord, clavichord, and piano.

ALLEMANDE

COURANTE

SARABANDE

GAVOTTE

POLONAISE

MENUET

BOURRÉE

GIGUE

CHRISTOPH WILLIBALD GLUCK

(July 2, 1714–November 15, 1787)

"Dance of the Blessed Spirits" from Act II of Orphée et Eurydice (1762 and 1774).

12.

Gluck is one of those composers of the second rank who, nevertheless, succeeded in writing a few first-class masterpieces. One of these is the opera *Orpheus and Eurydice,* not only an enchanting work but also a milestone in the history of opera. In it Gluck and his librettist* Calzabigi did away with many of the conventions of current operatic writ-, ing: the *secco* recitative,* the subordination to virtuoso singers, the lack of significant chorus numbers, and the stock situations and characters that made operatic personages little more than cardboard heroes, heroines, and villains.

The opera was first given in Vienna in 1762. When in 1774 it was taken to Paris, Gluck made several changes, adapting the title role from a castrato* alto to a tenor (the French had never liked castrati), and adding several ballet numbers, including the "B" section of this dance. No one has rivalled Gluck in his depiction of the serenity of a classical paradise, rather similar, one feels, to an eighteenth-century park. The Hades to which Monteverdi's Orpheus descends is a more sinister place altogether (see **37**), and with Gluck one wonders why Orpheus does not stay with his beloved in so charming a spot, instead of dragging her back to earth.

Of the composers represented in this book, none is particularly close to Gluck's style: if our Haydn symphony were only earlier, it might have served for comparison. There is something old-fashioned about this dance (even the middle section) that recalls the earlier Galant* era, reminding one of the milder moments of Rameau and C.P.E. Bach. By any standards, it is an exquisitely beautiful piece, and the pervasive figure of the "B" section (bars 40–42, etc.) lingers long in the memory. It has been suggested that the "flutes" should be alto recorders, since these are the traditional pastoral instruments, and since the key of F is more characteristic of recorder than of flute music (which tends more towards sharp keys). The tone of recorders would call for a less "romantic" performance than conductors usually give, which might be an improvement in itself.

Recordings: many, of the entire opera. The instrumental music only: RCA VICS-1435 (*Orfeo ed Euridice: Orchestral Music,* Rome Opera House Orch., Monteux, cond.)

Compare: 55, 57; the remainder of the opera; Monteverdi's *Orfeo*; the ballets and operas of Lully and Rameau; the music of Sammartini.

Ballet des Ombres heureuses.

FRANZ SCHUBERT

(January 31, 1797–November 19, 1828)

Waltzes from Opus 9 (published 1821).

13.

Schubert's Opus 9 contains eighteen of his many waltzes, strung together like so many pearls on a necklace. They are all pleasant and ideally suited to their humble purpose—that of accompanying social dancing and conversation—but now and then one will find a real beauty, such as No. 2. The titles (e.g., "Mourning" and "Longing" Waltz) were the publisher's, and Schubert thought them stupid: however could one have a sad waltz?

The second half of No. 2 contains an enharmonic* modulation:* the flats suddenly turn into sharps, and back again. The E♮ and F♭ in the bass are identical notes in sound, though not in function. It is interesting that the two halves of the Waltz end the same, and consist of only the two melodic cells

 and

in exactly the same arrangement. Such economy of means, yet such richness of sound!

Recordings: Turn. 34006 (*Schubert: Waltzes from Op. 9., D. 365 & Op. 50, D. 779, Hautzig)*

Compare: 15, 24, 35 (the "Libiamo" tune), **56;** Beethoven's and Mozart's *German Dances.*

FRÉDÉRIC CHOPIN

(March 1 or February 22, 1810–October 17, 1849)

Polonaise in C♯ minor, Op. 26, No. 1 (1834–35).

14.

Chopin is the only composer of the first rank who worked only in one medium—that of the piano—to the virtual exclusion of all others. He shunned the programmatic tendencies of his time, composing for the most part single "abstract" movements of a dozen different categories, such as this one and **15**. He took over from Beethoven a conception of the piano as primarily a singing instrument, and gave the sustaining pedal an indispensable part in the production of tone. More generally, he made explorations into new harmonic effects which were unsurpassed for boldness until Wagner's later works. His forms are generally simple (ternary form* being a favorite), but they contain music of immense emotional power and psychological insight.

Polonaise in C♯ minor was the first polonaise published by Chopin with an opus number, and the first of his seven great polonaises. Living in France as a voluntary exile, he wrote these works and his mazurkas as a homage to his native Poland, where in a far simpler form they were national dances. The vigorous opening and the strong dissonance on the first beat of the fifth bar give a sense of powerful forces only just kept in check by the quiet main theme. In the second section they keep bursting out in characteristic flourishes, but the central part (*meno mosso*) is lyrical and almost sentimental. It has a slow, decorated melody over repeated chords, similar to some of Chopin's nocturnes, and explores some strange harmonies. One can see from this section how Chopin used ornamentation as something essential to the structure, and not merely as a decorative effect. The cello-like solo in the left hand with the slower tune above it shows that Chopin could write counterpoint when he wanted to.

Recordings: many.

Compare: 11, 15, 72a; Chopin's other polonaises; Schumann, *Carnaval* of 1834, the year in which Schumann heralded Chopin's genius to the musical world; Liszt, *Années de Pélerinage*, Book I (1835/36).

Allegro appassionato.

FRÉDÉRIC CHOPIN
Waltz in C♯ minor, Op. 64, No. 2 (1847).

15.

This late waltz shows Chopin full of nostalgia and gentle melancholy. There is a curious contrast between the heavily emotional "A" section and the light-fingered refrain (*più mosso*). As in the preceding polonaise, a middle section in the major (*più lento*) provides a more *cantabile** element. Notice here how the rhythm of the melody is displaced from the main beats (bar 65f.), and subtly varied on its repeat (bar 82f.). The refrain, on the other hand, is absolutely unchanging: its sixteen-bar phrase is heard no fewer than six times. As often happens in Chopin, the left hand is restricted to accompanying chords, here in a typical waltz pattern.

Recordings: many.

Compare: 13, 14, 72a; Chopin's other waltzes and mazurkas; his *Fantasy Impromptu* which has the same key scheme as this and **14;** his *Prelude in D♭ major* which has the opposite one; the waltzes of Brahms, Johann Strauss, and Scott Joplin.

Klindworth:

SCOTT JOPLIN

(November 24, 1868–April 1, 1917)

The Entertainer Ragtime Two Step (1902).

16.

This piece dates from the time when popular music was beginning to diverge radically from "serious" music. Not so very long before, a "classical" composer such as Brahms or Johann Strauss could write tunes that found their ways into cafés and dance halls. But the music of Joplin's contemporaries was becoming less and less suitable for popular use and enjoyment. The concerns of composers such as Debussy and Schoenberg, obsessed as they were with the search for new modes of expression, were beginning to cut off the greater part of the public from the mainstream of music. The time was ripe for something new to fill the void, and it was the recently emancipated American blacks who provided it, in the form of ragtime, blues, and eventually jazz.

Ragtime developed originally from the "swing" with which black musicians would play marches and other popular pieces. Joplin's were not the first Rags to be published, but they did make a major contribution towards solidifying the conventions of the style: the syncopations and the uneven rhythmical patterns, most obvious of which are the displacement of the secondary beat from the fourth sixteenth-note of a 2/4 bar to the third (as at the very beginning of this Rag), and the division of the bar into three unequal beats containing 3 + 3 + 2 sixteenths (e.g. the beginning of the theme). The typical ragtime form, A B A C D, was borrowed from marches. In the case of a catchy "A" theme such as this one, it is tempting to repeat it between the "C" and "D" sections, or at the end. In actual practice, this may well have been done by the original musicians whose art was based so much on extemporization.

Recording: None. H-71248 (*Piano Rags by Scott Joplin*, Vol. I, Rifkin)

Compare: 15 (similar form), **26, 29, 30b, 43**; Joplin, *Maple Leaf Rag* and other works.

INTRO:

IGOR STRAVINSKY

(June 17, 1882–April 6, 1971)

"Introduction" and "Danses des Adolescentes" from *Le Sacre du Printemps* (1913).

17.

From time to time, a work of art will appear as if of its own volition, so far does it exceed the normal creative powers of one man. Monteverdi's *Orfeo*, Beethoven's Ninth Symphony, and Wagner's *Tristan und Isolde* are, perhaps, such works. *The Rite of Spring* is one of the few of the present century that seems to have this autonomy about it. Of course it is intensely Stravinskian: the use of the woodwinds and the simple folk-like melodies give him away from the very beginning. But there is also something universal and collective about it: a sense as of natural forces which were awaiting this opportunity to manifest themselves. The fact that today it makes sense to any educated Westerner means that our psychology must differ in some important respect from that of the people who found it so abhorrent in the first twenty years of its existence. Perhaps we have a new consciousness (thanks to Freud, Jung, and two World Wars) of the rhythms of sex, life, and death that this music so vividly evokes.

The first movement obviously describes the burgeoning of Spring. Never has the natural process been translated so faithfully into music: the creatures awake one after another and the sap bubbles up the tree trunks. Yet this is not naïve description à la Vivaldi (see **38**), but the very essence of the event, transferred to sound without the necessity for intervening words.

The second movement has been much analyzed on account of its irregular rhythm. It has the same overall form as the first: a gradual *crescendo,** much beloved of Russian composers. Another Russian trait is the continued repetition of the themes, without development, but in a kaleidoscopic variety of orchestra colors. The details of instrumentation are a source of endless delight: I will mention only the effects of the flute quartet between rehearsal Nos. 16 and 18, and the complicated subdivision of the strings at 30.

The third movement follows the end of this extract without a break, and the entire ballet lasts about 33 minutes. The last movement, "Danse sacrale," is the most shattering of all, and was absolutely without precedent when it appeared.

Recordings: many.

Compare: 63, 64, 66; the remainder of the work; Stravinsky's preceding ballets, *The Firebird* and *Petrouchka*; Bartók, *Allegro Barbaro* (1911—an anticipation); Prokofiev, *Scythian Suite* (1914—an imitation).

ВЕСЕННІЯ ГАДАНІЯ.
ПЛЯСКИ ЩЕГОЛИХЪ.

LES AUGURES PRINTANIERS.
DANSES DES ADOLESCENTES.

SONGS OF TWO ERAS

Three Musicians by Lorenzo Costa; the era of
Josquin des Prez

Bettmann Archive (London, National Gallery)

"God save the Queen" engraved by J. and G. P. Nichol
the era of Schumann and Foster.

Bettmann Archive

Music and poetry

A song may seem a simple thing: a musical trifle in comparison with a symphony, a Mass, or a ballet. Yet what could be more complex than the relations between poet, composer, singer, and listener? These four characters (and we will forget the accompanist, for now) enter into a psychological relationship of the utmost subtlety which can teach us something about music as a whole.

Consider first the poet. In the early days he would often be the composer, even the singer as well. Such has been the tradition with bards and epic singers of all nations and times, who carried in their capacious memories thousands of lines of their own and others' verses which they would recite or chant. The Medieval schools of troubadours,* trouvères* (see **1c**) and Minnesingers (see **18**) were not far removed from this tradition: they were poets first and composers second. Even with Machaut and Landini, the two greatest composers of the fourteenth century, this precedence held good. During festivities in Venice in 1364, Landini, himself a renowned organist, lost the organ-playing contest but was crowned with a laurel wreath for his poetry. And Machaut was a prolific poet whose influence was even felt abroad—by Chaucer, for one.

If early composers were frequently poets, they were even more often professional singers. A roster of those represented in this book would include Dufay, Josquin, and Palestrina, all members of the Papal Choir in Rome; Byrd, Lassus, and Monteverdi, who all worked as singers before (and, doubtless, after) their promotion to directoral posts; Dowland was probably, and Purcell certainly, an incomparable singer of his own songs. But of these singing composers, Dowland alone was possibly a poet as well.

Among the later composers, only Foster and Handy (**26, 29**) wrote their own words. This points up again the fact that the "serious" musical habits of the past tend to crop up in popular music: a field in which improvisation is still widespread, and in which people still write and sing their own songs. The classical composers have chosen, on the whole, to set works of comparatively minor poets (e.g. **25, 27**) or the more lyric poems of the great poets (**24, 28, 30a, 31**). Many have written music for "Where the bee sucks," Ariel's song in Shakespeare's *The Tempest*, but only a student or an amateur would try to set Hamlet's Soliloquy or T. S. Eliot's *Four Quartets*. One should always ask oneself, when intending to set a poem to music, "Am I improving the situation?" Obviously the poetry that plumbs the depths of Man and the Universe is best left unimproved. Music, in any case, has its own ways of doing this.

There are also songs in which the poem is no more than a hook on which to hang a good tune (**21, 23, 26, 29**). In some of these cases the composer may have commissioned or written words for music that was already in his head or on paper. But the manner in which music and poetry blend is one of the great mysteries of the arts. It raises the whole question of meaning in both.

Take the first song of Schumann's *Frauenliebe und Leben* (**25a**):

> Since mine eyes have seen him,
>   As if blind I seem;
> When I gaze around me
>   I see only him.
> Ever thus his image
>   Does my day-dream fill,
> Growing out of darkness,
>   Brighter beaming still.
>
> But for him no ray of
>   Light would mark my way.
> With my sisters gaily
>   I no more can play;
> In my lonely chamber

> I would weep and dream.
> Since mine eyes have seen him,
> As if blind I seem.

Schumann has improved Chamisso's mediocre poem by giving a beautiful musical interpretation to a man's egotistical fancy of a girl overwhelmed by her first love. Hear the hesitations in the accompaniment, the swellings of emotion in the voice part, and especially the passionate suspensions* in the last lines. But is it as simple as that? Compare lines 3–7 of the poem's two stanzas: how different they are! In the first she is perpetually enraptured by his image, while in the second she is losing rapport with her younger sisters, and prefers to weep in her bedroom. Different sentiments, certainly; yet the music is identical for both. Perhaps it expresses the *general* emotional tone, and not the incidental feelings of the girl's situation. As such, it makes us feel and share her sentiments far more strongly than the poetry alone could do.

If this explanation seems satisfactory, turn to the last song (**25e**). By now the lover has become a husband, and, alas, has died. "For the first time," sings the widow, "thou hast given me pain." And after words have failed her in her grief, the piano repeats a complete stanza from the first song. Do we then feel like young lovers again? On the contrary, we feel the almost unbearable poignancy of the contrast, as we think back to those early days when one wept not for sorrow but for sheer wonder and happiness. The music here "means" something quite different, yet the notes are exactly the same. If we were to hear this coda* under the impression that it was merely one of Schumann's many short piano pieces, how different our response would be!

This excursion proves that the meaning of music is not always in the notes alone. Any song, by definition, brings in another level of meaning: that of the words, which may far outweigh the contribution of the music to our total response. The case of *To Anacreon in Heaven* (**23**) is an extreme example of this. Most people believe that our National Anthem has a splendidly rousing and patriotic tune, celebrating the Defense of Liberty and the Victory of 1814. Is anything of this actually in the tune? Apparently not, for it was originally composed as a highbrow drinking song. To a Colonial gentleman, it would have summoned up visions of nothing nobler than mahogany tables set with bottles of port.

The relation of poet and composer is something that could be (and should be) discussed at length. Here, however, we should turn to the other persons involved: the singer and the listener. They should, ideally, be very cultured people, since they need to understand at least four languages: English, French, German, and Italian. But not only do most listeners not understand them: the singers often cannot even pronounce the songs they sing. Why, then, do we not translate all songs into English, so that everyone can sing and understand them?

There are two answers to this: first, many people believe that the actual sound of the words, quite apart from their sense, is an important ingredient of the song, and that to substitute the sounds of another language is to misrepresent both the composer's and the poet's intentions. It would be as unsuitable, they will say, to substitute a string quartet* for the piano accompaniment. This is the perennial objection to the translation of poetry, which certainly holds good when the poet's sound is superior to his sense. Singers will often add that English is the worst of all languages to sing, on account of its awkward consonant groups and dipthongs, its rhythm, which seldom accords with the typical metrical patterns of post-Renaissance music, and the fact that in singing one has to pronounce sounds which disappear in everyday speech. To hear these songs of Schubert (**24**), and Schumann (**25**) sung in their English translations would certainly support these complaints. Can any translation replace adequately the onomatopoeic effect of Rückert's words: *"Du bist die Ruh'"*? *"In thee is rest"* is ugly, *"Thou art sweet peace"* is little better. The soft *"oo"* sounds are an absolutely integral part of the music.

In the case of the Schumann songs, at least, a second objection to translation might well be raised, namely that one is far better off if one does not understand the German, since one will not be distracted from Schumann's beautiful music by Chamisso's embarrassing words. It is often a welcome ignorance that enables one to enjoy the human voice, finest of all instruments, with one's mind uncluttered by someone's "poetic" thoughts. In any case, one is sometimes unable to understand the words even of English songs; and apparently the Germans themselves have trouble understanding Wagner's operas on first hearing.

If one does not know the language of a song, one should take the opportunity of listening to the voice as an instrument, and enjoying its pure emotional quality which can be far more eloquent than words. But if one knows the language only slightly, and the poem is worthwhile, one can soon learn to associate sound with sense. This leads to the situation, actually the most difficult, in which one understands the words perfectly well. If one can really concentrate on the song, without daydreaming, one will find that there is almost too much going on. Should one try to visualize what the poem describes? This is unavoidable with Milton's and Tennyson's very pictorial poems (**30a, 31**), but others lend themselves to it less well. Dowland's anonymous verses and Rückert's poems (**22, 24, 28**) are psychological pictures, already interpreted by the music. Here it is the mood that one enjoys (or suffers), irrespective of the words, which serve mainly to focus our musical attention. Mood is paramount in the early songs (**18–22**), for here, even if one is at home in the language, one cannot share the emotional world of courtly love which most Renaissance and Medieval songs express. Perhaps the main pleasure is that of time-travel to a world utterly remote from our own.

The reader will notice two large gaps in the historical sequence of this chapter: about one hundred and fifty years between Binchois and Dowland, and over two hundred years between Dowland and Schubert. The first gap appears because in that period part-songs* were preferred to solo songs, and the second because in the seventeenth and eighteenth centuries the song-writing impulse was diverted almost exclusively into arias* for operas and cantatas.* "Songs" of those periods will therefore be found elsewhere (part-songs: **49, 50, 51;** arias: **32, 33, 34, 37**).

Suggestions for further reading On songs in general, see Donald Ivey, *Song: Anatomy, Imagery, and Styles* (New York, 1970); Elaine Brody and Robert A. Fowkes, *The German Lied and Its Poetry* (New York, 1971). On composers, see Diana Poulton, *John Dowland* (London, 1972), Maurice J. E. Brown, *Schubert: A Critical Biography* (New York, 1958) and *Essays on Schubert* (London and New York, 1966), Joan Chissell, *Schumann* (London, 1948), Eric Sams, *The Songs of Robert Schumann* (London, 1969), Norman Suckling, *Fauré* (London, 1946), Neville Cardus, *Gustav Mahler, His Mind and His Music* (London, 1965), John Kirkpatrick, ed., *Charles E. Ives: Memos* (New York, 1972), Eric W. White, *Benjamin Britten, His Life and Operas* (Berkeley, 1970). Oscar Sonneck, *The Star-Spangled Banner* (Washington D.C., 1914) and W. C. Handy, ed., *The Blues; An Anthology* (New York, 1926) are rare, but excellent backgrounds for **23** and **29**.

NEIDHART VON REUENTHAL

(ca. 1180–ca. 1240)

Maienzit

There were four schools of monophonic secular music in the Middle Ages:

18.

1. **Troubadours**	Southern France	End of 11th to end of 13th century
2. **Trouvères**	Northern France	Mid-12th to end of 13th century
3. **Minnesingers**	Germany	Later 13th to early 14th century
4. **Meistersingers**	Germany	Early 15th to late 16th century

From the musical point of view, the second and third groups are the most interesting, since their melodies have come down to us in the greatest number and variety (see **1c** for a trouvère melody, *Robin m'aime*). The composers were mostly aristocratic poet-musicians whose favorite subject was *Minne*: "Courtly Love." Neidhart is actually somewhat of an exception, since his poems tend to be earthier and more oriented towards Nature. The Meistersingers* were members of craft guilds who formed societies in imitation of the Minnesingers. Unfortunately they soon caused the art to stultify, constricted by rigid rules and bereft of the ideals of *Minne* which had inspired their more refined predecessors. They are aptly satirized in Wagner's opera *Die Meistersinger von Nürnberg* (see **36**). *Maienzit*, like almost all the songs of the German schools, is in "Barform" (A A B). There are several further verses, in which the tone degenerates to one of personal vilification, somewhat out of keeping with this spring-like melody.

Recording: Tel. S-9487 (*Minnesong and Prosody, c. 1220-1230*, Studio der Frühen Musik)

Compare: All plainsong melodies, **1c, 7, 19, 36;** trouvère songs.

1. May - en - zeit o - ne neidt freud - en geit wi - der streit sein wi - der - kum - en kan uns
2. Uff dem plan o - ne wan sicht man stan wol - ge - than licht - e präu - ne kan uns

al - len helf — fen. 3. Durch das gras sind sie schon uf - ge - drung - en und der walt man - i -
bey den gelf — fen.

gualt un - ge - tzalt ist der schalt — das er ward mit dem nie pas ge - sung - en.

GUILLAUME DE MACHAUT

(between 1300 and 1305–April, 1377)

Virelai: *Se je souspire.*

19

During the fourteenth century motets (see **1c**) were gradually abandoned as the favorite form for secular music, and replaced by
chansons* (French, "songs") in the *formes fixes* (French, "fixed
forms"). These were various ways of combining two strains, or sections, of music with poems of varying lengths and patterns. Nos. **19, 20,**
and **21** illustrate two of the three main forms, of which the simplest (not
represented) is called, in French, *Ballade,* in Italian *Madrigal:*

A a B

In this shorthand, the same letters mean the same music, but lower-case
letters mean that the words change. The next in length was the *virelai:*

A B b a A

This example, in two parts, shows Machaut's genius for simple but
beautiful melody. The fact that there are two further verses means that
the musical form of a complete performance would be:

A b b a A b b a A b b a A

One would therefore hear the first strain seven times, and the second
strain six times. We cannot underestimate the Medieval tolerance for
repetition, unsurpassed until Satie (see **67**).

Recordings: Dec. 79431 (*The Romance of Medieval France,* N.Y. Pro Musica, Greenberg, cond.); Arc. 3032 (*The Ars Nova in France,* Brussels Pro Musica Antiqua).

Compare: **1c, 2b, 4c, 5b, 6b, 18, 20, 21;** Machaut's other chansons and those of the trouvères.

1. Se je sou - spir par - fon - de - ment   et____
4. Qu'a vous tres a - mou - reu - se - ment   en -
5. Se je sou - spir *etc.*

ten - dre - ment pleure en re - coy,   c'est, par ma   foy,   pour vous, quant vo fai - tis corps
tie - re - ment doing et of - froy   le cuer de   moy   qui loing de vous e - sba - te -

gent,   da - me,   ne____   voy.   2. Vo - stre   doux main - tieng sim - ple et
ment,   n'a n'e - sba - noy.   3. et vo   ma - nie - re   sans   ef -

coy,   vo   bel__   ar - roy,   coint   et____   plai - sant,
froy,   pris   m'ont__ cil____   troy   si   dou - ce - ment.

FRANCESCO LANDINI

(1325–September 2, 1397)

Ballata: *Gram piant'agli ochi.*

20.

This piece by the foremost composer of the Italian *Ars Nova** is in the same fixed form as Machaut's *Se je souspir*. In Italy, however, the virelai form was known as the *ballata*, and this is not to be confused with the French ballade, the shortest of the fixed forms, whose Italian equivalent was the madrigal (A a B).

Although Landini was organist at San Lorenzo in Florence, we have no sacred music of his. (The main task of Medieval organists seems to have been improvisation on plainsong themes: see **2b**.) There are, however, over one hundred fifty of his secular works extant, constituting over a third of the surviving *trecento** pieces. They are largely songs in two or three parts in the Italian *formes fixes*: madrigal, ballata, and *caccia*.* This lovely ballata has words under the tenor and triplum,* and a wordless contratenor whose less mellifluous lines make it more suitable for an instrument than a voice. As often in Italian music (though more rarely in French) there are written-out trills and other ornaments, though those here are very mild in comparison with the coloratura* passages one sometimes finds (e.g. in **2b**). They are so plainly elaborations of typical phrases, e.g.:

that one is probably justified in applying similar ornaments elsewhere *ad libitum*.

The stock cadence* pattern, especially clear at the ends of the sections, in which a $^6_3$ chord expands to an $^8_5$, is sometimes varied by a decorative lowering of the upper part (e.g. the end of bar 11). This is the so-called "Landini cadence": a useful phrase, so long as one remembers that everyone else used it before, during, and for fifty years after his lifetime.

Recordings: Odyssey 32160177 (*Ballades, Rondeaux and Virelais,* Zurich Ancient Instrument Ensemble); Tel. S-9466 (*Frühe Musik in Italien, Frankreich und Burgund,* Studio der frühen Musik); Phi. 802904 (*Music from the time of Decameron,* Musica Reservata).

Compare: 1c, 2b, 4b, 5b, 6b, 19, 21; Landini's other songs and those of Jacopo de Bologna, his teacher.

Compare 1c, 2b, 4b, 5b, 6b, 19, 21; Landini's other songs and those of Jacopo de Bologna, his teacher.

Recordings: Odyssey 32160177 (Ballades, Rondeaux and Virelais, Zurich Ancient Instrument Ensemble; Tel. S-9466 (Fruhe Musik in Italien, Frankreich und Burgund, Studio der fruhen Musik), Phil. 802904 (Musik from the time of Decameron, Musica Reservata).

GILLES BINCHOIS
(ca. 1400–1460)
Rondeau: *De plus en plus.*

Binchois is the only composer of the early fifteenth century who is comparable to Dufay, and then only in his secular chansons. He excelled in the composition of these short songs, dealing with the refined sentiments of courtly love. The fact that after some time as a soldier he took holy orders was no obstacle to his pursuit of this worldly art: like Dunstable, Machaut, Dufay, and many Medieval artists and intellectuals, he derived his income largely from ecclesiastical posts which we would today call sinecures, i.e. well-endowed positions of which the actual work can be foisted onto a badly-paid substitute. Marxists could surely never bring themselves to enjoy the fruits of such exploitation! Yet we must face the fact that lovely music can, and often does, come from unlovely social conditions. We are all able now to enjoy music which in Binchois' day was reserved for the most exclusive social circles.

The melody of this *rondeau* is one of those tunes that speaks to us directly: there is nothing antiquated or crabbed about it. The rondeau is the longest of the *formes fixes:*

A B a A a b A B

Rondeaux commonly had only one verse, however, unlike the several of ballades and virelais.

21.

Recordings: Tel. S-9466 (*Frühe Musik in Italien, Frankreich und Burgund,* Studio der frühen Musik); Pleiades P-251 (*Early and Late Fifteenth Century Music,* University of Chicago) Bach Guild BG-634 (*Music at the Burgundian Court*); Amadeo AVRS-5028 (*Music at the Burgundian Court,* Brussels Pro Musica Antiqua)

Compare: 4c, 5b, 19, 20; chansons of Dufay, Busnois, and Ockeghem.

De plus en plus se re-nou - vel - le

De plus en plus

De plus en plus

Ma dou - ce dam-me gen - - te et bel - - -

- le Ma vou-len - té de vous ve - ir

De plus en plus se renouvelle,
Ma douce damme gente et belle,
Ma voulenté de vous veir:
Ce me fait le très grand désir
Que j'ay de vous oir nouvelle.

bar	
1	Ne cuidies pas que je recelle
9	Com à tous jours vous estes celle
18	Que je veul de tout obeyr:
1	De plus en plus se renouvelle
9	Ma douce damme gente et belle.

1	Hélas, se vous m'esties cruelle,
9	J'aroye au cuer angoisse telle,
18	Que je voulroye bien mourir:
25	Mais ce seroit sans déservir,
29	En soustenant vostre querelle.

(Repeat verse 1)

JOHN DOWLAND

(December, 1562–January 21, 1625)

Flow, my tears or *Lachrymae* (before 1595; publ. in *The Second Book of Songs or Ayres,* 1600).

22.

For fifty years this song and its arrangements enjoyed popularity in Europe comparable to that of a present-day pop song. Dowland identified with his "hit" (and with the sentiments expressed in it) to such an extent that he even signed his name "Jo. Dolande de Lachrimae" in a fellow musician's visiting book. The foremost lutenist of his time, he worked as a court musician for kings and princes, mainly in Europe, and never lacked good employment or fame. His ayres* for voice and lute were printed, and many times reprinted—this a real rarity for the time—and his lute pieces were repeatedly included in textbooks, anthologies, and manuscript collections. Despite this worldly acclaim, Dowland was famous for a melancholic disposition such as this song epitomized and as was fashionable in his day. But his musicianship is also illustrated here: a gift for long-breathed melodies with great rhythmic variety, a way of making the accompaniment more than just a background (e.g. the imitations in bars 11–12, 19), and a sense of climax rare for his time.

Lachrymae (Latin, "tears") was the original name of this piece, first composed as a pavane for lute alone. The words were written probably later by a gentleman of rank who preferred to remain anonymous. Among the many arrangements which were made are Dowland's own beautiful *Lachrymae, or Seven tears, figured in seven passionate pavanes* (1605) for lute and five viols: one of these is a straight transcription, and the others take off in different directions from the opening notes. Many other composers paid homage to Dowland by beginning pavanes and other pieces with the same phrase.

Beneath the accompaniment part is seen the original tablature* for lute. Here the six lines represent the strings g' d' a f c G (with low D represented by occasional ledger lines*), and the letters the frets: a for an open string, b for the first fret (a semi-tone* higher), c for the second, and so forth. Above the staff are the rhythmical signs, like the tails of eighth- and sixteenth-notes. This is actually a far more efficient notation for lute (or guitar) than the usual staff, since it indicates fingering which otherwise must be laboriously worked out. (Note for guitarists: if one tunes the G-string down to F♯, one has the equivalent of a lute, tuned a minor third low, and can play this piece from tablature.) It was customary to support the lowest line with a bass viol, thus anticipating the Baroque continuo* texture. Alternatively, the ayres were often issued with optional parts for other voices, making even a *capella** performance possible.

Recordings: RCA VICS-1338 (*Lachrymae, or, Seven Tears . . . with diuers other Pauans, Gallards, and Almands . . .*, Schola Cantorum Basiliensis); MCA 2505 (*Elizabethan and Jacobean Ayres, Madrigals,* New York Pro Musica Antiqua).

Compare: 9b, 37, 51; arrangements for keyboard by Byrd and Farnaby in *The Fitzwilliam Virginal Book,* Vol. II, pp. 42, 472; consort arrangement in Morley, *Consort Lessons;* Gibbons, *Lord Salisbury's Pavane* (in *The Fitzwilliam Virginal Book,* Vol. II, p. 479, called simply "Pavane"), which uses the same opening.

VOICE

Flow, my tears, fall from your springs! Ex - iled for ev - er, let me mourn; Where
Down, vain lights, shine you no more! No nights are dark e-nough for those That

LUTE

night's black bird her sad in - fa-my sings, There let me live for -
in de - spair their lost for - tunes de - plore. Light doth but shame dis -

- lorn. Nev - er may my woes be re - liev - ed, Since pi -
- close. From the high-est spire of con - tent - ment My for-

dwell, Learn to con-temn light.   Hap - py, hap - py they

that in hell Feel not the world's de - - - spite.

1
Flow, my tears, fall from your springs!
Exiled for ever let me mourn;
Where night's black bird her sad infamy sings,
There let me live forlorn.

2
Down, vain lights, shine you no more!
No nights are dark enough for those
That in despair their lost fortunes deplore.
Light doth but shame disclose.

3
Never may my woes be relieved,
Since pity is fled;
And tears and sights and groans my weary days
Of all joys have deprived.

4
From the highest spire of contentment
My fortune is thrown;
And fear and grief and pain for my deserts
Are my hopes, since hope is gone.

5
Hark! you shadows that in darkness dwell,
Learn to contemn light.
Happy, happy they that in hell
Feel not the world's despite.

ANONYMOUS

To Anacreon in Heaven (ca. 1770).
Words by Ralph Tomlinson.

This facsimile shows an early edition (late 1770s) of a song which was destined far to exceed its original fame. This is, of course, the tune of the National Anthem, *The Star-Spangled Banner*. But it began as the theme song of the Anacreontic Society of London, a club which met once a fortnight at the Crown and Anchor Tavern in the Strand. Its members were gentlemen from all professions—and none—who enjoyed singing. The evening would begin at eight p.m. with a two-hour concert, after which, to quote a contemporary account, "the company adjourns to a spacious adjacent apartment, partakes of a cold collation, and then returns to the concert-room, where the remainder of the evening is totally devoted to wit, harmony, and the God of wine." No doubt the songs grew more ribald as the evening progressed.

23.

To Anacreon in Heaven, which always opened these proceedings, became so well known that it was soon published in Ireland (from where this version comes) and in the United States, as "The Anacreontic Song." By 1814, when Francis Scott Key wrote *The Star-Spangled Banner*, the tune was an obvious choice. Similar adaptations of popular tunes to new purposes have occurred throughout musical history, from Luther's re-wording of *Innsbruck, ich muss dich lassen* to the numerous modern college songs sung to *Far Above Cayuga's Waters*.

The tune has a notoriously wide range, which becomes more comprehensible in its original context: the first half has the range d–f♯', suitable for a "second tenor," and the second half is in the high tenor range f♯–a'. In the first verse, at least, it would suit the words to divide the two halves between two singers, so that one gives the narration and the other impersonates the cheerful Greek poet. It is interesting to see the other changes which the tune has undergone, notably the sharpening of the first G in order to give more force to the cadence.

Recordings: many, with Key's words.

Compare: 26, 29, for other "national" songs; **12, 34,** for roughly contemporary pieces; *God Save the Queen* ("America"); the *Marseillaise;* glees and catches of Purcell and others; eighteenth century hymns.

The ANACREONTIC Song

Sung by Mr. Incledon with great Applause.

DUBLIN. Published by E. RHAMES, at her MUSICAL CIRCULATING LIBRARY, Nº 16, Exchange Street

VIVACE To ANACREON in Heav'n, where he sat in full Glee, a few Sons of Harmony sent a Petition, that

he their inspirer and Patron wou'd be; when this Answer arriv'd from the Jolly old GRECIAN, Voice

Fiddle and Flute, no longer be mute, I'll lend you my Name, and inspire you to boot: and be—

—sides I'll instruct you, like me, to intwine the MYRTLE of VENUS with BACCHUS'S VINE.

2

The news through OLYMPUS immediately flew,
When OLD THUNDER pretended to give himself airs:
If these Mortals are suffer'd their scheme to pursue,
The Devil a GODDESS will stay above stairs.
Hark! already they cry
In transports of joy,
Away to the Sons of ANACREON we'll fly,
And there, with good fellows, we'll learn to intwine
The MYRTLE of VENUS with BACCHUS'S VINE.

3

The YELLOW HAIR'D GOD and his NINE fusty MAIDS
From HELICON's Banks will incontinent flee;
IDALIA will boast but of tenantless Shades,
And the BIFORKED HILL a mere Desert will be.
My Thunder, no fear on't,
Shall soon do its errand,
And soundly I'll swinge the Ringleaders I warrant:
I'll trim the young Dogs, for thus daring to twine
The MYRTLE of VENUS with BACCHUS'S VINE.

Ye Sons of ANACREON, then, join hand in hand,
Preserve Unanimity, Friendship and Love;
'Tis yours to support what's so happily plann'd
You've the Sanction of GODS, and the FIAT of JOVE.

4

APOLLO rose up, and said, Prythee ne'er quarrel
Good KING of the GODS, with my Vot'ries below;
Your Thunder is useless — then shewing his Laurel
Cried, Sic evitabile Fulmen, you know.
Then over each head
My Laurels I'll spread,
So my Sons from your Crackers no mischief shall dread,
Whilst snug in their Club-room, they jovially twine
The MYRTLE of VENUS with BACCHUS'S VINE.

5

Next MOMUS got up, with his risible Phiz,
And swore with APOLLO he'd chearfully join.
The full tide of harmony still shall be his,
But the SONG, and the CATCH, and the LAUGH shall be mine.
Then JOVE be not jealous
Of these honest fellows.
Cried JOVE, We relent, since the truth you now tell us:
And swear by OLD STYX that they long shall intwine
The MYRTLE of VENUS with BACCHUS'S VINE.

6

While thus we agree, — Our Toast let it be
May our Club flourish, happy, united and free!
And long may the SONS of ANACREON intwine
The MYRTLE of VENUS with BACCHUS'S VINE.

FOR THE GUITAR.

FRANZ SCHUBERT

(January 31, 1797–November 19, 1828)

Du bist die Ruh', Op. 59, No. 3 (published 1826).
Words by Friedrich Rückert.

24.

Although the shortest-lived (and probably the shortest) of all great composers, Schubert produced an amount of music which is well-nigh incredible. His fame, negligible in his lifetime, increased after his death and has never suffered eclipse, perhaps because there is nothing that anyone can possbily dislike either about the man or his music. In its purity and beauty it seems to be a direct gift from God.

In his six hundred or so *Lieder,** Schubert avoided the (to us) excessive length of some of his instrumental works, and created many of the greatest songs of all time, such as *Erlkönig, Gretchen am Spinnrad,* and *Heidenröslein. Du bist die Ruh'* embodies a mood peculiar to Schubert and found frequently in his instrumental slow movements, in which there seems to be a profound stillness behind the music. The harmonies at such times are of the simplest kind, although Schubert knew as well as anyone how to twist tonality* in ingenious ways (see the development section of **56**).

There is some debate about whether the voice's note in bar 70 should be f♭ or d♭. The original edition had f♭; the early editors assumed that it was a misprint for d♭, as appeared in bar 56, but later ones restored the f♭ for the expressive effect. The editors of the official Critical Edition believe that d♭ is correct because of the unchanging accompaniment. If the authorities disagree to this extent, we can surely make our own decision.

Recordings: Ang. S-36341 *(Schubert Songs: "Trout" and Other Songs,* Fischer-Dieskau); and many others.

Compare: 13, 25, 27, 28, 40, 56; Schubert's other songs; is there any generic difference between the single ones and those in cycles?

mein Aug' und _ Herz. _

Kehr' ein bei mir, und schlie _ sse du   still hin _ ter

dir die Pfor _ ten zu.   Treib' an _ dern Schmerz _ aus die _ ser _

Brust!   Voll sei dies Herz _ von dei _ ner _ Lust, _ von dei _ ner _

Lust. _

ROBERT SCHUMANN

(June 8, 1810–July 29, 1856)

Five songs from *Frauenliebe und Leben* ("Woman's Love and Life"), Op. 42 (1840). Words by Adalbert von Chamisso.

25.

Schumann's fame rests principally on his short piano pieces, his songs, and a few symphonic works. They occupied him approximately in that order. His piano works date from his ten-year friendship and courtship of Clara Wieck, the first woman to be a wholly successful concert pianist; his songs celebrate their eventual marriage in 1840, during which year he wrote no fewer than 140. But much of his later activity was directed into operas and oratorios* which are now forgotten. His last years were tragic, as he was increasingly troubled by mental disorders, possibly originating from a syphilitic infection in early life.

These songs, dating from the happiest time of his life, illustrate the flow of beautiful melody with which all the early Romantics were gifted, and the concentration on small forms which was in a way a reaction against Beethoven's expansion of symphonic architecture. But Beethoven had also written the first Romantic song-cycle,* *An die ferne Geliebte* ("To the distant beloved"), and it was this, even more than his symphonies and sonatas, that influenced his immediate successors.

Schumann's songs differ from Schubert's in the more important role given to the piano (e.g. the postludes* to all of these songs) and in their subjectivity. The choice of poems and the strongly emotional way in which they are set show that Schumann wore his heart on his sleeve. The forms are simple, but allow of delightful subtleties such as the last return of the theme in the "wrong" key in **25c**. Example **25e** is a rare example of recitative used in a Lied.

Recordings: RCA LSC-3169 (*Leontyne Price Sings Robert Schumann*); Oiseau S-293 (*Schumann: Frauenliebe und Leben, Op. 42/Hugo Wolf: Songs*, Watts, Parsons, piano).

Compare: 24, 26, 27, 40; Schumann, *Dichterliebe* (for the man's side of the story); piano works, especially *Carnaval; Spring Symphony;* Song-cycles: Beethoven, *An die ferne Geliebte;* Schubert, *Die Schöne Müllerin, Winterreise;* Berlioz, *Nuits d'été.*

a.

„Seit ich ihn gesehen."
"Since mine eyes have seen him."
(Chamisso.)

Original key B flat

Sonst ist licht- und farb-los al - les
But for him   no   ray of light would

um mich her,   nach der Schwestern Spiele nicht be - gehr' ich mehr, möchte
mark my way,   With my sis - ters gai-ly   I   no more can play, In my

lie - ber wei - nen still im   Käm - mer - lein,__ seit ich
lone - ly cham - ber   I would   weep __ and   dream. Since mine

ihn __ ge-se-hen,   glaub' ich blind zu sein.
eyes __ have seen him,   as if blind I   seem.

b.

„Er, der Herrlichste von Allen."

"He, the best of all."

Original key E flat

(Chamisso.)

Innig, lebhaft.
Vivace, con affetto.

Er, der Herr-lich-ste von Al - len, wie so
He, the best of all, the no - blest, O, how

mil - de, wie __ so gut! Hol - de Lip - pen, kla - res
gen - - tle, O, __ how kind! Lips of sweet-ness, eyes of

Au - ge, hel - ler Sinn und fes - - ter Muth.
brightness, brave of heart and clear __ of mind!

So wie dort in blau - er Tie - fe hell und herr - - lich je - - ner
As from bound-less depths of a - zure bright and glo - - rious shines __ yon

Stern, al - so Er ____ an mei-nem Himmel hell und herr - lich, hehr, und
star, So shines he ____ from out my heav-en, bright and glo - rious, high _ and

fern!
far.

Wand - - le, wand-le dei - ne Bah - nen, nur be - trach - ten dei - - nen
On - - ward speed thy course ex - alt - ed; far be - low as I re -

Schein, nur in De - - muth ihn be - trach - ten,
main, On thy ra - - diance hum - - bly gaz - ing,

se - lig nur, und trau - - rig sein._____ Hö - re nicht mein stil - les
thrills my heart with joy   and   pain._____ Know   thou not, when for thy

Be - ten,   dei - nem Glü - cke nur __ ge - weiht,   darfst mich nie - dre Magd nicht
wel - fare   low in si - lent prayer I bow;   I for thee am all too

ken - nen, ho - her Stern der Herr - lich - keit,_____ ho - her Stern der Herr - lich-
low - ly, lof - ty star of glo - ry thou,_____ lof - ty star of glo - ry

keit.   Nur die Wür - dig - ste von Al - len   darf be - glü - cken dei - ne
thou! 'Tis a - lone the best, the wor - thiest   by thy choice should fa - vor'd

Wahl, _____ und ich will die Ho - he seg-nen vie-le tau - - -send-
be, _____ And a thou-sand times I'll bless her, who is thus___ be-lov'd by

mal; will mich freu - en dann und wei - nen, se - lig, se-lig bin ich
thee. Shedding tears, al-tho' re - joic - ing, hap - py, happy then my

dann, _____ soll-te mir das Herz auch bre-chen, brich, o Herz, was liegt ___ dar-
lot: _____ E'en tho' my poor heart be bro-ken, break, O heart, it mat - - ters

an?
not.

Er,   der Herr-lich-ste von Al - len,   wie so mil — de, wie___ so
He,   the best of all, the   no - blest,   O, how gen — tle, O, ___ how

gut!   Hol - de Lip - pen,   kla - res   Au - ge,   hel - ler
kind!   Lips of sweet - ness,   eyes of bright - ness,   brave of

Sinn und fes - ter Muth, ___   wie so mil - de, wie so gut.
heart and clear   of mind, ___   O, how gen - tle! O,   how kind!

C. „Ich kann's nicht fassen, nicht glauben."

"I can not, dare not believe it."

Original key C minor

(Chamisso.)

d.

Der Ring.

The Ring.

(Chamisso.)

Original key E flat

Innig.
Con molto affetto.

Du Ring an mei-nem Fin-ger, mein gol-de-nes Rin-ge-
Thou ring up-on my fin-ger, My beau-ti-ful ring of

lein,   ich__ drü-cke dich fromm an die Lip__-pen, dich
gold,   My__ lips on thee fer-vent-ly lin__-ger, And

fromm an die Lip-pen, an das Her__-ze mein. Ich hatt' ihn aus__-ge-
close the dear treasure to my heart I hold. My child-hood's dream had

träu__-met, der Kind-heit fried-lich schö-nen Traum, ich
van__-ish'd, A joy-ous dream__ se-rene and bright; A-

fand al-lein mich ver-lo-ren im ö-den, un-end-li-chen
tone I seem'd as if ban-ish'd To des-o-late re-gions of

Raum. Du___ Ring an mei___nem Fin___ger, da
night. Thou___ ring up-on my fin___ger, Hast___

hast du mich erst be-lehrt, hast mei___nem Blick er-
giv'n to glad thoughts a birth, For-bid-dest clouds to

schlos-sen des Le-bens un-end___li-chen, tie___fen Werth. Ich
lin-ger, Trans-form-est to rap-ture my life on earth, And

will ihm die-nen, ihm le___ben, ihm an___ge-hö-ren
I'll live for him and near___ him, Will al___ways his re-

„Nun hast du mir den ersten Schmerz gethan."
"Now for the first time thou hast giv'n me pain."

Original keys D minor, B flat (A. von Chamisso.)

English version by Dr. Th. Baker.

Op. 42, № 8.
Composed 1840.

Adagio.

Nun hast du mir den er-sten Schmerz ge-than, der a-ber
Now for the first time thou hast giv'n me pain, Ah, and so

traf. Du schläfst, du har-ter, un-barm-herz'-ger Mann, den To-des-
sore! Thou sleep-est, cru-el, un-com-pass-nate man, To wake no

schlaf. Es bli-cket die Ver-lass'-ne vor sich hin, die Welt ist
more. Be-fore me, all for-sa-ken where I bow, The world's a

leer, ist leer. Ge-lie-bet hab' ich und ge-lebt, ich bin nicht
void, a void; I lov'd and liv'd for thee a-lone, and now My

le - bend mehr. Ich zieh' mich in mein Inn'- res still zu-rück, der
life's de-stroy'd. I si-lent-ly with-draw with-in my breast, The

Schlei - er fällt, da hab' ich dich und mein ver-lor-nes Glück, du mei-ne
veil doth fall; There I have thee and ev-'ry joy I lost, O thou, mine

Welt!
All!

Adagio.

Tempo wie das erste Lied.
(Larghetto.) Tempo as in the first song.

STEPHEN FOSTER

(July 4, 1826–January 13, 1864)

My Old Kentucky Home, Good-night (1853).
Words by the composer.

This famous song is given here in its original version. Just as the sixteenth-century lute songs were often published with parts for additional voices (see commentary to **22**), so the nineteenth-century sentimental ballads often had a chorus for three or four voices in harmony, of which the one designated "Air" (here the second soprano) was the only indispensable one.

26.

Foster's genius, like that of many popular songwriters, is almost impossible to analyze. Any attempt to do so is hindered by the fact that we have known these tunes ever since we can remember, and thus cannot compare them impartially to similar but less successful ones. But one can say that he had the gift to be simple—something denied to many greater composers (but not to the greatest ones). In this sense, he is in no way inferior to the Schubert of *Heidenröslein* or the Schumann of *Du Ring auf meinem Finger* (**25d**). He could not possibly have written a good sonata, but fortunately he never bothered to try.

Notice the various ways in which the principal melody begins: BBG (Introduction), B/BBG ("The sun"), A/BBG ("The corn"), D/BBG ("By'n by"), GA/BBG ("We will sing"). Each has its own purpose and effect.

Recordings: many.   **Compare: 13, 16, 24, 25, 27, 29.**

merry, all happy and bright: By'n by Hard Times comes a

knocking at the door, Then my old Kentucky Home, good night!

CHORUS

Weep no more, my lady, oh! weep no more to-day! We will sing one song For the

Weep no more, my lady, oh! weep no more to-day! We will sing one song For the

old Kentucky Home, For the old Kentucky Home, far a_way.

old Kentucky Home, For the old Kentucky Home, far a_way.

2ᵈ V. They hunt no more for the possum and the coon On the meadow, the hill and the shore,   They

sing no more by the glimmer of the moon, On the bench by the old cabin door.   The

day goes by like a shadow o'er the heart, With sorrow where all was de_light: The

time has come when the darkies have to part, Then my old Kentucky Home, good-night!   Chorus.

3ᵈ V. The head must bow and the back will have to bend, Wherever the darkey may go: A

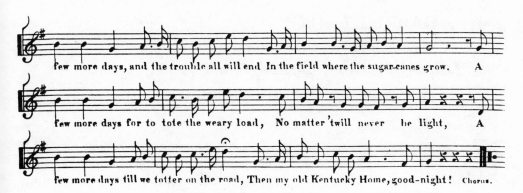

few more days, and the trouble all will end In the field where the sugar-canes grow.   A

few more days for to tote the weary load, No matter 'twill never   be light,   A

few more days till we totter on the road, Then my old Kentucky Home, good-night! Chorus.

GABRIEL FAURÉ

(May 12, 1845–November 4, 1924)

Les Berceaux, Op. 23, No. 1 (1882).
Words by Sully Prudhomme.

27. Fauré was one of those late Romantic composers who was content to cultivate a limited range of expression, generally keeping to the small forms. Just as one can contrast the "Classical" Brahms with the ultra-Romantic Wagner, so in French music the aristocratic Fauré represents the opposite pole from the headstrong Berlioz.

This song does not pretend to be much more profound than Foster's (**26**): it is a first-class specimen of the drawing-room romance beloved of amateur singers in the nineteenth century. As such, it is no less beautiful than Schumann's songs (**25**), and no more sentimental. The wide-ranging tune is a model of balanced construction: the first section describes a downward arc, the second an upward one, and the third encloses them both. But it was principally Fauré's harmony that was to influence the younger French composers, Debussy and Ravel. The harmonies of this song are interesting, particularly in the middle section: such harmonic twists had been in use for a century, but only now had they achieved the status of standard devices, to be inserted as casually as they are here.

Recordings: West. XWN 5502 (*The Complete Songs of Gabriel Fauré*, Monmart, Dutey, Mollet, Gouat, Janopoulo, piano)

Compare: 24, 25, 26, 28, 30a, 35, 36; Fauré's Verlaine songs; his major works, e.g. *Requiem* and the Piano Quintets; songs of Debussy and Ravel.

pleu _ rent, Et que les hom _ mes cu _ rieux

Ten _ tent les ho _ rizons qui leur _ _ _ rent! _

Et ce jour là _ les grands _ vaisseaux,

Fuy _ ant le port qui di _ mi _ nu _ e, Sen _ tent leur mas _

GUSTAV MAHLER

(July 7, 1860–May 18, 1911)

Um Mitternacht (1902).
Words by Friedrich Rückert.

28.

This is one of a set of five songs to words by Rückert which Mahler wrote between his Fifth and Sixth Symphonies. Although the symphony was the medium to which he devoted most of his time—or spare time, since he was one of the greatest conductors of his day—some of his most perfect creations are songs. The *Rückert* Songs can be performed with piano, but their accompaniment is really intended for orchestra and they gain immeasurably from its color and sustaining power. On the last pages of this song the piano part cries out for the sound of real brass, timpani, and harps.

Mahler was a deeply religious man. Born a Jew, he converted to Roman Catholicism in 1897 on becoming director of the Vienna Court Opera: a politically necessary move, but doubtless undertaken with sincerity. He remained much concerned with God and death, the major themes of all his works. Rückert's poetry must have echoed his own thoughts and feelings, especially in a poem such as this one with its description of spiritual anguish and resignation.

The texture* is quite different from that of most songs: there is little continuity, and no accompaniment figures such as Schubert, Schumann, and Fauré almost invariably use. In the orchestral version, instruments drift in and out, and the voice seems to be just one color among many others, the total effect scarcely exceeding chamber music* dimensions until the apotheosis.

Recordings: many.

Compare: 24, 25, 27, 30a, 31; the other four *Rückert* Songs; Mahler, *Kindertötenlieder* (also on texts by Rückert), Fourth Symphony, *Song of the Earth;* orchestral songs by Wagner (*Wesendonck Lieder*), and R. Strauss (*Four Last Songs*).

WILLIAM CHRISTOPHER HANDY
(November 16, 1873–March 28, 1958)
St. Louis Blues (1914).
Words by the composer.

29.

If Scott Joplin (see **16**) was the first to solidify the rhythmic conventions of black musicians, W. C. Handy, "The Father of the Blues," was the first to make available something of their characteristic melody and harmony. The well-known "blue notes" are minor thirds (and sometimes sixths and sevenths) used in otherwise major surroundings: thus in a piece such as this one, which is in G major, the blue note will be a B♭, used in place of a B♮ (e.g. the note on "sun"). Often the minor third will slide up to the major third. In such cases it is conventionally written differently, so that here it appears as an A♯ leading to a B♮ (see the first note of the song, and the chorus). This progression, in turn, suggests the most characteristic blues cadence:

IV   I

(See bars 10–11, 14–15, etc.)

The combination of ragtime rhythms with blues harmonies and melodies led directly to the development of jazz in the 'teens and twenties, a phenomenon that arose parallel to Schoenberg's Twelve-Tone System* (see **66**) and the Neo-classic movement of Prokofiev (see **62**), Stravinsky, and others. Of the three movements, it is jazz and its further developments that has obviously captured the attention and allegiance of the majority of people; and this is as one would expect, for jazz and pop are the inevitable music of the industrial masses of the twentieth century.

Recordings: many.

Compare: 16, 26, 29, 42; various musicians' treatment of the blues, especially Bessie Smith and Louis Armstrong.

Piano

I hate to see—— de ev'-nin' sun go down——
Been to de Gypsy to get ma for-tune tole——
You ought to see—— dat stovepipe brown of mine——

Hate to see—— de eve-nin' sun go down.——
To de Gypsy done got ma for-tune tole.——
Lak he owns de Di-mon Jos-eph line.——

Cause my ba-by,— he done lef dis town——
Cause I'm most wile— 'bout ma Jel - ly Roll——
He'd make a cross - eyed o' man go stone blind——

Feel - in' to-mor - row lak— Ah feel to - day——
Gyp - sy done tole— me, "don't— you wear no black"——
Black-er than mid - night, teeth— lak flags of truce——

Feel to-mor - row lak— Ah feel to - day——
Yes she done tole me "don't— you wear no black"——
Black - est man in — de whole St. Louis——

I'll pack my trunk— Make ma get a - way—— St. Lou - is
Go to St. Louis— You can win him back—— Help me to
Black-er de ber-ry— Sweet - er is the juice—— A-bout a

wo - man —— Wid her dia - mon' rings —— Pulls dat
Cai - ro —— make St. Louis by ma - self —— Git to
crap game —— he knows a pow'-ful lot —— But when

man roun' — by her a-pron strings —— 'Twant for
Cai - ro —— find ma ole friend Jeff, —— Gwine to
work-time comes he's on de dot —— Gwine to

pow-der —— an' for store bought hair —— De
pin ma self close to — his side —— If ah
ask him —— for a cold— ten spot —— What it

man I love— would not gone no where.—
flag his train— I sho' can ride.—
takes to git it— he's cer - t'n - ly got.—

CHARLES IVES

(October 20, 1874–May 19, 1954)

30.

a. *Evening* (1921).
   Words by John Milton.
b. *Charlie Rutlage* (1920–21).
   Words from a newspaper, 1891.

The two sides of Charles Ives, the sentimental Romantic and the aggressive Modernist, are sometimes hard to reconcile, and Ives himself would have laughed at any attempt to do so. Nevertheless, he is one of the hardest composers to understand: how did he choose his notes? Why did he write as he did? These and other questions often prevent one from enjoying the music itself.

But there is nothing problematic about these two songs, at least for our generation. *Evening* is a beautiful picture, with Impressionistic whole-tone chords* (bar 4) and those quiet, high notes in the piano part that Ives loved to touch gently with the left hand. *Charlie Rutlage* is a dramatic setting which does not shy away from illustrating the climax of the poem with appropriate noises: the singer shouts and the pianist hammers with fists. There is something poignant yet rather funny about the return to a normal, folksy mood at "his relations in Texas."

Both songs contain musical quotations—something which Ives used very frequently and which is becoming more and more popular among composers today (see **72a**). *Charlie Rutlage* quotes a real cowboy song in the piano part ("Whoopee . . "), and *Evening* quotes Lowell Mason's hymn tune *Bethany* (sung to the words "Nearer, my God, to thee") in bar 3 and again at the end. Otherwise, neither song is remarkable for its melody. Ives seems to achieve all he needs by means of harmony and rhythm. What one remembers, above all, is atmosphere.

Recording: None. 71209. (*Charles Ives: Songs/Toehr: Four Songs from the Japanese/Schurmann: Chuench'i*, Nixon, McCabe, piano)

Compare: 29, 31, 64; Ives, *General William Booth enters Heaven; Concord* Sonata; genuine cowboy songs.

Evening

Charlie Rutlage

brave,__While Charlie Rutlage makes the third to be sent__ to his grave, Caused _____

faster (half spoken)   *recite__following the piano*

by a cow-horse falling, While run-ning af-ter stock; 'Twas on the spring round up, A

faster

(octs. ad lib.)

(hold back)

place where death men mock, He went for-ward one morn-ing on a

(hold back here)   (Whoopee ti yi yo, git a-long lit-tle dogies,

cir-cle through the hills, He was gay and full of glee, and

Whoopee ti yi yo, etc.)

*In these measures, the notes are indicated only approximately; the time of course, is the main point.

BENJAMIN BRITTEN

(born November 22, 1913)

Nocturne, from *Serenade for Tenor Solo, Horn, and Strings,* Op. 31 (1943).
Words by Alfred, Lord Tennyson.

31.

Britten has achieved his position as the premier composer of England by writing music that is fresh, original, and yet comprehensible to lovers of "classical" music. He rarely abandons tonality, and never ceases to write beautiful melodies. Much of his music springs from concern for the oppressed (*Billy Budd, Voices for Today*), for children (*The Little Sweep, Children's Crusade*), or for peace (*War Requiem*). Of his more abstract music, several works are inspired by sleep and the night. This *Serenade* has a later companion piece, *Nocturne,* for tenor, strings, and several different obbligato* instruments; then there are *Night-Piece* for piano and *Nocturnal* for guitar. The *Serenade* is a cycle of six songs whose texts, all by different poets, deal with aspects of evening or nightfall, and incidentally display Britten's wide knowledge and excellent taste in literature. The conception of the work is most original: the use of the horn as obbligato instrument, the framing prologue and epilogue in which it plays only on the notes of its natural harmonic series,* and the unified variety of the songs are things that only Britten would have thought of.

This song is a wonderful evocation of evening. Its three verses are most ingeniously varied, with an abrupt shift to C major for the hushed, elfin horns of the middle verse, and an inspired raising of the vocal line in the last, where the bass joins in imitation. The unification of all the melodies through chains of thirds is exemplary.

Recordings: Dec. 710132 (Bressler, Froelich, Waldman, Musica Aeterna Orch.); Lon. 26161 (Pears, Tuckwell, Britten, London Symph. Orch.); Ang. S-36788 (Tear, Civil, Marriner, North. Sinf.)

Compare: 27, 30a, 33, 34 (obbligato instruments); the remainder of the *Serenade;* Britten, *Les Illuminations, Nocturne, Peter Grimes, The Turn of the Screw, War Requiem;* English song cycles: Vaughan Williams, *On Wenlock Edge;* Tippett, *Boyhood's End.*

BAROQUE OPERA

Servio Tullio by Agostino Steffani, as produced in Munich, 1685.
Note the exaggerated perspective and the stylized gestures.

Music and drama

4

If a song is complicated enough, an opera* is even more so: for here the dimension of drama is added to the complex of music, poetry, singer, and listener. The singer is no longer someone in evening dress on an empty stage, but a character in a story, arousing in us sympathies, antipathies, and a host of other reactions. And yet opera has been, from its inception, one of the most popular forms of entertainment. Without a laborious analysis of why this is so, I would say simply that opera takes one out of oneself. Not until the advent of movies (which have in a way superseded it) has there been anything so calculated to remove one to a fantasy land where one can witness incredible comedies and tragedies, and yet emerge unscathed from one's seat at the end of the performance. We love these vicarious experiences because they enrich our lives and remove, for a while, the heavy burden of our own personalities. "I lost myself in it," we say of an absorbing novel or play, thereby admitting that we are not always our own favorite company.

To enjoy an opera to the fullest, one should experience it as it was intended: complete, and in live performance. The noblest entertainment ever devised deserves more than a casual response, so I would ideally treat it as follows: I would buy as good a ticket as I could afford, long enough beforehand to get to know both plot and music, if I did not already know them. On the day of the opera I and my companion(s) would dress attractively and dine out before the performance, eating an excellent dinner but not a large or bibulous one, because that might make us fall asleep during the slower numbers. We would arrive in time to admire the opera house, its situation and decoration (assuming that it were somewhere pleasant like Paris or Lincoln Center). And then for three hours we would give ourselves into the hands of the composer, the librettist, the conductor, the singers, and the orchestra. Afterwards we might have a light supper by candlelight, and discuss the pleasures of what we had just seen. I describe this traditional opera-going ritual knowing full well that it will raise some supercilious smiles. But we have few enough rituals nowadays, and should be thankful for what we can get. Ritual heightens the emotional tone of what is happening, whether it be a religious, aesthetic, or political event, and to despise it is merely to betray a fear of living to the full.

Of course one need not, and many cannot, go to these lengths in order to enjoy opera. An evening with a recording, even of excerpts, and a score can be an immense pleasure. But one cannot stress too much the hedonistic and aristocratic aspects of opera. It has always been the favorite entertainment of leisured people, at least until modern times, and if many such people are fools and snobs, many others have been true connoisseurs and generous patrons. Actually, none of the operas represented in this chapter were written for court presentation. They are all "popular" to some degree, and no doubt that has contributed to their survival and continuing success. On the other hand, their characters are all larger than life; there are two kings (Ariadeno in **32** and Bertarido in **33**), a prince (Tamino in **34**), and a knight (Walther in **36**). Even the very human drama of *La Traviata* (**35**) takes place in high society. The characters in opera, as in Greek tragedy and much of Shakespeare, are royal or noble because they are not supposed to be individuals like you or me: they are archetypal figures, symbolizing the basic human relationships and actions that underlie our lives. They are, admittedly, oversimplified—Violetta and Tamino, Lear and Oedipus, are hardly credible as people—but this is to enable us to see in them more clearly the forces that govern our lives and make us the way we are.

If music can reinforce the impact of a poem, it can do even more to a drama. In a spoken play, we learn about the characters from what they say, and naturally that takes time and words. In an opera, a few bars of music alone can speak volumes. We know

something about Erisbe's character from her sprightly ritornello*
(see the beginning of **32**), and we feel Bertarido's tragic mood
(see **33**), before the singers even open their mouths. Imagine
what a stage director could do in the way of entrances during
these introductions.

Dwelling for a moment on the two extracts from Baroque
operas, it is worth comparing the scores themselves. They certainly *look* extremely different. This is because *Rodelinda* (**33**) is
taken from a scholarly edition, and *Ormindo* (**32**) from a performing edition. The distinction is due to the fact that much
written music before 1750 demands a contribution from the performers in the way of ornamentation, realization of the continuo,
and even choice of instruments. A scholarly edition should show
exactly what the composer wrote, and distinguish from this
whatever the editor has added. A performing edition provides
what is necessary to recreate a plausible performance. Look at
the different treatments of recitative. On p. 245, we see what
Handel gave his performers: for this piece a line for the singers,
and a line for the harpsichord, cello, and bass (or other continuo
instruments). The words are the original Italian ones, without
translation. Compare a recitative of *Ormindo* (rehearsal
Nos. 38–39): this editor, working from a similar source, has amplified it with notes such as the harpsichordist *might* have added
on the spur of the moment. Elsewhere he has included the violin
parts in the keyboard arrangement so that one cannot distinguish
them; he has added vocal ornaments, and provided English and
German translations.

The disadvantage of a scholarly edition is that most people
cannot put it up on the piano and read through it with enjoyment, as they can with the score of *Ormindo*. The disadvantage
of a performing edition is that the scholar often cannot tell what
the composer originally wrote. There has never been a satisfactory compromise between the two, but these two editions certainly represent extremes in both directions. The formidable appearance of the Handel scores must have deterred people from
examining them, and may have contributed to the eclipse of his
operatic music. Yet musicologists* interested in Baroque opera
must regret that the only accessible score of Cavalli's should be
so full of editorial additions, subtractions, transpositions,* and
the like, with nothing to tell them where Cavalli stops and

Raymond Leppard, the editor, takes over. Mr. Leppard would reply that only thanks to his machinations has Cavalli been revived at all; and his performances and recordings have certainly given far more pleasure than anyone's scholarship.

There are several things about Baroque opera that we cannot revive at all, but they are worth bearing in mind. Why does ex-King Bertarido sing in a woman's voice? Is it part of his disguise? No: if one were to leaf through Handel's operas, one would find dozens of alto and even soprano heroes, competing with their wives and daughters in vocal altitude. The favorite voice of the period was, in fact, the male castrato. Many promising choirboys succumbed to irrevocable loss in the hope (or their parents' hope) of a brilliant career, such as that of the fabulous Farinelli who virtually ruled Spain during the incapacity of his patron, King Philip V. To thicken the plot, it was common for male sopranos and altos to sing the women's roles as well; in Rome it was, in fact, compulsory, since no woman was allowed on the stage. And then, to make it worse, the operas teem with disguises (usually trans-sexual) and mistaken identities. It is certainly a strange affair. But then the music is (or was) a minor consideration. The principal singers were the main attraction, and the stage designers earned far more than most composers. This is understandable when one considers that an opera may have contained half a dozen sets, each as elaborate as the one shown at the head of this chapter, and some of them may have had moving parts (known as "machines") such as ships, fountains, and clouds (from which the gods descended at convenient times—hence the phrase "Deus ex machina"). Present-day opera budgets forbid such visual delights, and in any case Cecil B. de Mille has raised our standards of the spectacular above the level of cardboard clouds and creaking machinery.

The extracts from Mozart, Wagner, and Verdi represent the greatest of all operatic composers. They have this in common: in each extract the story actually requires a song. Alfredo (**35**) has had a few drinks and needs no prompting to sing of the consequences. We have probably heard the tune before, and the rest of the company knows it well enough to join in—in harmony, even. The scene that follows, on the other hand, is ordinary conversation rendered in song. Walther (**36**) is carried away by a different intoxication: his love for Eva and the excitement of a moment which he (and we) have been awaiting throughout the opera. He enters the Mastersingers' competition with a song of an entirely new and unorthodox kind, and despite the hostility and jealousy of a reactionary rival, he is acclaimed by all the folk and carries off the prize. It is no secret that Wagner identified this story with his own career. Verdi and Mozart had no such axes to grind, since they did not think of themselves as revolutionaries. Their business was to make a living by giving pleasure; and if *The Magic Flute* (**34**) is instructive as well as entertaining, pieces such as this duet and Tamino's song of thanksgiving are exquisitely enjoyable on any level.

The dramatic aspect of opera is strongest in the scenes by Handel and Mozart. The former shows the deposed king lurking by his own tombstone, and enduring the sight of his wife visiting it, she believing him to be dead. What a predicament! But their suppressed emotions break out into music that proves Shelley's dictum: "Our sweetest songs are those that tell of saddest thought." Mozart's *finale* is dramatic in a more direct way: things are happening fast. The princely hero, Tamino, is seen approaching the stronghold of Sarastro, whom he thinks has wickedly kidnapped his sweetheart Pamina. In fact, Sarastro has done her a good turn in removing her from the influence of her mother, the Queen of the Night. We hear Tamino's incomprehension at the words of the inscrutable priest, and his joy as he hears that Pamina is not only alive, but perhaps close by in the care of the bird-man Papageno. Mozart uses the Magic Flute and Papageno's echoing panpipes* as delightful musical "props."

From *Ormindo,* I offer an early and a late scene in order to show the deepening of Erisbe's character. At the beginning, her dalliance with the young princes Ormindo and Amida compensates for the boredom of her marriage to the aged King Ariadeno. But by the end she is much more serious: a passing fancy has turned into a love stronger than death. I should add that this touching scene is not the end: Ariadeno is appalled when he sees the two "corpses" whose execution he has ordered, and shares in the general relief when the deadly poison turns out to have been merely a sleeping draught. He is so happy that he resigns both throne and wife to the lucky Ormindo, and goes into gentlemanly retirement such as befits aging monarchs.

The scene of Verdi's is a beginning; that of Wagner's is an end. One shows a paradise of conviviality and the first stirrings of love, marred only by the serpent of Violetta's illness which is to bring the opera to such a heartbreaking conclusion. The other shows the culmination of Walther's (and Wagner's) mastery in one of the most sublime of all melodies. Such "highlights" spoil us and may make us impatient during the less exciting parts, which can be tedious, especially in Wagner. But if we were eighteenth-century Italians, we would not be worried by them: there would be conversation, chess, spaghetti, and who knows, perhaps even flirtation in our private box. We would attend only to what pleased us.

Suggestions for further reading Donald J. Grout, *A Short History of Opera* (2nd ed., New York and London, 1965) is long and comprehensive; Joseph Kerman, *Opera as Drama* (New York, 1956), brief but brilliant. On Cavalli and his time, see Simon Towneley Worsthorne, *Venetian Opera in the Seventeenth Century* (Oxford, 1954). The bibliography of the other composers is immense (see Grout, above, for details). In this context, see Winton Dean, *Handel and the Opera Seria* (Berkeley, 1969) and Paul Henry Lang, *George Frideric Handel* (New York, 1966); Edward J. Dent, *Mozart's Operas* (2nd ed., London, 1960) and Jacques Chailley, *The Magic Flute, Masonic Opera* (New York, 1971); Ernest Newman, *Life of Richard Wagner* (New York, 1933–46) and, for the light it sheds on Wagner in general, Robert Donington, *Wagner's Ring and Its Symbols* (New York, 1969). Alexandre Dumas *fils'* novel, *La Dame aux Camélias* ("The Woman of the Camelias"), the basis for *La Traviata,* is worth reading; the best introduction to the operas is Julian Budden, *The Operas of Verdi: From Oberto to Rigoletto* (New York, 1973), which will hopefully be continued to include the later works.

FRANCESCO CAVALLI

(February 14, 1602–January 14, 1676)

Excerpts from Acts I and II of *L'Ormindo* (1644). Words by Giovanni Faustini.

32.

Cavalli was one of the most important operatic composers of the generation that followed Monteverdi. He was trained under the older master and eventually succeeded to the same post at St. Mark's in Venice. Being church musicians, however, did not prevent him and Monteverdi from composing primarily secular music: *Ormindo* is one of over forty operas which Cavalli wrote for the Venetian stage.

The opera house, in the seventeenth and early eighteenth centuries, was more than just a theater: it was a social center for people of all classes, the humbler ones in the pit and the higher orders in tiers of boxes which, if small, were comfortably furnished with armchairs and even fireplaces. Even those who had no taste for music or theater found it convenient to lease a box for the social advantages it offered, and night after night during the long Carnival season (December 26 to Shrove Tuesday) people would go to hear their favorite singers, or merely to meet their friends and business associates. Much high politicking, one suspects, went on in the privacy of these tiny rooms.

This opera shows how Cavalli did his best to keep the attention of his audience on the stage. There are frequent changes of mood and speed, as the musical texture alternates between aria and recitative.* The first extract has five such changes before the longer final section (rehearsal No. 39 to end). But Cavalli cleverly maintains continuity by musical cross-references, such as the return of the initial ritornello at 40, after which it infects the vocal part as well as the accompaniment. Even the recitatives have motives in common: the pattern of a rising triad and one note occurs in the passages immediately after rehearsal Nos. 37 (e' g' b' c''), 38 (f' a' c♯'' d''), and 39 (f' a' c'' d'').

The story is almost self-explanatory: Erisbe is the young "Queen of Morocco and Fez," and Mirinda is her waiting-woman, the traditional recipient of regal confidences. The "delightful princes" Ormindo and Amida are enjoying a flirtation with the queen. But in the course of the opera it becomes a more serious affair, at least for Ormindo; and we meet him again after he has been captured while trying to elope with Erisbe. (Osmano is the commander of the king's forces.) This long recitative is in the Monteverdi tradition, full of expressive harmonies. The beautiful final duet is written in a favorite form for passionate laments, the ground bass.*

Recordings: Argo ZNF–8/10 (Cavalli: *L'Or-mindo,* Carcisanz, Van Bork, Howells, Ber-bié, Allister, Wakefield, Cuénod, London Phil., Leppard, cond.)

Compare: 33, 37; Cavalli, *La Calisto;* Monte-verdi, *L'Incoronazione di Poppea* (1642); Cesti, *L'Orontea.*

Mirinda:
vec-chio ag-ghiac-cia-to, ag-ghiac-cia-to ed___ im-po-ten-te.___
old man so de-cre-pit, so de-cre-pit and___ cold as win-ter.___
Grei-se auf-zu-op-fern, der er-kal-tet und___ im-po-tent ist.___

38

ERISBE / Erisbe:
Ti giu-ro, io ge-le-re-i, fi-da Mi-rin-da, a la-to del con-sor-te ge-
Mi-rin-da, you can i-ma-gine how I would freeze by the side___ of my frost-bit-ten
Ich schwör dir, ich müsst' er-frie-ren, treu-e Mi-rin-da, zur Sei-te mei-nes Gat-ten er-

Erisbe:
-la-to se dop-pia-men-te A-mo-re, non m'ac-cen-des-se il co-re.___
hus-band, if lit-tle Cu-pid had not in-flamed my heart twice___ o-ver.___
-star-ren, wenn nicht zwei-fa-che Lie-be mit ih-rer Glut mich er-wärm-te.

Erisbe:
O prin-ci-pi, prin-ci-pi di-let-ti e-gual-men-te voi sie-te d'E-ris-be in-na-mo-
Oh, prin-ces twain! Oh, de-lightful prin-ces! For your lov-ing E-ris-be you both in e-qual
O Jüng-lin-ge, heiss-ge-lieb-te Prin-zen! Der ver-lieb-ten E-ris-be be-deu-tet ihr in

41

ERISBE

Se mi cin-ge, se mi strin-ge dop-pio lac - - - cio e dop-pio_
*If my ea - ger heart is tied in dou - ble knot _____ and dou - ble_*
Wenn mich zwei-fach bin-det, dop-pelt schnürt der Fes - - - seln fe - ster.

mf

Erisbe

no - do, il con-ten-to dop-pio sen-to, dop-pia gio - - ia io_
fet - ter; I en - joy a dou-ble plea-sure, what on earth _____ could.
Kno - ten, fühl ich dop-pelt Wohl-be-ha-gen, wird mir zwei - - fa-che_

Erisbe

pro - - vo e go - - do,   il con-ten-to dop-pio
please _____ me bet - - ter?   I en - joy a dou-ble
Lust _____ ge-bo - - ten,   fühl ich dop-pelt Wohl-be -

Erisbe

sen-to; il con-ten-to dop-pio sen-to, dop-pio gio — — ia io pro — —
plea-sure, I en-joy a dou-ble plea-sure, what on earth _____ could please _____
-ha-gen, fühl ich dop-pelt Wohl-be — ha-gen, wird mir zwei — — — fa-che Lust ____ (ja_

42 **Ritornello**

Erisbe

— — — — — vo e go — do. _____
me bet — ter? _____
zwei — — fa-che_ Lust) _____ ge-bo — ten.

f leggiero

Co - no - sco, co - no - sco gl' ap - pa - ra - ti, tu, tu m'ar -
I know, yes, I know____ what this means. Friend, it is
Ich ah - ne, ich ah - ne, was du vor - hast. Du bringst mein

-re - chi la mor - te e pro - fe - rir non l'o - si?
death that you bring me and have no heart to tell me.
To - - des - ur - teil und wagst nicht, mir's zu ver - - kün - den.

OSMANO

A te que-sta che mi ri ve - le - no-sa be-van-da ed
The King charged me to serve you with this mur-der-ous po - tion, which
Dies Gift schickt dir der Kö - nig. Erst sollst du da-von trin-ken, der

ORMINDO

Ch'io mo-rir deg-gia è
That I must die___ is
Mein Le - ben ist ver-wirkt, ge -

Osmano

al - la bel-la E-ris-be il Re - ge man - da.
he has sent for you and the fair E - ris - be.
Rest ist für E - ris - be. So be - fiehlt er.

Ormindo

giu-sto, con vi-o-len-to sfor-zo a l'o - nor d'A - ri-a - de-no in-si-die
jus-tice; I laid my snares with cun-ning and im - pa - tience for A - ri-a - de-no's
-recht ist's. In wil-dem Un - ge-stüm hab' ich die Eh - re des Kö-nigs mit Füs-sen ge-

Ormindo

te - si, con le ra-pi - ne mie trop-po, trop-po l'of-fe - si.
ho-nour; and with the heart I stole, too much, too much I wronged him;
-tre-ten; ich kann für mein Ver - gehn kein Er - bar - men er-war - - ten.

Erisbe

Son que-ste, son que-ste le sue fa-ci ch'ar - der, ch'ar - der do-ve-a-no in -
Are these, are these in-deed her tor-ches, shin - ing, shin - ing and glit-ter-ing a -
Sind die-se, sind die - se ih-re Fak-keln, die___ mit strah - len-dem Glan-ze un-ser

p   *poco cresc.*   *p*

Erisbe

- tor - no, in - tor - no a no-stri let - ti, ch'ar - der do - ve-a-no, per in -fiam-
-round us, a - round us for our wed-ding, shin - ing and glit-ter-ing to light our
E - he-bett hell um-leuch-ten soll-ten, lo - dernd uns-re See-len, uns-re glühn-den

p   *poco cresc.*

62

Erisbe

-.mar - ci mag-gior-men-te i pet - ti? Oh, oh di su - per-bo e di-spie-
way o - ver the clouds we are tread-ing? Oh! Oh, that a god, in his most un-
Her - zen um - so - mehr zu ent-flam-men? Ach! Du hast ver - ra - ten uns, mit-leid-

mf

Erisbe

- ta - to nu - me, tra - di - tri - ce, tra - di - tri - ce na - tu - ra, em -
-feel - ing blind-ness, should be - tray us, should be - tray us both with such en -
- lo - se Gott-heit. Vol - ler Tük - ken ist dein lok - ken-des Leuch-ten, grau -

mf > *p*

✳ *Optional cut to fig.* **62**.

GEORGE FRIDERIC HANDEL

(February 23, 1685–April 14, 1759)

Excerpt from Act I of *Rodelinda* (1724–5).
Words by Antonio Salvi, adapted by Nicola Haym.

33.

During the eighty years that elapsed since the preceding opera, the form of opera became solidified into something as rigid as the sonata form of the Classic period, yet as capable of individual variation. The basic plan of an *opera seria** is an alternation of recitatives with arias: things happen in the recitatives, and in the arias the characters comment upon how they are affected thereby. Some variety is provided by occasional duets, trios, choruses, and instrumental numbers, but the solo aria in ABA (*da capo**) form is the heart of the opera. There may be as many as sixty such arias in a single work.

In this extract we can see most of the forms found in Baroque operas:

Sinfonia (instrumental prelude or interlude)

Recitativo accompagnato or **stromentato** (the voice accompanied by strings): "Pompe vane di morte!"

Aria in **da capo** form: "Dove sei"

Recitativo secco (the voice accompanied by the continuo instruments alone) "Ma giuage Unulfo"

Aria in da capo form with flute obbligato (the second "A" section slightly different from the first, hence written out in full): "Ombre, piante"

Recitativo accompagnato: "Ombra del mio bel sol"

This gives a brief taste of the vast amount of Italian opera Handel wrote between 1711 and 1737, when, tired out by business and financial wrangles, he turned to the composition of English oratorios. The popularity of his later works such as *Messiah* has given the public an unbalanced view of his art. But the difficulties of reviving Baroque opera in enjoyable form are such that his reputation as an operatic composer must rest mainly on extracts and recordings.

Recording: 3-West. 8205 (Handel: *Rodelinda*, Stich-Randall, Forrester, Young, Isepp, Vienna Radio Orch., Priestman, cond.)

Compare: 32, 34, 38, 53, 54, 55; the remainder of the opera; Handel; *Xerxes, Samson;* the operas of Alessandro Scarlatti.

-per_bo   il ge_nio al _ tie_ro   voi di _te,   ch'io son mor_to,   mà ri_sponde   il mio   duol,   che non è

ve_ro.   „Ber_ta   ri _ do fu Rè;   da Gri_mo_al_do vin_to fug _ gì;   prez_zo de_gli Un_ni

(*Legge l'iscrizione.*)

gia_ce.   Ab_bia l'al_ma ri _ po_so,   e'l ce_ner   pa_ce."   Pa_ce   al ce_ner mi _ o? A_stri ti _

_ran_ni!   dun_que fin ch'a_vrò   vi _ ta   guer_ra a_vrò con gli sten_ti,   e con gli af_fanni. Do_ve

SCENA VII.

RODELINDA, che tiene per mano FLAVIO, e detti indisparte.

WOLFGANG AMADEUS MOZART

(January 27, 1756–December 5, 1791)

Excerpt from Act I of Die Zauberflöte (1791). Words by Emanuel Schikaneder.

34.

In *Die Zauberflöte* (*The Magic Flute*) Mozart raised the native German *Singspiel* ("sung play") to the heights generally reserved for Italian opera. *Singspiele* were somewhat similar to present-day musicals: much spoken dialogue, humor, and sentiment, interspersed with songs and other musical numbers. *The Magic Flute* has all of this, but it also contains some of Mozart's most beautiful music, and carries a profound meaning behind its sometimes ludicrous, sometimes mysterious story.

The tale, written by a theater director, comic actor, and fellow Freemason of Mozart's, tells of the search of Prince Tamino for Princess Pamina (Act I), and of the trials they must undergo before they are united (Act II). Tamino is accompanied by the bird-man Papageno, who is sometimes a help but more often a responsibility, and at first helped, but later threatened, by the Queen of the Night (Pamina's mother) and her servants. As No. 7 begins, Tamino has been separated from Papageno, who has managed to find Pamina. This love duet, the only one in the opera, is the more touching for being sung by two people who are *not* in love with one another, but who comfort each other's loneliness as they long for their respective partners.

The form is simple: A A' (bar 18) coda (bar 33). The second verse is beautifully ornamented, and the coda is a prime example of how cleverly Mozart can delay a final cadence: notice the ways in which he avoids it at the potential stopping points of bars 40, 44, and 46.

No. 8, of which only a part is given here, contains a remarkable and dramatic accompanied recitative. Tamino is led to the stronghold of Sarastro, whom he at this stage believes to be an evil wizard who has kidnapped Pamina. But we can tell from the demeanor of Sarastro's priest that we are not dealing with a villain, and Tamino's aria (*Andante*) shows that he, too, is feeling the serenity and holiness of the place. In fact, Pamina has been rescued from her mother's evil influence, so that she and Tamino may undergo a quasi-masonic initiation and be united on a higher level at the end of the opera.

Like most fairy stories, *The Magic Flute* can be enjoyed as a delightful tale, or interpreted as an esoteric allegory. If it is understood in the light of Freemasonry, which at this time was a serious, religious, and even an occult affair, it emerges as the most spiritual of all Mozart's works. Yet it is seldom heavy: there is a popular, folklike atmosphere about it that explains why it was an immediate and tremendous success: by 1800 it had played in eighty-five towns, and by 1833 it had even reached New York.

Recordings: many. 3-Lon. 1397 (Mozart: *Die Zauberflöte,* Lorengar, Deutekom, Prey, Fischer-Dieskau, Vienna Phil., Solti, cond.) has delightful spoken dialogue (in German).

Compare: 32, 33, 35, 36, 37, 40, 58; the remainder of the opera: Mozart's other Singspiel, *Die Entführung aus dem Serail;* his other operas; Beethoven, *Fidelio* and Weber, *Der Freischütz* (the next great German opera).

No. 7. Duet

Weib, und Weib und Mann rei - chen an die Gott - heit an,

Weib, und Weib und Mann rei - chen an die Gott - heit an,

an die Gottheit an, _____ an die Gottheit an. *(Exit.)*

an die Gottheit an, an die Gottheit an. *(Exit.)*

(Change of scene. A grove, in the middle of which stand three temples.)

No. 8. Finale

Larghetto

(The Three Spirits lead Tamino in.)

1st & 2nd Spirits

Zum Zie - le führt dich die - se Bahn, doch

3rd Spirit

Zum Zie - le führt dich die - se Bahn, doch

Tamino
Ja, ich will gehn, froh und frei, nie eu-ren Tempel sehn.

Priest
Erklär dich nä-her mir, dich

Tamino
täuschet ein Be-trug. Sa-ra-stro wohnet hier? das ist mir schon genug.

Priest
Wenn du dein Leben liebst, so re-de: bleibe da! Sa-rastro hassest du?

Tamino
Ich haß ihn ewig,

Priest
ja! So gib mir dei-ne Gründe an.

Tamino
Er ist ein Unmensch, ein Ty-rann!

Priest
Ist das, was

Tamino
du gesagt, er-wie-sen? Durch ein unglücklich Weib bewiesen, das Gram und Jammer nie-der-

GIUSEPPE VERDI

(October 10, 1813–January 27, 1901)

Excerpt from Act I of *La Traviata* (1853).
Words by Francesco Maria Piave.

At the ultimate operatic party, we discover how Verdi can build a whole movement out of one fine tune, and at the same time introduce a hint of the personal relations which are just about to develop. One delightful feature of opera is the way in which it can transform the "rhubarb, rhubarb" of a stage crowd into a musical accompaniment (see the end of No. 3). Another is the fascinating borderline between operatic music and "real" music, such as that of the band in No. 4 whose cheerful sounds contrast so ironically with Violetta's seizure. This waltz provides an adequate background to the lovers' first conversation, but when Alfredo becomes serious (bar 181), "ideal" music has to take over from the "real."

35.

Think how banal this scene would be in a spoken drama, especially the end of it, where the two voices sing together:

> *Violetta:* You must forget me.
> *Alfredo:* Violetta, I can't!
> *Violetta:* You will.
> *Alfredo:* I won't.
> *Enter Gaston.*

In music, things are not so cut-and-dried. The sentiments may be discordant, but their music harmonizes so perfectly that we can sense the unconscious tie that is already binding the two characters. As it is, they fall in love, live together, quarrel, and are reunited at Violetta's deathbed.

Compared to this drama, the other operas represented here are all fairy tales, devoid of real suffering and real passion. What *La Traviata* lacks, however, is the moral seriousness and the quasi-religious undertone of Wagner's operas. Only Mozart, it seems, could combine the best of both Italian and German characteristics; after him, the two streams were never to meet again.

Recordings: many.

Compare: 32, 33, 34, 36, 40; the remainder of the opera; Verdi, *Il Trovatore, Aida, Otello;* Puccini, *La Bohème,* which is in many respects modelled on this opera.

Nº 3. "Libiamo ne' lieti calici,,.

Drinking-song.

prò__ di - vi - -de - re il tem-po mio gio - con - do; tut -
love__ and friend - ship You all are so__ free - ly__ giv - ing. Life

_to è fol - li - à, fol - li - a nel mon - - -do ciò che non è pia -
__holds no meaning and is not worth liv - - -ing If not__for pleas-ure a -

cer. Go - diam, fu - ga - ce e__ ra - pi - do è il gau - dio del - l'a -
lone. So come, en - joy your__ hap - pi - ness In breath-less crowd-ed__

mo - re; è un fior che na - sce e__ muo - re, nè più si può go -
hours,__ For love, like ten - der__ flow - ers, Is swift - ly dead and__

der.__ Go - diam! c'in - vi - ta, c'in - vi - ta un fer - -vi - do ac -
gone.__ My friends,__ em - brace this al - lur - ing oc - ca - - sion, Let's

Nº 4. "Un dì felice, eterea.„

Valse and Duet.

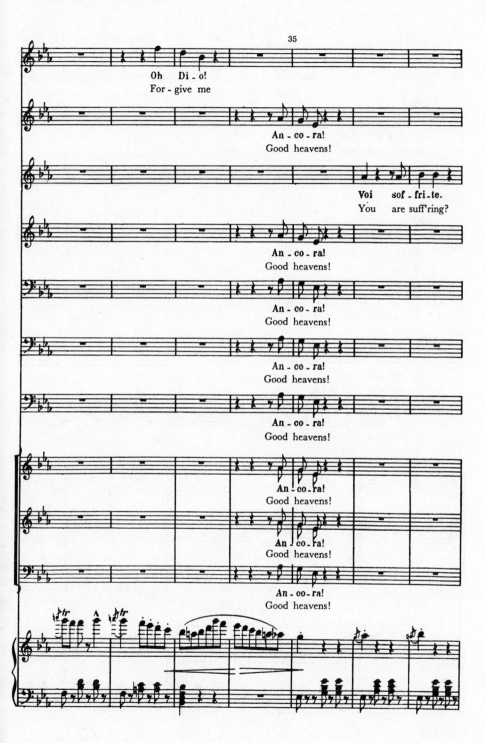

RICHARD WAGNER

(May 22, 1813–February 13, 1883)

Excerpts from Act III of *Die Meistersinger von Nürnberg* (1862–67).
Words by the composer.

36.

Wagner, more than any other composer until Bartók, developed Beethoven's methods of building large structures from the metamorphoses of small motives. In Beethoven's work this is most obvious in the Fifth Symphony, where the rhythmic unit UUU– generates so much of the material. But the developments of the great song theme of the Ninth Symphony are equally impressive (see **46**). Wagner brought these methods to bear on the opera, which had formerly been rather a disjointed form, relying on the dramatic action to hold together the many separate movements. His most famous invention was that of the *Leitmotif* (German, "leading-motive") as used in the four-opera cycle *Der Ring des Nibelungen*. Here all the major characters, objects, and ideas have their own motives, out of which Wagner weaves an almost symphonic texture rich in meaning and allusion. But this was not his only method. He interrupted the writing of the *Ring* to complete two unconnected operas, *Tristan und Isolde* and *Die Meistersinger von Nürnberg*, each of which was organized in a different way around the same principle of metamorphosis. In *Tristan* the "cell" is a chord, and in *Meistersinger* it is a tune, first adumbrated in the overture and brought to an apotheosis in the final scene.

The first extract shows Walther trying out a song which he has dreamed, and intends to enter for the Mastersingers' competition (see commentary to **18**). The winner will be rewarded with the hand of Eva, the goldsmith's daughter, who is already in love with Walther. Hans Sachs, the cobbler and a veteran Mastersinger, encourages him. But the malevolent Town Clerk, Beckmesser, also has his eye on Eva, and is determined to fault the young knight's song. Tensions are therefore very high when we come to the actual competiton. But Beckmesser, who sings first, makes such a fool of himself that we can sit back and relax when Walther stands up to sing.

The second extract is his Prize Song (*Preislied*). Carried away by emotion, he extends his original tune into a marvellous new melody, stirring all the listeners to admiration, bringing relief to the goldsmith Pogner, and confirming Sachs' faith in him. This aria is almost unique in Wagner's works, and shows that he could write a tune to match the best of Italian opera—but only when there was a proper dramatic reason for doing so.

Recordings: many.   **Compare: 34, 35, 40, 46;** the remainder of the opera; the singing competition in Wagner's earlier *Tannhaüser;* his other operas.

SACHS.

weiss ich noch nicht, so gut ihr's ge-reimt, was ihr ge-dichtet, was ihr ge-träumt.
still I know now, though clear was your theme, but half your po-em, and half your dream.

WALTH.

„A-bend-lich glü-hend in himm-lischer
"Sun-set was gild-ing with hea-venly

Gluth verschied der Tag, wie dort ich lag: aus ih-ren Au-gen Wonne saugen Ver-
light the dy-ing day, as there I lay; my heart on fire, with one de-sire, from

lan-gen einz'-ger Macht in mir nur wacht! Nächt-lich um-
eyes so won-drous bright, to drink de-light. Night clo-ses

WALTH.

däm - mert der Blick mir sich bricht: wie weit so nah' be-schienen da zwei lich-te
round me   and   darkens the   place: a - far yet near, two stars ap - pear, in day's de-

cresc.

Ster - ne aus der Fer - ne, durch schlanker Zwei - ge Licht, hehr mein Ge - sicht.
clin - ing, soft-ly   shining, where branches in - ter - lace, down on my   face.

mf   dim. - - - - piùp   pp poco cresc.

P.   ✛   P.   ✛   P.   ✛   P.   ✛

Lieb-lich ein Quell   auf stil - ler Hö - he dort mir rauscht; jetzt schwellt er
There on   a   height, a   bubbling fountain at my   feet, from earth out-

p   cresc. -

an sein hold Ge - tön', so stark und   süss ich's nie er - lauscht: leuchtend und
pours its lim-pid stream, with swelling   tone, so full and sweet.   Sparkling and

f   dim. -

P.   P.   ✛

(Walther beschreitet festen Schrittes den kleinen Blumenhügel.)
(Walther firmly steps on to the mound.)

Sehr mässig.

(sehr lang)
(molto ten.)

WALTH.

„Mor - gen-lich   leuch-tend   im
"Bathed   in   the   sun- light   at

(anschwellend.)
(cresc.)

ro - si - gen Schein, von Blüth' und Duft ge-schwellt die   Luft,   voll al - ler
dawn - ing of   day, while blossoms   rare made sweet the   air,   with beauties

(An dieser Stelle lässt Kothner das Blatt, in welchem er mit den andern Meistern eifrig nachzulesen begonnen, vor Ergriffenheit unwillkürlich fallen, er und die Uebrigen hören nur noch theilnamvoll zu.)
(Kothner, who with the other Masters had begun to follow the written words of the song, deeply moved, here lets the paper fall. He and the rest listen with interest.)

WALTH. 20 (wie entrückt.) *(in ecstasy.)*

Won — nen nie er-son-nen, ein Garten lud mich ein, dort un-ter ei-nem
teem — ing past all dreaming, a garden round me lay, and there beneath a
ein wenig zurückhaltend

sehr ausdrucksvoll dim. *p sehr zart.*

25
Wun-der-baum, von Früch-ten reich be - han-gen, zu schau'n in sel' - gem
wondrous tree, where fruits were rich-ly throng-ing, my bliss-ful dream re -

30
Lie - bestraum, was höchstem Lust - ver - lan-gen Er - fül - lung kühn ver -
vealed to me the goal of all my long-ing, and life's most glor-ious
Allmählich wieder in etwas bewegterem,

cresc. *dim.* *p* *cresc.*

(zart.)
(tenderly.)
hiess, das schön - ste Weib: _____ E - va im Pa - ra -
prize, a wo-man fair: _____ E - va in Pa - ra-
frühern Zeitmass.

f *dim.* *pp*

WALTH.

A - bend-lich däm-mernd um-schloss mich die Nacht; auf stei-lem Pfad war ich ge-
Dark-ness had fall-en and night closed me round; on ston-y road my foot-steps

naht zu ei - ner Quel - le rei - ner Wel - le, die
trod, where on a mount - ain rose a fount - ain that

lo - ckend mir ge - lacht: dort un - ter ei - nem
lured my feet with its sound: there un - der - neath a

Lor - beer - baum, von Ster - nen hell durch -
lau - rel tree, where stars like fruit were

THE EMBARKATION FOR CYTHEREA by Antoine Watteau, 1717
(Painting in Berlin, ehem. Staatliche Museen). This painting was
the inspiration for Debussy's *L'isle joyeuse* (42).

The virtuoso

According to the Oxford English Dictionary, a virtuoso is one who "excels in, or devotes special attention to, technique in playing or singing." Technique in music means, I suppose, the process of transforming an idea into communicable sounds. This can occur on two levels. For a composer, technique is a matter of formulating precise directions that will enable performers to re-create the sounds which he hears with his mental "ear." For a performer, it is a matter of making the physical and mental operations which this re-creation requires. Some of these operations are quite extraordinarily complex, and it is their mastery that makes a musician into a virtuoso. But not every musician need raise his technique to the highest level. It is all too easy to place excessive importance on technical matters, and to forget that technique should serve the musical idea, and not vice versa.

Each of the pieces in this chapter has its own peculiar difficulties, requiring skill of the highest order. The piece by Liszt (**41**) will probably seem, superficially, the most awe-inspiring in its display of virtuosity, because it requires extremely fast yet accurate movements on the part of the player. But the breath and voice control demanded by Monteverdi's and Donizetti's songs (**37, 40**) and the inspired partnership of Satchmo's trumpet with Earl Hines' piano (**43**) are as impressive to the connoisseur. Bach's organ *Passacaglia and Fugue* has perhaps the least claim to this company, since it is in the repertory of every serious organist. But since it is probably the greatest work written for the instrument on which Bach himself was an acknowledged virtuoso, it is worth investigating its special difficulties.

Any pianist who has played fugues from Bach's *Well-Tempered Clavier** knows the problems involved in keeping track of the three or four simultaneous melodic lines. The modern mind is happier in "vertical" than in "horizontal" thinking, and it does not easily split in four! The fingers must have complete independence from one another, as they constantly have to skip from one line to the next (whereas in a choir of voices each member sticks to his own line). But at least the pianist or harpsichordist can sit tight while his hands do the work. The unfortunate organist has to use his feet as well: something that seems particularly terrifying to a pianist. And on top of it, he has to disengage a hand every now and then in order to grab one or more of perhaps seventy stops.* An organist certainly has to work hard in a piece such as **39**; and if he is trying to sound musical and not mechanical, all the voices, including the pedals, must be carefully phrased,* and both their independence and interdependence emphasized.

In Vivaldi's *Autumn* (**38**) the solo violinist does not need to make any mind-splitting contortions, but he must be in the fullest control of his instrument. An out-of-tune note or a fumbled run will stick out sorely in this transparent music, whereas our organist could have dropped a few notes without undue harm. *Autumn* is of course not a profound work: it is music for entertainment, and it must sparkle from beginning to end with precision and wit. (Virtuosi are often short on the latter, having had to practice for long hours when they were children and should have been playing games.) For someone merely to struggle through this concerto would be as embarrassing as for a comedian to forget his punch lines. The soloist has to sail over the scales,* arpeggios,* and double-stops* as if they were the easiest thing in the world. To bring off a comparatively simple work such as this one requires a special kind of virtuosity, in which a light touch is combined with absolute security of technique. It is no Himalaya of the violinist's repertory (as is the Schoenberg Concerto—see **66**), but the talents of a top-flight virtuoso are not wasted on it.

Even top-flight virtuosi cannot always sing Lucia's famous "Mad Song" (**40**) with more than a cursory regard for the notes: how often the chromatic scale* in bar 17 degenerates into a scoop, the figures in 28-30 into chirrups! Alternatively, the second verse (21f) may sound merely like an exercise in vocalization. But a good coloratura can work wonders with it, and, if she can act as well, can convey the sinister atmosphere as the festivities are interrupted by the advent of a madwoman and a murderess, singing to herself in tones of unearthly beauty. Coloratura singing always has something rather surreal about it: it is far closer to our own speech than the music of an instrument, yet utterly remote from normal discourse. Hence its appropriateness to heroes (**37**), madwomen, and high-class courtesans with hearts of gold (**35**).

Liszt's *Hungarian Rhapsody No. 2* (**41**), on the other hand, is impersonal and is simply intended to thrill through its obvious difficulty. It serves here as a monument to one of the supreme virtuosi of all time. Liszt the composer has been relegated to the second rank, but Liszt the pianist was second to none in his day. The reaction of the audiences at his concerts of the 1830's and '40's was unmatched until the Beatles' era: ladies would sigh, shriek, throw their jewels onto the stage, or faint dead away. After the concert, there would be a mad scramble for relics, which the hero would usually encourage by nonchalantly leaving his gloves behind on the piano.

Liszt was already a fine pianist by the standards of his day when in 1831 he heard Niccolò Paganini, a violinist whose playing was so extraordinary that people said he was in league with the Devil himself. Resolving to do for his own instrument what Paganini had done for the violin, Liszt proceeded to raise keyboard virtuosity to a new height. A piece such as **41** would have terrified the virtuosi of Beethoven's day. But just as athletic records are continually being broken, so pianists continually attempted to outdo each other in technique. If something became too easy, they would gladly make it more difficult: Leopold Godowski, for instance, arranged some of Chopin's more demanding Études (Studies) for the left hand alone.

In the nineteenth century the piano virtuosi enjoyed fame comparable to that of sports, movie, and rock stars today. They paid for this by a lowering of standards—not of technique, of course, but of taste. Liszt's favorite concert pieces were not the great works of the keyboard literature—Bach, Mozart, Beethoven, and Chopin—but his own operatic transcriptions, in which he would embellish popular songs with pianistic fireworks. If we were to seek a parallel today, it would not be the work of Horowitz and Rubinstein, but something more like Liberace playing hits from *Oklahoma*. Our taste nowadays is both better and worse: our serious virtuosi do not fool around with the notes as the Romantic pianists did, yet we have a new world of popular music which has outdone even the nineteenth century in vulgarity.

The *Hungarian Rhapsody* has some splendid tunes, but its musical content is hardly commensurate with its technical difficulty. Debussy's *L'Isle joyeuse* (**42**), on the other hand, could not exist without the virtuoso pianism which it requires. The *Hungarian Rhapsody* has been simplified so that an amateur or child could enjoy playing the tunes, but *L'Isle joyeuse* is already as simple as it could ever be. (If it had been written fifty years earlier, no doubt someone would have arranged it for the left hand, or in double octaves.) This illustrates how Debussy differed from practically every composer before him: they thought in melodies and harmonies, then put them into sound; he thought in pure sound, and then put it into notes. The melodies of *L'Isle joyeuse* are less important than the textures and sonorities; and these can only be achieved on the piano by certain rather tricky means.

The virtuosity of Schoenberg's *Violin Concerto* (**66**) has a similar *raison d'être*. The solo violin part is horrendously difficult, but it is in no sense a display piece. Schoenberg's ideas were such that they inevitably produced music difficult to play. In this work the challenges arise from the facts that the violin was invented and developed in an era when music was tonal,* and that Schoenberg's music is atonal.* Considering that the tuning and form of the violin were decided upon at about the period of Palestrina, it is quite amazing that a work so distant from its roots can still be played upon it. But whereas the solo part of Vivaldi's concerto (**38**) is conceived in total sympathy with the instrument, exploiting its strongest points, it almost seems that Schoenberg writes "against" the violin, forcing it to the (temporary) limits of possibility in his quest for expression. Certainly it requires a new kind of player. Yet the same was true in Liszt's day, too: *plus ça change.* . . .

The piano and the violin are the instruments for which the

most virtuoso music has been written. But in the Baroque period (ca. 1600–1750) the most favored and fêted virtuosos were not players but opera singers. The prototype of all singers is Orpheus himself, the mythic hero of Thrace who "with his lute made trees, And the mountain-tops that freeze, Bow themselves when he did play" (*King Henry VIII*). And the prototype of all musical dramas is Monteverdi's first opera, *Orfeo* (1607). To those who love mythology and early music, nothing could be more solemn and moving than the moment when this archetypal virtuoso sings the song that is to gain him entrance to Hades, denied to other mortals (**37**).

This piece also illustrates the reason for the absence of any earlier virtuoso music. It will be noticed that the singer is given two different parts, one very simple and the other extremely elaborate. The latter is supposedly·Monteverdi's suggestion of what a singer was expected to do with the former. Usually he did not bother to write it out, but left the elaboration to his performers, for this was an era of improvisation, in which the performer contributed almost as much as the composer. The great Baroque singers would have been incapable of singing only the notes in front of them: nor would their composers expect, or their audiences want, them to do so. In many situations the composer provided no more than the framework, which the performer would fill in as his skill allowed. And the same thing sometimes happened in the Renaissance: there survive a few examples of sixteenth-century madrigals—in themselves staid, uncomplicated pieces—as they were performed by virtuosi, in which the original notes are scarcely perceptible among the welter of added figuration (see commentary to **51**).

This arrangement had the happy result that up to a point everyone could enjoy the same music. Beginners could stick to the written notes, and the more advanced could ornament and decorate as their skill (and taste) allowed. The same thing survives in jazz: a tune such as *St. Louis Blues* (**29**) is material alike for the rawest amateur and the top professionals. *Weather Bird* (**43**) is an example of what happens when the very best performers get together. Needless to say, they would never have done it the same twice running (and the same would probably go for Monteverdi's singer), and the notes of this transcription have not the binding, unalterable status of notes by Schoenberg or Debussy. Here again we find that popular musicians have kept alive something that their "serious" brethren have forgotten.

Virtuosity is attractive because it excites admiration on the part of the audience and feeds the ego of the performer. Yet there is also, for the same reason, something rather repulsive about it. In etiquette books of the Renaissance, gentlemen were advised not to become too good at music, lest they lose thereby their amateur status and descend to the level of those who entertain for money. And King Louis XIV remarked, when he was presented with a "virtuoso" who could simultaneously play, sing, and dance three different airs, that what the man did was certainly difficult, but that it was not pleasing. Perhaps we give our virtuosi more adulation than they are worth. When we were children we were led to believe that show-offs were obnoxious. Are we now being encouraged, as adults, to worship them? I would suggest an attitude of respect for the hard work that goes into achieving virtuosity, but if the result is not pleasing *musically* then that work is wasted. If a virtuoso cannot move us by his rendition of a simple piece, he is no musician. But to hear a consummate artist, with all the technique in the world at his fingertips, play a simple work (to hear Horowitz play a Haydn sonata, perhaps) is to experience something as close to perfection as is possible in this sublunary world.

Suggestions for further reading For a marvellous account of virtuosi and their ways, see Harold C. Schonberg, *The Great Pianists* (New York, 1963). Angus Heriot, in *The Castrati in Opera* (London, 1956) documents the previous generation of *prime donne*. On the composers, see Denis Arnold and Nigel Fortune, eds., *The Monteverdi Companion* (New York, 1968), Walter Kolneder, *Vivaldi* (Berkeley, 1971), Phillipp Spitta's monumental foundation-stone of Bach research, *Johann Sebastian Bach* (New York, 1951—reprint of 1885 edition), Alan Walker, *Franz Liszt, the Man and His Music* (New York, 1970), Edward Lockspeiser, *Debussy, His Life and Mind* (London, 1965–66). On Louis Armstrong, see Gunther Schuller, *Early Jazz* (New York, 1968).

Other peaks of virtuosity: Dowland's *Fantasias* for lute; Bach's works for unaccompanied violin; Beethoven's *Hammerklavier* Sonata, Op. 106; the songs of Schoenberg and Webern; piano music of Boulez, Stockhausen, and Xenakis.

CLAUDIO MONTEVERDI

(baptized May 15, 1567–November 29, 1643)

"Possente Spirto" from Act III of *L'Orfeo* (1607). Words by Alessandro Striggio.

37.

Orpheus has lost his wife Eurydice and is descending to Hades in order to bring her back to life: with the help of his music and various Immortals he is successful. Thus in short goes this allegory of man's own destiny which holds a special place in the history of opera. Peri and Caccini, the grandfathers of the art, had used the same story in their *Eurydice* of 1600, and it was to be used many years later by Gluck in another epoch-making work (see **12**).

Monteverdi's score, published in Mantua two years after the first performance there, is an isolated landmark in the history of orchestration because it gives precise directions for instrumentation, something that was usually left to be worked out during rehearsals (e.g., in **32**). This aria, in which Orpheus implores the infernal boatman Charon to carry him across the waters of Lethe, gives an idea of the wealth of tone color employed in the opera. There are first, the foundation or continuo instruments, specified at the head of the score ("Orpheus, to the sound of an organ with wooden pipes, and a long-necked lute, sings only one of the two parts.") These improvise appropriately on the chords of the accompaniment. Then there are the "obbligato" instruments, whose parts are fully written out: two violins for the first verse, two cornetti* for the second, a harp for the third, and two violins and cello for the fourth. The final peroration is for voice and continuo alone.

This song is, perhaps, the highlight of the greatest of early operas. In our day the strangeness of the sound may have as much attraction as its beauty—which might be said of much early music. But Monteverdi chose to make the climax of the song the simplest part, where Orfeo, having displayed all the skill of a virtuoso singer and all the resources of his "orchestra," resorts to a chaste plainness in his final plea. The singer should make this the most moving part of all.

Recordings: 3-Tel. SKH-21 (*Monteverdi: L'Orfeo,* Vienna Concentus Musicus, Munich Capella Antiqua, Harnoncourt, cond.)

Compare: 22, 32, 33, 34, 44; the remainder of *Orfeo;* Monteverdi's *Lamento d'Arianna* and his late opera, *L'incoronazione di Poppea;* the corresponding event in Gluck's *Orphée et Eurydice.*

ORFEO AL SUONO DEL ORGANO DI LEGNO, E UN CHITARRONE CANTA UNA SOLA DE LE DUE PARTI.

Claudio Monteverdi: *Orfeo*

1) *Nell'originale é cosi:*

già mai per huom mor - tal non vas - si. O de le
this day no mor - tal foot hath trod - den. Oh glor - ious

per huom mor - tal non vas - si. O de le
no mor - tal foot hath trod - den. Oh glor - ious

1) *A questo punto finisce la variazione: le due parti si riuniscono.*

lus - trous eyes, eyes of my lov'd one, a sin - gle glance from you my life re -

lu - ci mie lu - ci se - re - ne, s'un vo - stro sguar - do può tor - nar - mi in

- stor - eth: Ah who would de - ny me so - lace for my sor - row?

vi - ta, ahi chi nie - ga il con - for - to a le mie pe - ne,

ANTONIO VIVALDI

(March 4, 1678–July 28, 1741)

Autumn: Violin Concerto in F major, from The Four Seasons, Op. 8, No. 3. (before 1725).

38.

Vivaldi, Bach's great contemporary in Italy, was the prime mover in the ascendancy of the solo concerto over the *concerto grosso* established by Corelli (see **53**). Natural selection has allowed only the fittest of his 221 violin concertos to survive, foremost of which are those fortunate enough to be equipped with attractive programs describing the Four Seasons. In *Autumn*, we see the Baroque mind at its most literal: music, like poetry, is thought of above all as a descriptive art. A sonnet, whose lines appear from time to time in the score, provides the moods and the pictures which the music so charmingly illustrates, but the whole is governed by the standard form which Vivaldi used for concertos: three movements, fast, slow, and fast. This scheme, derived from the Italian opera overture, remained that of all concertos through the nineteenth century.

Almost any modern composer would die of embarrassment before descending to such naïve description as we have here. But that need not prevent us from enjoying the clumsy peasant dance and the inebriated violin part of the first movement, and the highly chromatic* slumber of the second. Are we to assume in the "hunt" of the last movement, the usual double meaning of hunting imagery, in which the chase and kill also represent the seduction of women? One hopes not, for Vivaldi's profession was that of a priest (who, however, scarcely ever said Mass, "for reasons of health") in charge of the music at the Seminario musicale dell'Ospitale della Pietà, a Venetian institution for orphaned girls.

Recordings: many.

Compare: 33, 53, 54, 59, 61; Bach's violin concertos; "picturesque" music of the Baroque, e.g. the *Biblical* Sonatas of Johann Kuhnau; Couperin's and Rameau's harpsichord pieces; Haydn, *The Seasons* (oratorio); Telemann, *Die Tageszeiten* ("The Times of Day").

Ballo e Canto di Villanelli

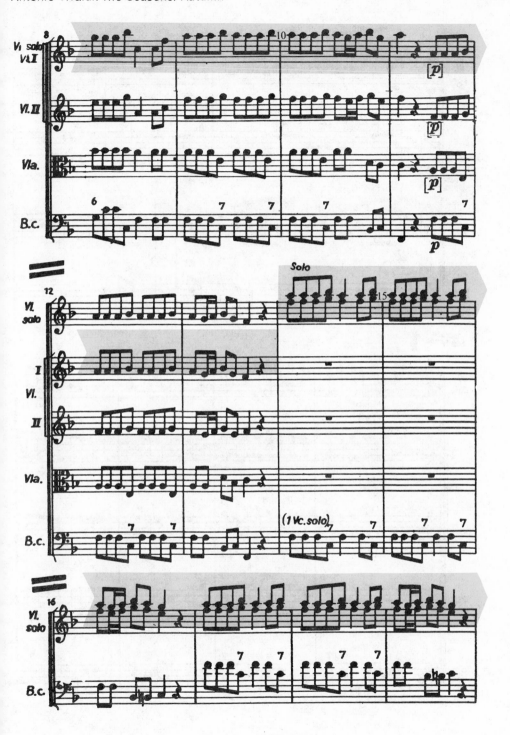

*) in print Allegro assai

ƒ Allegro molto

II

Ubriachi dormienti. Fà ch'ogn'uno tralasci e balli e canti L'aria

ch' temperata dà piacere, E la Staggion ch'invita tanti e tanti d'un

dolcissimo Sonno al bel godere.

*) in print Adagio molto

*) These dynamic marks have been aligned in the score for uniformily.

III

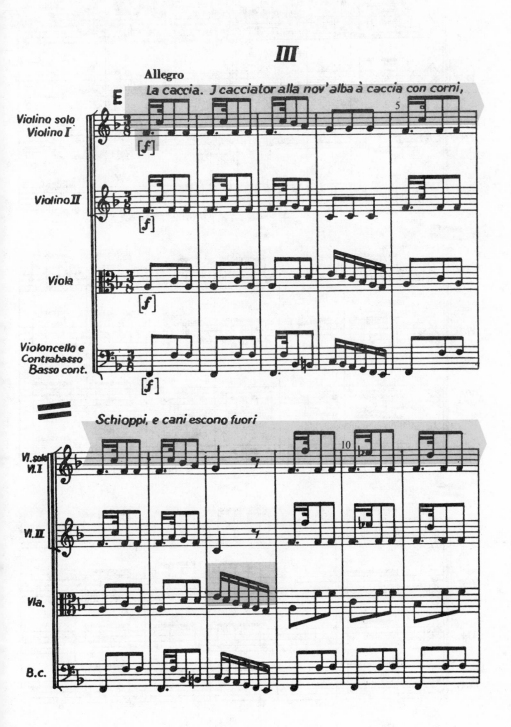

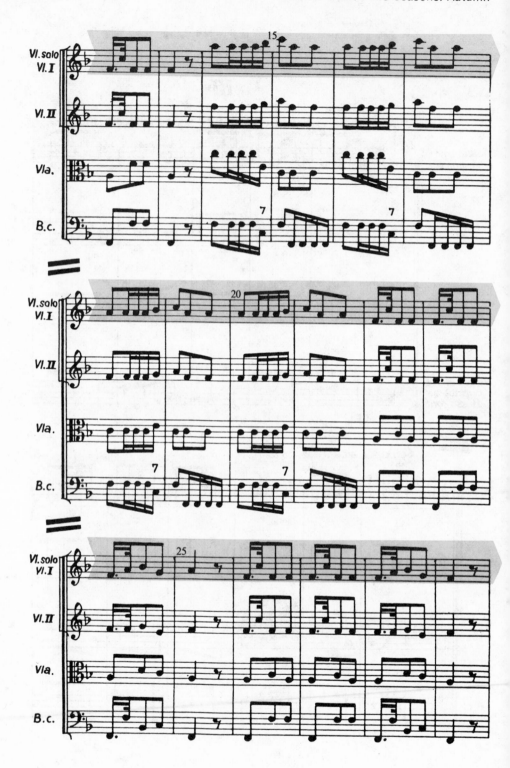

F La Tiera che Fugge

Fugge la belua, e seguana la traccia

G *Già Sbigottita, e lassa al gran rumore de'Schioppi e cani, ferita*

*) A in print

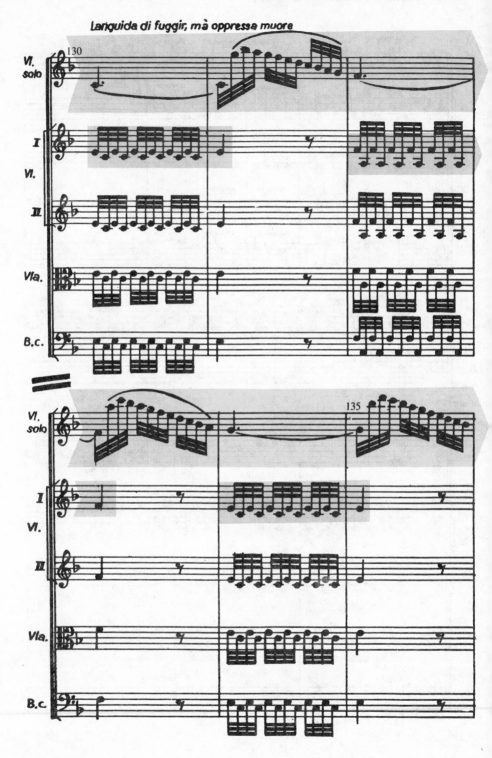

JOHANN SEBASTIAN BACH

(March 21, 1685–July 28, 1750)

Passacaglia and Fugue in C minor, BWV 582 (between 1708 and 1717, or after 1723).

The *passacaglia** is the simplest of variation forms, and hence the one that demands most imagination from the composer who wishes to make a major work of it. The theme in this piece stays in the pedal part for the first eleven statements, then suddenly sings out in the highest voice. In variations XIV-XVI it is hard to see the theme in the score, but by this time the ear is so imbued by its sound that one will probably be singing it, at least internally, along with the music. From variation XVII to the end it returns to the bass.

    Most *fugues** begin with an unaccompanied statement of their theme or "subject." In this fugue, however, we already know the subject so well that Bach can omit this convention and begin with two parts: the subject and the *countersubject* that generally accompanies it (in the left-hand part). Moreover, since the passacaglia has been entirely in regular eight-bar phrases, he reduces the theme to an irregular five bars. The fugue begins with an *exposition*, in which each voice in turn has the subject. The remainder of this and any fugue consists of alternating *statements* and *episodes;* in a statement, the subject is sounded once or more, while in an episode it is absent (though fragments of it may remain). The following plan of this fugue illustrates the incidence of statements (S) and episodes (E), together with the keys and voices in which the subject appears:

39.

	EXPOSITION				S	S
bar nos.	168	173	180	185	191	197
voice no.	2	1	4	3	2	3
key	C mi.	G mi.	C mi.	G mi.	C mi.	E♭ ma.

		E	S	E	S	E	S	E	S	E	S	E	S
bar nos.	204	208	213	220	225	233	237	245	250	255	260	271	276–end
voice no.	2		4		3		1		4		1		
key	B♭ ma.		G mi.		C mi.		G mi.		F mi.		C mi.		

Recordings: many.

Compare: 9b, 11, 32, 52; Bach, Chaconne for violin solo; other fugues; Purcell, Chaconne for Strings; Beethoven, Variations in C minor, Op. 32; Buxtehude, Prelude, Fugue and Chaconne; Brahms, passacaglia from Symphony No. 4, and Webern, Opus 1.

GAETANO DONIZETTI
(November 29, 1797–April 8, 1848)

"Alfin son tua" from Act III of *Lucia di Lammermoor* (1835).
Words by Salvatore Cammarano, after Sir Walter Scott.

40.

The calm and beauty of this famous aria are deceptive. The scene in the opera is a wedding reception given for Lucy (Lucia) and her new husband, Arthur. But Lucy is in love with another man, Edgar, whom her family has wronged. Mad with grief, she has just stabbed Arthur to death. Her old servant announces this terrible news to the assembled company, then Lucy herself appears and, to their horror, goes through an imaginary marriage with Edgar. (Their comments are omitted in this edition.) Her idyllic cloud-cuckoo-land contrasts ironically with the harsh reality of the situation, making this one of the most powerful scenes in Romantic opera. It is a favorite display piece for coloratura singers, and various conventions have grown up around it involving cadenzas, ornaments, and extra high notes, though these occur mostly in the remainder of the scene, which is not given here.

It was in Italian opera of the early nineteenth century that the traditions of Baroque opera had their last fling, and in these conventions we still retain something of that golden age when the singers reigned supreme and the composers were employed to enable them to display their powers. This did not, of course, prevent Donizetti, or Handel, from being very successful in their own rights. But it is worth keeping in mind that the audience for their operas was not entirely so highbrow as the average opera audience in America today: it included the kind of people who today prefer Broadway shows. And in Italy, at least, they did not hesitate to express passionately their like or dislike of what they heard. Virtuosity must have been really rewarding in those days.

Recordings: many.

Compare: 25, 33, 34, 35, 37; the remainder of the "Mad Scene"; arias from operas by Rossini and Bellini (e.g. "Casta Diva" from Bellini's *Norma*); "mad scenes" from Alban Berg, *Wozzeck* and Britten, *Peter Grimes*.

Lie . to gior,no!oh   lie . to! Al . fin son tu . . a   al . fin sei
Day of rapture!oh   rap ture! At   last I'm thine, love   at   last thou'rt

mi . . o,   a   me ti   do _ na,   a   me   ti   do . na un
mine,   love,   Heav'n smiles up . on   us,   And love's de . light's have

Di . . o   Ah! _____ O . . gni pia.cer piu' gra . to,
won   us   Ah! _____ Ah!   we're no more di . vid . . ed,

si,   o . gni pia . ce . . . . re   mi   fia _____ con . te . . di
no,   no more di . vid . . . . ed,   'Tis heav'n _____ to   be _____ with

vi.so, con te,   con   te. _____ Del   ciel _____ cle . men . . te,   del
thee   with thee, with   thee _____ my   own _____ for ev . . er,   By

FRANZ LISZT

(October 22, 1811–July 31, 1886)

Hungarian Rhapsody No. 2 (1847).

41.

In his major piano works Liszt opened up new vistas in piano technique, making the instrument a virtual orchestra in itself. It is good to remember that he used to play in his concerts not Beethoven's sonatas, but his symphonies, and that he was not averse to putting orchestral directions (*quasi corno, quasi oboe*) in his piano music. At the beginning of this rhapsody one can imagine the bite of a gypsy violinist's bow; and the air of the *Lassan* is obviously on the G-string.

One difference between Liszt's use of ornamentation and Chopin's is well illustrated here: Liszt will break the rhythm (bar 24) to accommodate some flashy passage-work, whereas Chopin nearly always subordinates such things to the prevailing meter. This reveals something of the difference in attitudes of the two great Romantic piano composers: Liszt is nothing if not "effective," especially in live performance, but Chopin's is the more serious musical mind. These rhapsodies were for Liszt the equivalent of Chopin's polonaises and mazurkas: evocations of a homeland which could not do justice to his genius. (Liszt left Hungary in 1821; Chopin moved to Paris at the age of twenty.)

This piece is a *Verbunko*, a popular Hungarian dance form consisting of a slow introduction (*Lassu*) and a fast section (*Friss*), reputedly danced in an extremely wild manner by soldiers wearing swords and spurs. Most of Liszt's favorite tricks are used here, including repeated notes (bar 142), double octaves (bar 264), and rapid chromatic chords (bar 344).

After a brilliant concertizing career, Liszt settled in Weimar, Goethe's town, to further the cause of modern music. Here he devoted much effort to publicizing and producing the operas of Wagner, and turned from piano music to the writing of symphonic poems.* In his later years he returned to Budapest and also resided in Rome, where he took minor religious orders and was always surrounded by a throng of admirers. Having grown up with the early Romantic composers, he lived to witness the whole course of Wagner's career, and, in his late piano pieces, to anticipate harmonic developments of the twentieth century.

Recordings: many.

Compare: 14, 15, 42; Liszt, *Transcendental Studies,* late piano works; symphonic poems: *Mazeppa, Orpheus;* Brahms, *Hungarian Dances;* Bartók, Rhapsodies (same form).

Friska

CLAUDE DEBUSSY
(August 22, 1862–March 25, 1918)
L'Isle joyeuse (1904).

42.

If the eighteenth century was above all the century of form, the nineteenth was that of harmony. During the Romantic period, composers such as Wagner and Strauss expanded the conventional harmonic system to the utmost by the use of discords and irregular juxtapositions of chords. Debussy took the next logical step by abandoning the conventions of "common practice" in favor of a free harmonic field in which chords were able to "be themselves," rather than to imply and require other chords, as had always been the case.

The very first chords of this piece (bar 3) are discords, and traditional standards would demand that they be resolved directly or indirectly into concords. But Debussy does not so resolve them: he just leaves them hanging. Actually this short cadenza is already in an irregular scale: the whole-tone scale,* which Debussy often used and which is incompatible with conventional harmonies. After the double bar, the harmonies are unconventional in another way: they do not change. The low A is sounded almost continuously for many bars on end, and in the second section (bar 28f), by which time most composers would have modulated, the harmonies are still founded firmly on A.

Debussy is no less revolutionary in form. Unlike most French composers, he uses free forms, newly invented for each piece. It would be futile to describe this piece in terms of A's and B's: the form is an organic one, arising from the metamorphoses of the principal motives (bars 1, 9, and 21–22), and the contrast of the whole-tone scale with A major. The two main A major sections (un peu cédé) stand out from their surroundings as moments of ecstatic relaxation, where one can really sing (or think) along with the melody. Notice the rhythmic effect in the first one, where the left hand plays five notes to a bar against the right hand's two or three chords. This is difficult to play, but it gives an inimitable rubato* effect.

The title refers to a picture (see Plate 5) painted in 1717 by Jean Antoine Watteau, entitled L'Embarquement pour Cythère ("The Embarkation for Cytherea"). Cytherea is the mythical island of Venus or Aphrodite, the Goddess of Love. In this magnificent picture, gallants and their ladies are seen entering a gilded boat, manned by cupids, which will take them to the isle where love knows no bounds and no end to its delights. Debussy's piece is the response of a very sensuous composer to this incomparably sensuous painting: it has the same fantastic, erotic quality about it, marred only by the ending which is, I think, too violent—and far too soon.

Recordings: DG 139458 (Vasary); complete collections of Debussy's piano music played by Frankl, Webster.

Compare: 27, 41, 61, 64, 72; Debussy, *Préludes; L'après-midi d'un faune; La Mer;* Ravel, *Gaspard de la nuit;* Scriabin, later piano works.

Tempo: très animé jusqu'à la fin.

LOUIS ARMSTRONG

(July 4, 1900–July 6, 1971)

Weatherbird (1928).

43.

This is a rare instance of a performance by jazz virtuosi which can be transcribed more or less exactly and reproduced as chamber music by other players. The early jazz musicians rarely dispensed with the rhythm section to create a pure duet such as this one, in which Armstrong was accompanied by the pianist Earl Hines.

It was Armstrong who, more than any other man, really "made" jazz in the decade following 1923. His inspired improvisations, with their skillful and varied ornaments, his sense of exactly how far one can go counter to the beat without losing it (which is the essence of "swing"), and his complete mastery of his instrument made him a figure to be reckoned with for all those who followed after him. Most of them were content merely to borrow his ideas, which became the *lingua franca* of classic jazz. It is amazing to recall that this piece, here set out in black and white, was actually a one-time affair: an extemporization that would never have sounded exactly the same again, had it not been captured on a recording.

Recording: P6 11891 (The Smithsonian Collection of Classic Jazz)

Compare: 16, 29; Armstrong's *West End Blues* and other works; early jazz by Jelly Roll Morton, Sidney Bechet, Duke Ellington; later jazz virtuosi: Art Tatum, Miles Davis, Charlie Parker, John Coltrane.

THE ENTRY OF THE BLESSED INTO PARADISE by Luca Sig-
norelli, circa 1500 (Fresco in Orvieto Cathedral). Instruments,
clockwise from the top: guitar, harp, lute, tambourine, viola da
braccio, viola da braccio or guitar, tambourine, 2 lutes.

6

The grand manner

Most composers have tried from time to time to create something so magnificent and sublime that it leaves its audience breathless and awestruck. When the right intersection of genius and history occurs, the result is a transcendent masterpiece such as Bach's Mass or Beethoven's Ninth Symphony (see **45, 46**). No one will dispute the status which these works have attained, and that is sufficient reason for including them here. But not all such attempts succeed. Some composers try to say the Ultimate Word almost every time they open their mouths, and, naturally, sometimes they fail. Berlioz, Wagner, Bruckner, and Mahler are the composers who most consistently wrote on a grand scale (discounting a few second-rate megalomaniacs), and none of them achieved the consistently high quality of Bach, Mozart, and Chopin, to name some composers who have their ups and downs, but never embarrass with excess.

Grandeur in music, however, requires noise first and inspiration second. Everyone knows how the mere sound of a brass band can raise goosebumps. The final word on brass bands is surely spoken by Berlioz, when in the Dies irae of his Requiem (**47**) the large orchestra and chorus are amplified by no fewer than four bands, one at each point of the compass. And in case we should think that this is the best he can do, Berlioz throws in, at Tuba mirum, sixteen timpani as well. Unfortunately, the size of this book does not allow for reproduction of the full score. The noise which Berlioz makes at this point deafens one to the musical sense, if any; as with "hard rock," we just lose ourselves in the sheer volume, irrespective of the notes. Where the composer's skill does show is in the inexorable build-up, and in the following movement, *Quid sum miser,* which is in a way more impressive than all the sound and thunder. Here the orchestra is virtually silent: voices, oboe, English horn, and basses call to each other, infinitely lonely, over the vast spaces created by the maelstrom of the *Dies irae.*

Brahms impresses more by the adamantine quality of his musical thought than by noise alone. One feels that a profound mind is at work behind this movement (**48**), constructing an edifice stone by stone with impeccable logic. There are three distinct moods, yet they seem to make up a coherent whole. Actually, the first themes of each section all feature a broken triad,* and several subsidiary motives are based on the same figure. Such inner consistency, perceived unconsciously by the listener, is the mark of a great composer. It makes each part, however different, sound like the inevitable outcome of what came before. (See commentaries to **60, 63**.)

Domine ad adjuvandum (**44**) is a magnificent sound, but otherwise it is hardly comparable to the other pieces in this chapter. Monteverdi did not intend it as a self-contained piece, but merely as a "curtain-raiser" for what was to follow. He had used almost identical music, without the voices, as a prelude to his opera *Orfeo* three years earlier, and we can assume that what we have here is really a written-out fanfare, such as brass instruments of the time might have played on all sorts of occasions. As such, it gives a brief vision of splendiferous ceremonial at cathedrals and courts of the late Renaissance.

Despite their titles, both Bach's *B minor Mass* and Beethoven's *D minor Symphony* end in the key* of D major.* This is partly because for a long time D was the favorite key for trumpets. In the days before the universal adoption of valves* for brass instruments (which were invented in 1813), trumpets and horns could only play the notes of a single harmonic series, which roughly describes an arpeggio and a scale in a given key. Most works of the Baroque and Classic eras which make extensive use of trumpets are in the key of D (though a couple of famous exceptions are Bach's second *Brandenburg Concerto* in F and Haydn's *Trumpet Concerto* in E♭). By Berlioz's time valves were widespread, and consequently trumpets could play in any of the twenty-four keys, although the military band keys of B♭

and E♭ were particularly favored (e.g. the entry of the brasses on a chord of E♭ in **47**). Trumpets and kettledrums are of course the traditional instruments of kings and princes, as well as of war, and they are an essential part of many pieces composed in what I call the "grand manner." Over the years, the key of D has become so associated with them that to some people it seems even now to have a sound of brightness and splendor about it. Rimsky-Korsakov and Scriabin, two late nineteenth-century composers who gave lists of color-key correspondences, both thought of D as yellow (practically their only point of agreement); and the color of brass instruments might have something to do with this.

Bach's *Sanctus* (**45**) opens to the unforgettable sound of trumpets and drums, while the sixfold chorus sings words originating from the Book of the Prophet Isaiah in the Old Testament:

> In the year that King Uzziah died, I saw also the Lord sitting upon a throne, high and lifted up, and his train filled the temple. Above it stood the seraphims: each one had six wings; with twain he covered his face, and with twain he covered his feet, and with twain he did fly. And one cried unto another, and said, "Holy, holy, holy is the Lord of hosts, the whole earth is full of his glory." (Ch. VI, vv. 1–3)

A prominent English musician, whom I knew as a boy, said that when he died he expected to see the gates of Heaven open with this music, and God the Father to appear enthroned with Jesus Christ on His right hand and Johann Sebastian Bach on His left. I hope he will not be disappointed. One certainly could not wish for anything more splendid than the *Sanctus,* nor more joyous than the angelic dance of the *Pleni sunt coeli.*

Beethoven (**46**) cannot give us an immediate vision such as Bach could. Being a Romantic artist and an individualist, he begins by showing us the birth pangs, as it were, of his vision. The first sound we hear is Chaos (that which perhaps precedes the creation of a world), and then come the strivings of the cellos and basses, blundering about like large beasts in their search for a theme. They are trying to sing a recitative together, which is something essentially soloistic and vocal; no wonder it sounds odd. The rest of the orchestra offers them, one after another, ideas from the preceding three movements, but each one is rejected. When the fourth theme is offered, however, it is clear that they approve: they actually exclaim with delight. And then they begin to sing the famous tune. First it comes without accompaniment. Then it moves up an octave* and the violas take it over (notice the delightful bassoon part here). Up another octave, and the violins play it in sensuous harmony. Then, and only then, come the trumpets, and the celestial gates are attained. Beethoven, you see, describes a *process*, whereas Bach described a *state*. After this incredible scenario, we are thrown back again into Chaos, but this time it is not animals (i.e., instruments) that emerge, but Man. What audacity, not only to introduce voices into a symphony, but to make them wait so long before singing!

Everyone must make his own exploration of the remainder of this movement, itself the size of a whole Haydn symphony. It is sometimes compared to masterpieces in the other arts, such as *Hamlet* and Michelangelo's *Last Judgement*. But the "comparable" works almost always seem to be tragic, or at least awesome, whereas this piece, like so many of Beethoven's, is radiant with joy and what Dante calls, in his *Paradiso*, "L'amor che muove il sol e l'altre stelle"—the Love that moves the Sun and all the Stars.

Suggestions for further reading On Monteverdi's *Vespers,* see the introduction to Denis Stevens' (incomplete) edition (London, 1961). George Marek, *Beethoven; The Biography of a Genius* (New York, 1969) is one of the most readable of countless lives-and-works. See also Martin Cooper, *Beethoven, the Last Decade, 1817–1827* (London, 1970). Jacques Barzun, *Berlioz and the Romantic Century* (3rd ed., New York, 1969) is more social than musical history of the time. On the composers, see A. E. Dickinson, *The Music of Berlioz* (New York, 1973) and Karl Geiringer, *Brahms, His Life and Work* (2nd ed., New York, 1961).

For other manifestations of grandeur, one might investigate Thomas Tallis' 40-part motet *Spem in alium,* the massive works of Orazio Benevoli (1605–72), French opera of the period around 1800, Liszt's *Faust Symphony,* Richard Strauss' tone poems, Schoenberg's *Gurrelieder,* and Stockhausen's *Gruppen* for three orchestras, in addition to the composers and works mentioned in this chapter.

CLAUDIO MONTEVERDI

(baptized May 15, 1567–November 29, 1643)

"Domine ad adjuvandum" from *Vespers of the Blessed Virgin* (published 1610).

44.

Monteverdi lived at the juncture of two periods and made them both his own. The early seventeenth century was a time of much heated debate between adherents of the "old" style of the Renaissance, based on counterpoint, consonance, and the equality of parts, and the "new" style of the Baroque, based on free expression including dissonance, and the polarity of melody and bass. In 1610 Monteverdi published a large collection of vocal music which proved him master of both styles: there was a Mass in strict six-part counterpoint in the Roman tradition, five Psalms for choir and instruments in a style favored by the composers of the Venetian school, and four sacred songs for solo voices which were closer to the new operatic monody* that had originated in Florence, as well as two Magnificats, a hymn, and a sonata.* His intention in putting out this extravagant advertisement of his skill was simple: he wanted a new job, and hoped above all for that of organist and musical director of St. Mark's Cathedral in Venice, the most coveted musical appointment in all Italy. His trouble and expense were, as it happened, repaid by this very appointment which he held from 1613 until the end of his life, but not until some very difficult years had passed, full of uncertainty, financial difficulty, and ill health.

Vespers (Latin *vespera*=evening) is one of the Offices, or Hours, of the Roman Catholic liturgy (see Chapter 1), and it was often celebrated with great splendor, especially on the feasts of the Virgin: Nativity, Annunciation, Visitation, Purification, and Assumption. Monteverdi sets here the invitatory response, common to all the Hours, with a "joyful noise" of instruments and voices entering with triumphant effect after a plainsong intonation, sung by the officiating priest. The Psalms and other items that follow are, naturally, much longer and more complex, yet this fanfare tells us something valuable about the kind of music that was more usually improvised than written down.

Recordings: 2-CSP CM25-763 (Monteverdi: *Vespro della Beata Vergine*, Gregg Smith Singers, Ft. Worth Boys Cho., Col. Baroque Ens., Craft, cond.); 2-Tel. S-9501/2 (same title, Vienna Boys Cho., Hamburg Monteverdi Cho., Vienna Concentus Musicus, Jurgens, cond.); 2-Van. C-10001/2 (same title, Accademia Monteverdiana, Stevens, cond.)

Compare: 8 a & b, for the origin of this homophonic, chordal style in dance music; the remainder of the Vespers; the very similar prelude to Monteverdi's *Orfeo;* polychoral* works of Giovanni Gabrieli and Heinrich Schütz.

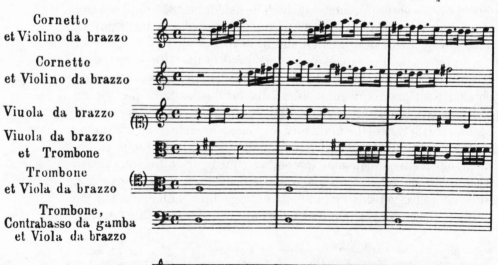

20

.tu - i   Sanc - - .to .

.tu - i   Sanc - - .to .

.tu - i   Sanc - - .to .

.tu - i   Sanc - - .to .

.tu - i   Sanc - - .to .

.tu - i   Sanc - - .to .

35

50

JOHANN SEBASTIAN BACH

(March 21, 1685–July 28, 1750)

Sanctus from *Mass in B minor, BWV 232 (1733–38)*.
Words from the Roman Rite.

45.

This Mass was conceived not on a liturgical scale, but on an operatic one. The five Ordinary movements (see introduction to Chapter 1) are subdivided into twenty-four, each a full-sized chorus or aria: the Sanctus alone has two further movements after this one. Like Monteverdi's great collection of 1610 (see **44**), the work was partly composed as an advertisement—in this case for the Elector of Saxony, a Catholic prince from whom Bach hoped for a post as Honorary Court Composer. In 1733 he submitted the Kyrie and Gloria (which constituted a complete Mass setting in Bach's own Lutheran church), and in 1736 was rewarded with the position. The remainder of the Mass was finished by 1738.

In this sublime movement we can see the typical large orchestra of the Baroque. Still under the influence of the "whole consort" ideal of the Renaissance (see commentary to **52**), the instruments are grouped in families. The two violins and viola, together with the cellos and basses which play the continuo line, constitute a four-part string consort. The three trumpets and timpani are the "brass" choir: although pitched in D, they are customarily written in the basic key of C. The three oboes would have been supported by their close relative the bassoon, also playing the continuo line. In actual performance, the string parts would each have been played by several instruments, and the woodwind parts perhaps doubled as well. Binding these groups together with the six-part chorus would be the organ, improvising chords from the continuo part.

By Haydn's time the conception of the orchestra as a massing of instrumental choirs had changed. In **58** and **59** the strings carry the musical argument to which the winds add occasional color. The decline of trumpet playing after Bach's day is very apparent from a comparison of these parts—played, of course, on a valveless trumpet—with those of **59**.

The *Pleni sunt coeli* is an accomplished fugue in which some entries are doubled at the third (e.g. S.II and A.I at bar 66, T. and B. at 72). Although there is some variation in the number and independence of parts, the movement is regularly divided into statements and episodes (see commentary to **39**). In order to clarify the structure, I have highlighted all the statements, although they are not always the most interesting things that are happening.

Recordings: many.

Compare: 5, 39, 44, 46, 47, 48, 53; the remainder of the Mass; Bach's *Christmas Oratorio* and Orchestral Suites; Handel, "Hallelujah" from *Messiah,* which shows vividly the contrast between these two masters; Beethoven, *Missa Solemnis.*

LUDWIG VAN BEETHOVEN
(December 16 or 17, 1770–March 26, 1827)
Fourth movement of Symphony No. 9 in D minor,
Op. 125 (1817-23).
Words by Friedrich von Schiller.

46.

Haydn wrote 104 symphonies, and Mozart 25 piano concertos: Beethoven wrote nine and five respectively, and each one is imbued with a personality of its own. This sums up one of the major revolutions which Beethoven effected; for the serious composers who followed him, there was no going back to the days when one could churn out symphonies by the half-dozen, and concertos by the score.

In Mozart's and Haydn's time, the symphony was above all entertainment (see commentaries to **58** and **59**), and to keep the audience's attention it usually began seriously and became more frivolous as it proceeded. A rough psychological plan of its four movements would be something like this:

I	II	III (Minuet)	IV
Cerebral	Serene	Hearty or Suave	Effervescent

As far as one can generalize about nine very different individuals, one can say that Beethoven made two major changes to the shape of the symphony: he substituted the rapid *scherzo** for the minuet, and transformed the last movement from a frolic into the climax of the whole work. The last movement of his last symphony is, fittingly, the apotheosis to end all apotheoses. Some guidelines to its beginning are given in the introduction to this chapter; here it will be useful to map out the remainder.

The symphony as a whole has the plan: first movement, scherzo, slow movement, finale. This differs from the normal ordering in that the scherzo is placed before, instead of after, the slow movement. Here, as in Beethoven's *Hammerklavier* Sonata, Op. 106, the scherzo provides some relief between the very concentrated first and slow movements. Now the finale of the Ninth Symphony is a microcosm of the whole symphony, for it, too, consists of four major sections:

	I	II	III	IV
	Introduction and Song	March and Fugue (Scherzo)	Slow movement	Finale
	Allegro	**Allegro assai vivace**	**Andante maestoso**	**Allegro energico**
bar nos.	11	331	594	654

The scherzo, true to its name, begins with a joke. After the surprise of the preceding chord, the first low B♭'s sound as if they might herald a profound slow section. But they turn out to be the off-beats of a march for military band, complete with "Turkish music"* and a cheerful *Heldentenor* as the Captain. There is more humor in the juxtaposition of this march with a fugue, the "heaviest" of musical forms.

The slow section, with its more religious text and its wonderful musical evocation of the starry skies, is a short and self-contained entity. It is only afterwards that all the threads are pulled together (bar 654), when the slow theme is combined with the first one, in the rhythm of the march. This double development is followed by two single ones: of the song theme (bar 763), and of the "slow" theme (bar 851), after which a short coda gives the *coup de grâce* to the already exhausted musicians.

Recordings: many.

Compare: 45, 47, 48, 60; the remainder of the symphony; Beethoven's other symphonies; his *Missa Solemnis;* the symphonies of Anton Bruckner and Gustav Mahler.

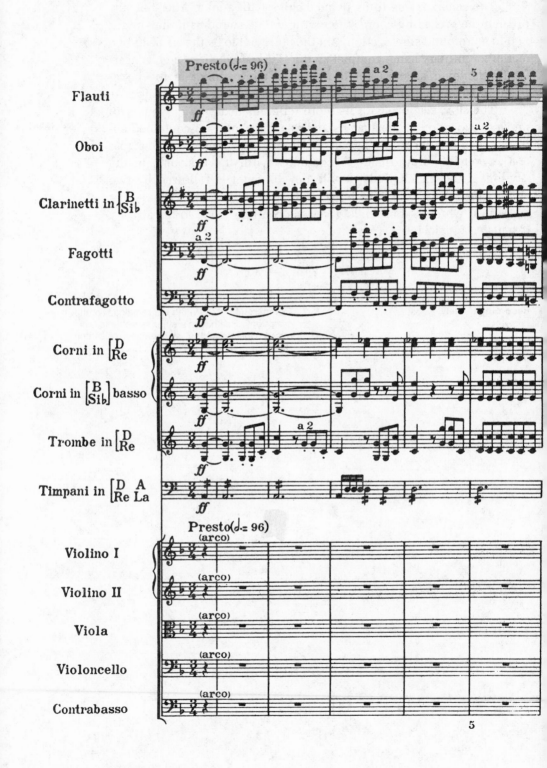

*) *Selon le caractère d'un Récitatif, mais in Tempo*

O Freun - de, nicht die - se Tö-ne!
O friends, no more these sounds con-ti-nue,

streng ge-teilt; al - le Men-schen werden Brüder, wo dein sanf-ter Flü-gel weilt.
par-ted wide, All __ man-kind are brothers pligh-ted where thy gen-tle wings a-bide.

Andante maestoso (♩ = 72)

Seid umschlungen, Mil - li - o - nen! Die-sen Kuß der ganzen
O ye mil - lions, I____ em-brace ye! Here's a joy-ful kiss for

W. Ph.V. 30

Adagio ma non troppo, ma divoto ($\natural$ = 60)

Ihr stürzt nie-der, Mil - li-
O__ ye millions kneel be-

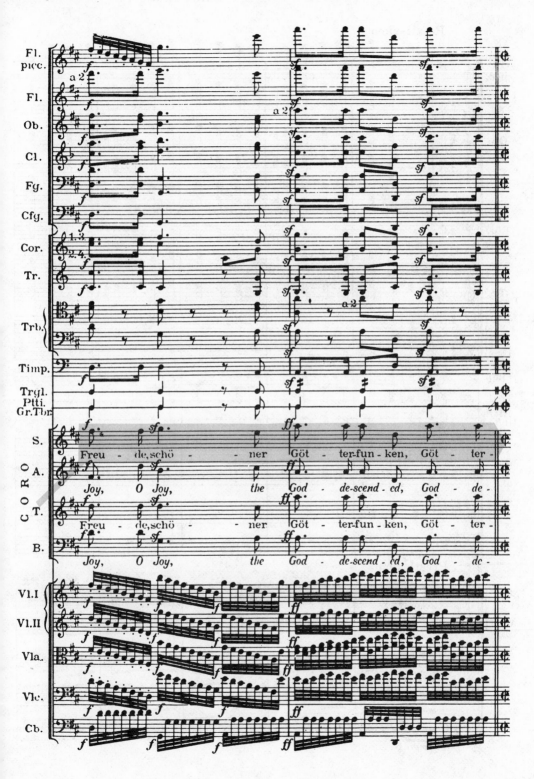

HECTOR BERLIOZ
(December 11, 1803–March 8, 1869)

Dies Irae and *Quid sum miser* from *Grande Messe des Morts* (1837).

Words from the Roman Rite, possibly by Thomas of Celano, 13th century.

47.

Berlioz is a problematic composer. Of the early Romantics, Schumann, Chopin, Mendelssohn, and Liszt, he alone lost no time in taking up the challenge of Beethoven's major works. He accepted the tacit assumptions that from now on an artist must be satisfied with nothing less than masterpieces, and that he is there to educate and impress his public, rather than to serve them up, like a cook, with the sort of music they expect and like. But he wrote no chamber music, no piano pieces such as poured from his contemporaries (he could not play the piano) and only a handful of songs. He concentrated on choral, orchestral, and operatic works: like Victor Hugo's novels and Eugène Delacroix's canvases his compositions are large in scale and ambitious in content. He is the perfect early Romantic artist: gifted, or cursed, with an excess of sensibility, passion, and ambition, and pouring it all into forms which bend and break under the strain. There was no hope for Classicism after Berlioz.

The setting of words from the Requiem Mass (Mass for the Dead) was his first official commission, and was performed with enormous forces at Les Invalides in Paris. Berlioz begins the magnificent sequence, the *Dies Irae*, in a pseudo-plainsong manner, then harmonizes it in two parts (B) and in three (D). In the next section he uses his chorus in a plainly orchestral manner: see the trumpet-like entries of the sopranos, and the tenors' figurations that seem like a string part. The third time the tune comes around (modulation to D minor) the sound is fuller still, but this is nothing to the entrance of the brass bands at the *Andante maestoso*.

The Last Trump is described by the bass voices (*Più Largo*) in a kind of non-melody typical of Berlioz: unaccompanied, this line would be feeble in the extreme. As it is, the timpani virtually drown it. Then, at *Liber scriptus* (N), the brass bands and voices combine with overpowering force and continue to lift the roof off until the last quiet peroration (R).

In the *Quid sum miser* that follows, the fragmentation of the Dies irae theme and the emaciated counterpoints are overwhelmingly effective, yet there is also a kind of clumsiness in the notes themselves, which writers on Berlioz have frequently commented upon.

Recordings: many.

Compare: 45, 46, 48; Berlioz, *Te Deum;* Requiems of Mozart, Verdi, Fauré, Britten.

Dies irae.

Quid sum miser.

JOHANNES BRAHMS

(May 7, 1833–April 3, 1897)

"Behold, all flesh is as the grass," from *A German Requiem* Op. 45 (1857–68).
Words from the Bible: I Peter 1, 24; James 5, 7; I Peter 1, 25; Isaiah 35, 10.

48.

Brahms was primarily an instrumental composer, and it is therefore fitting that this choral piece should have been first written (1857–59) as a movement for a symphony. Only after the death of Brahms' mother in 1865, which prompted the composition of the Requiem, were the words added, and the movement was completed by the following year.

Brahms was not a Roman Catholic, and avoided the text of the Latin Requiem Mass which Mozart, Cherubini, Berlioz, and others had set before him. Instead he chose Biblical texts for his seven movements, all of which deal with Man's relationship with death, yet which avoid all Church dogma and even avoid mention of Christ. Sometimes the brevity and suffering of earthly life are emphasized, but more often is the certainty of a happier life beyond the grave. This splendid movement displays both moods. It begins with a slow movement in ternary form,* possibly inspired by the slow movement of Beethoven's Seventh Symphony but with an elegiac atmosphere that is Brahms' own; it must be the only funeral march ever written in triple meter. There follows a tremendous episode which, although not a real fugue, continually uses imitations and *stretti.** Brahms had so absorbed himself in the study of Bach and Handel that such contrapuntal thinking had become second nature to him.

It is fascinating to compare this movement with Berlioz's *Dies Irae* (**47**), and to see the difference between a composer who is rampant with new ideas yet deficient in technique, and one who is a consummate technician yet content to remain within his tradition.

Recordings: many.

Compare: 35 (also completed 1868), **39** (similar bass line and textures), **45, 46, 47;** the remainder of the Requiem; Brahms' four symphonies; his Piano Concerto in D minor, which also embodies ideas from the early symphony of which this was part; the Requiems of Verdi and Fauré.

CHAMBER MUSIC by Dirk Hals (Dutch, first half of the 17th century). Three singers, recorder, lute, and large bass viola da gamba. Note the part-books, and the violist's unusual position, standing and reading from the floor.

The music of friends

Chamber music, which is the subject of this chapter, is the antithesis of the Grand Manner: it is private music, written for the pleasure of the players as much as for the listeners. Much of it is out of place in the concert hall, and out of tune with the usual performer-audience relationship. The examples of chanson (**49**)· madrigal (**50** and **51**), fantasia (**52**), and duo-sonata (**54**) may never have been performed on a stage until the twentieth century. They would normally have been played or sung in private homes by people who enjoyed making music; and if anyone had come to listen, they would probably have been competent enough and willing to join in the next piece.

Throughout the centuries, music has been used as an agreeable way of passing the time, and especially as an activity for evening, when the candles were lit and the day's work was done. Countless pieces which today we regard as concert fare, including all the Classic piano sonatas, violin sonatas, and string quartets, were intended above all for such occasions. But the times have changed. We can now hear music played by professionals at the turn of a switch, so why go to the trouble of becoming amateur performers ourselves? We do not need to entertain ourselves in the evenings, since we have the television. Our machines, in fact, have all but killed real chamber music in America. In Europe and especially in Germany, the situation is better: somehow it seems that the level of popular taste has not sunk so low, so that their television is often worth watching, and there is a thriving industry supplying simple *Hausmusik* ("music for the home").

Listening, after all, is not the same as playing. This is not to say that it is worse—but it is different. There is a special pleasure in playing an instrument or singing in a choral group, however elementary, which one cannot get from listening or watching. This must derive partly from the basic satisfaction of creating something oneself, in this case musical sounds—and it could as well be a piece of knitting or a well-painted window-frame—and partly from doing something in happy cooperation with other people (like a successful team game).

In order to illustrate the best of each genre, I have chosen pieces here that need a moderate or even a high degree of skill for their performance. But each one would have found a ready audience of competent amateurs. Josquin's, Lasso's, and Luzzaschi's pieces (**49, 50, 51**) are three of hundreds of chansons and madrigals composed during the sixteenth century for French and Italian speakers, respectively. English, German, Spanish, and Flemish speakers also had their appropriate part-songs. But in calling the pieces by this term, we do them an injustice: they are not only singable by one person to a part, but also playable by virtually any combination of instruments, with or without voices. Many chansons were published with words on the title page such as "suitable for voices or instruments." Madrigals were frequently arranged for harpsichord or lute, or turned into elaborate solos for cornetto or viol. So these are potentially instrumental as well as vocal pieces.

Instrumental ensembles of the Renaissance were commonly known, in English, as "consorts." They might be of two kinds: whole consorts and broken consorts. The instruments which made up a whole consort were all of the same family, but of different sizes: for example a group of recorders or viols (**52**), or one of the more exotic families such as krummhorns* or racketts.* A broken consort, on the other hand, contained instruments of different families, e.g. two viols, a flute, and three plucked instruments (lute, etc.), to cite a favorite combination of ca. 1600 (see **9a**). Most musicians could play a dozen instruments, so the variety of sound was enormous. Nowadays we hear too much Renaissance music sung *a capella,* * which is often the least interesting way to hear it.

While in a sense the scoring of Renaissance music was a free-for-all, there were some marked preferences. Italian madri-

gals which emphasize the poetry (**51**) are best sung by solo
voices. English fantasias (**52**) in which each part is of equal importance and activity should be played, if possible, by whole
consorts. But, as another prominent English musician reputedly said, "If a thing is worth doing, it is worth doing
badly" (R. Vaughan Williams). No better motto could be found
for chamber music enthusiasts—so long as no one is forced to
listen to the results.

Handel's Sonata in F (**54**) has been played badly, and well,
by thousands of flutists completely ignorant of the fact that it is
primarily intented for alto recorder. But even in Handel's day
there was some leeway in the choice of instruments, and both are
acceptable in this case, just as oboe, flute, and violin may inter-
change in some of his other works. I give my own "interpretation" of the work, as it might be ornamented by extremely competent amateurs. A similar treatment might have been given to
Corelli's concerto (**53**), for we know that the solo parts in his
works were embellished both by himself, as a violinist, and by
other performers. As it is, all the parts, including the continuo,
are left as he wrote them. In the terminology explained in the
previous chapter, No. **53** is given in a scholarly edition, No. **54** in
a performing edition.

It may surprise some that I include a concerto in a chapter
on chamber music. But Corelli's (**53**) is at the same time a piece
of chamber music: a trio sonata* for two violins and continuo.
The instruments of the *concerto grosso** can be omitted entirely,
and scarcely a note will be lost. We have the permission of
eighteenth-century authorities to perform a concerto such as this
one in any of the following ways, and more:

Concertino 2 violins or 2 oboes
(soloists) cello   bassoon
harpsichord or organ

Concerto grosso Omit, or 2–24 violins
(orchestra)   1–6 violas
                         1–6 cellos
                         1–4 basses
                         add extra harpsichord,
                         organ, lutes, *ad libitum*.

In about 1730 some of Corelli's Opus 6 were even published in
London with the title: *Six concertos for two Flutes and a Bass,*

with a Through Bass [continuo] *for the Harpsichord, Neatly transpos'd from ye great Concertos;* other arrangements were frequent throughout the century. The enormous success of these concertos must have been due, in part, to this adaptability.

Rameau's collection of trios (**55**) is written for one of the most common small combinations of the Baroque: one violin, a harpsichord, and a bass viol. Usually such a group would play music similar to Handel's sonata (**54**): the high instrument would have all the tunes, the low instrument a continuous bass line, and the harpsichord would play along with the bass, filling in chords as he went. Rameau's work is totally different. Here the harpsichordist is the principal performer, and his part is written out exactly. The violin (or flute) and viol (or second violin) play subsidiary parts which, says Rameau (eager to make yet another selling point?), may be omitted altogether. Just as the orchestra can drop out of Corelli's concerto, leaving a trio sonata, so these pieces can be reduced to harpsichord solos.

By 1800, this kind of adaptability was obsolete. Advances in technique had given to each instrument its characteristic music, untransferable to any other instrument. Specialization had made one person an oboist, another a flutist, whereas in Handel's day the same person might have played both and been a fair fiddler and organist as well. Consequently chamber music now settled down into certain fixed combinations:

without piano	**String Trio**	**String Quartet**	**String Quintet**
	violin	2 violins	2 violins
	viola	viola	1–2 violas
	cello	cello	1–2 cellos
with piano	**Piano Trio**	**Piano Quartet**	**Piano Quintet**
	violin	violin	2 violins
	cello	viola	viola
	piano	cello	cello
		piano	piano

Other groupings were relatively rare, and usually the result of a special commission from an otherwise excluded player, e.g. the famous clarinettist Anton Stadler (Mozart's Clarinet Quintet). It would have seemed absurd to Schubert to invent an entirely new combination, as do many modern composers, and then go around looking for people to play in it: he was there to supply the players with material, not they to satisfy his whims. Consequently he joined the great Classical and Romantic composers, from Haydn to Brahms, in writing much of his chamber music for the most popular of all the traditional combinations, the string quartet (**56**).

A string quartet is, of course, a "whole consort," and when necessary it can sound like a single instrument of immense range and versatility (e.g. the opening of **56**). On the other hand, it contains four distinct characters who can enter into a multitude of different relationships (e.g. the trio of **60**, where each in turn has the melody).

Compared to the sound of a string quartet, a trio sounds thin and a piano quintet overloaded, though each has its purpose. (The second fiddle may fall ill, or an important pianist may happen by.) Beethoven, in his last years, virtually abandoned all other media and concentrated entirely on string quartets. This fragment of Schubert's, written at the age of 21, precedes Beethoven's incomparable late works, but in its own way is a jewel in a genre which has seen many masterpieces.

The later nineteenth century was more a time of opera and orchestral music than of chamber music, as composers' ambitions waxed and the desire to impress became stronger than the will to please. Hence the symbolic gap: the historical sequence is resumed with the movement from Bartók (**63**), a composer who, more than any other, revived the string quartet as a vehicle for the profoundest thoughts.

Suggestions for further reading W. W. Cobbett, *Cyclopaedic Survey of Chamber Music* (2nd ed., London, 1964–65) is an invaluable reference work. Alec Robertson, ed., *Chamber Music* (London, 1957) contains many fine essays on the period since 1700. For the background to **49–52**, see the introduction to Helen Hewitt, ed., *Canti B* (Chicago, 1967), James Haar, ed., *Chanson and Madrigal* (Cambridge, Mass., 1964), Alfred Einstein, *The Italian Madrigal* (Princeton, 1949), Walter L. Woodfill, *Musicians in English Society* (New York, 1969). Marc Pincherle's *Corelli: His Life, His Music* (New York, 1969) is brief; Cuthbert Girdlestone's *Jean-Philippe Rameau* (New York, 1969) long and thorough. On performance practice in the Baroque and earlier times, see Thurston Dart's excellent summary, *The Interpretation of Music* (London, 1954) and Robert Donington's copious works, *The Interpretation of Early Music* (London, 1963) and *A Performer's Guide to Baroque Music* (London, 1973). On Schubert, see Otto E. Deutsch, ed., *Schubert, Memoirs by His Friends* (New York, 1958) and Jack A. Westrup, *Schubert's Chamber Music* (Oxford, 1969). On practical chamber music-making, see M. D. Herder Norton, *The Art of String Quartet Playing* (New York, 1966).

JOSQUIN DES PREZ
(ca. 1450–August 27, 1521)
Basiez-moy (published 1502).

49.

This is an early example of a form that was to dominate the field of secular music for half a century. In contrast to the chansons of Machaut (see **19**) and of the fifteenth-century Burgundian school (see **21**), the sixteenth-century chanson abandoned the *formes fixes* (see commentaries to **19, 20, 21**) in favor of through-composed and ternary forms, and the soloistic, treble-dominated* texture in favor of equality of all the voices (usually four). The use of imitation followed naturally from this, and led in some cases to the most thorough kind of imitation—the *canon.* * This chanson is a double canon, i.e. there are two canons going on simultaneously, between the top two and the bottom two voices. This kind of musical ingenuity is difficult to compose, but was a favorite diversion of the Netherlands school of composers: Ockeghem, Obrecht, Josquin, etc. The middle section incorporates a tune which is also found in a monophonic chanson collection of a slightly earlier date. This points up the easy-going system of musical borrowing, and the close interaction between the most refined composers and the world of popular song.

The first publication of this song was in Ottaviano Petrucci's *Canti B* (i.e. his second song collection). The year before, Petrucci had issued the very first printed collection of part-music, *Harmonice Musices Odhecaton A*. The fact that Petrucci was a Venetian, yet made his debut with books of Franco-Flemish chansons, shows how the composers from the Netherlands had come to dominate European music. But Petrucci was soon to turn to the publication of Italian *frottole*, the form from which the Italian madrigal (**50, 51**) was eventually to emerge.

The small accidentals above the notes are editorial additions. It was customary until about 1600 for performers to inflect certain notes, according to a system of rules and conventions which they and the composers understood better than we do. Such alterations were known as *musica ficta* (Latin, "made-up music"), as opposed to the music that was actually written or printed. In this piece the added accidentals occur mainly at cadences and would almost certainly have been sung. The disparity of key signatures is due to the fact that the canon is "at the fourth;" the two parts of each pair are a fourth apart and hence in different "keys."

Recordings: None. 71261 (*Josquin Des Prez: Chansons, Frottole & Instrumental Pieces;* Nonesuch Consort, Rifkin, cond.) Amadeo AVRS 6233 (*Instrumentalmusik am Hofe Maximilians I,* Concentus Musicus); Arc. 629517/8 (*La musique flamande*); 3-Sera. S-6052 (*Seraphim Guide to Renaissance Music*).

Compare: **4d, 21, 50, 51;** Josquin's *Salve Regina,* a more extensive piece composed on the same principles; the six-part version of the same piece also in *Canti B;* chansons of Jannequin, Sermisy, Certon, Crequillon; Italian *frottole*.

ORLANDO DI LASSO

(1532–June 14, 1595)

Matona mia cara (published 1581).

50.

So international was this composer that one hesitates whether to call him Roland de Lassus (as he was in his native France), Orlando di Lasso (as the Italians called him), or Orlando Lassus, as he appears as a composer of Latin church music. To complete the picture, he worked from 1556 until his death at the Bavarian Court in Munich. Immensely prolific, he wrote in every vocal style of his day: chanson, madrigal, Lied, motet, and Mass. This is one of his more frivolous pieces, included in order to show the range of Italian vocal music of the late sixteenth century: it represents the polar opposite to Luzzaschi's madrigal (**51**).

The singer is supposed to be a German soldier, attempting to seduce an Italian lady. The Italians derived much amusement from the speech and habits of German mercenaries, at least after they had forgotten the Sack of Rome by the German Emperor's troops in 1527. This translation bears hardly any relation to the original Italian, which has been sung cheerfully by countless modern choirs in blissful ignorance of the fact that it is grossly obscene.

Recordings: Tel. S-9462 (*Alte Madrigäle . . .*, Monteverdi-Chor); RCA Vic. S-1231 (*Sixteenth Century Love Songs,* Rome Polyphonic Chorus) o.p.; many others. Mace MC S9062 (*Music of the Renaissance,* Walther von der Vogelweide Chamber Choir of Innsbruck).

Compare: 3b, 8a & b, 49, 51; Lassus' other songs, of all kinds; the *Frottole* and *Canti carnalieschi*.

LUZZASCO LUZZASCHI

(1545–April 11, 1607)

Quivi sospiri (published 1584).
Words by Dante Alighieri.

51.

This composer is best known for his 1601 collection of madrigals for solo voices and keyboard, which contain the only extant examples of keyboard accompaniments from the Renaissance period, and also show fantastic ornamentation of the vocal lines such as the great singers of the time must have improvised. (They were written for three virtuoso sopranos at the Court of Ferrara.) Luzzaschi was also a fine composer of ordinary madrigals in the "expressive" tradition of Cipriano de Rore (his childhood teacher), Giaches de Wert, Marenzio, and the more celebrated Gesualdo. This highly chromatic piece is unusual for its time in setting a passage from Dante. The madrigalists neglected the riches of the *Divine Comedy* in favor of the lighter verse of Dante's younger contemporary, Petrarch. But no fewer than seven composers set the "Quivi sospiri" passage, showing an odd predilection for the gruesome, while the whole of that incomparable work was available to them. At least it lends itself well to the intense and passionate style of the later madrigal, with its emphasis on faithful expression of the text. Chromaticism in music has traditionally been used to express grief; here it appears both melodically and in bizarre juxtapositions of unrelated chords.

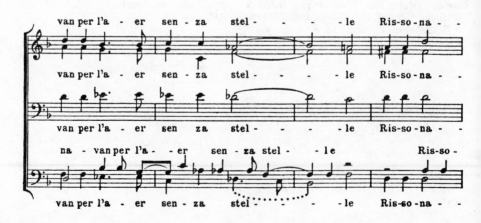

WILLIAM BYRD

(1543–July 4, 1623)

Browning Fantasia à 5 (before 1578?).

Byrd, chief composer of a golden age, excelled in all the genres of his time. He wrote an abundance of church music, both Latin and English, madrigals, accompanied songs, canons, chamber music for viols, and keyboard music. This fantasia, best suited to viols (see commentary to no. **55**), shows his skill in constructing a long, monothematic, "seamless robe" of counterpoint. The title is traceable to a popular song beginning: "The leaves be green, the nuts be brown, they hang so high, they will not come down." These words will be found to fit the music at the points indicated in the score by the small number 1–20. With admirable ingenuity, Byrd weaves this simple tune into counterpoint of increasing complexity. The structure of the piece is most easily understood through rhythm. The entries of the voices gradually speed up until the ninth entry of the theme:

52.

bar	part	
1	1	
14	4	
21	5	
26	1	
28	2	

At bar 34 the pace slows down for a time. Then at the end of bar 53, quite suddenly, the rhythms become extremely complex. By bar 56 we have the following meters striving against each other:

part	meter	
1	$\frac{12}{8}$	displaced by one eighth-note
2	$\frac{6}{4}$	
3	$\frac{12}{8}$	on the beat
4	$\frac{6}{4}$	
5	$\frac{12}{8}$	

At bar 61 all is calm again, though the entries are more frequent and the motives spikier, and another "rhythmic crescendo" begins. The fastest notes of all come in bar 69, and the activity continues in full spate until the closing bars where Byrd maintains the tension with some characteristic English cross-relations.* The most dissonant one of all is reserved for the very last bar, where it has a striking effect.

This brief description shows that one must analyze sixteenth-century pieces in an entirely different way from later ones. The harmonic and thematic forms of Baroque and Classic music are quite irrelevant here.

Recordings: Tel. S-9511 (*English Music for Recorders and Viols*, Brüggen Consort)

Compare: 3b, 4d, 9b, 49, 50, 51; Byrd, *Browning* à 3; *Masses* in three, four, and five parts; fantasies of Gibbons, Jenkins, and Purcell (for later developments in the genre).

ARCANGELO CORELLI

(February 17, 1653–January 8, 1713)

Christmas Concerto Grosso in G minor, Op. 6, No. 8 (1712).

53. Corelli resembles Chopin in the single-mindedness with which he worked throughout his life in a single medium, and brought it to at least a temporary perfection. His chosen field was that of music for stringed instruments and continuo. He wrote for only three different combinations: one violin and continuo (twelve sonatas, Opus 5), two violins and continuo (48 sonatas, Opus 1–4), and string orchestra (twelve concertos, Opus 6—but see the introduction to this chapter on their adaptability to smaller ensembles). This neat repertory is divided equally between works intended for the Church (sonatas and concertos *da chiesa*) and those written for secular use (*da camera,* "of the chamber"). The latter contain some dance movements and resemble suites,* while the church pieces are collections of from four to nine "abstract" movements (some of them, as here, mere bridge-passages) making much use of imitative textures.

The *da chiesa* pieces were played in Church before, after, and even during the Mass. But of course they were not restricted to this use. This concerto, "made for the night of the Nativity," is the only one to end with a slow movement, but the famous *pastorale* is, as the score says, an optional addition. Both Bach and Handel were to write similar movements in the "Pastoral Symphonies" of the *Christmas Oratorio* and *Messiah*. The remainder of the movements fall into the conventional four sections of the church style:

I **Slow (Vivace - Grave),** solemn, and unornamented, with imitation and suspension.

II **Fast (Allegro)**, in binary form, usually fugual texture.

III **Slow (Adagio - Allegro - Adagio)**, less solemn than I.

IV **Fast (Vivace - Allegro)**, mainly homophonic texture.

Recordings: many.

Compare: 33, 38, 54; earlier concertos by Torelli; later ones by Bach (*Brandenburg Concertos*), Handel (*Grand Concertos,* Op. 6), and Vivaldi.

Pastorale ad libitum

GEORGE FRIDERIC HANDEL

(February 23, 1685–April 14, 1759)

Sonata in F major, Op. 1, No. 11 (published 1724).

54.

This *sonata da chiesa* (see commentary to **53**) is one of a collection of twelve sonatas for a solo instrument with continuo part "for the Harpsichord or a Bass Violin" (i.e. cello). Two of these are for oboe, three each for violin and flute, and four, including this one, for alto recorder. It is not known exactly when they were written. Handel later incorporated material from this sonata into an organ concerto: the kind of borrowing which was common in his day, even between composers. The long lines of the *Larghetto* bespeak the composer of "Dov'è sei" (see **33**) and "I know that my Redeemer liveth," from *Messiah,* while the jolly second and fourth movements look to the *concerti grossi* and the operatic overtures.

In this ornamented arrangement, which derives from practical experience of both the solo and the harpsichord parts, my contribution consists of the small notes, and Handel's of the large ones. The ornaments in the fast movements are intended only for the repeats.

Recordings: DG ARC 2533060 (Handel: *Sonatas, Op. 1 for Flute; Sonatas for Flute,: "Halle",* Linde, Richter, J. Koch); RCA VICS-1429 (same title, Linde, recorder, Leonhardt); Tel. S-9421 (same title, Brüggen, recorder, Leonhardt).

Compare: 10, 11, 33, 38, 53, 55; Handel's trio sonatas and concertos, especially the Organ Concerto, Op. 4, No. 5; Bach's flute and violin sonatas; recorder music of Telemann and Loillet.

JEAN-PHILIPPE RAMEAU

(September 25, 1683–September 12, 1764)

a. *La Livri*

b. *La Forqueray*

from *Pièces de Clavecin en Concert* (1741).

55.

Rameau began his musical career as an obscure provincial organist and writer of learned theoretical treatises. But at the age of fifty, to everyone's amazement, he suddenly began a second career as an opera composer, in which capacity he revolutionized French operatic taste and gave rise to some lively controversies. These "Pieces for Harpsichord in Ensemble," consisting of sixteen pieces in five suites, represent the best of Rameau's chamber music, presumably written over the several preceding years. They admit us to an ultra-refined world in which one must play with consummate taste or not at all. Handel's sturdy music can survive almost any treatment, but much of the beauty of Rameau's is on the surface: like a piece of Rococo furniture, it is exquisitely decorated and polished, even though its shape may not be particularly interesting.

A contemporary of Rameau wrote in 1764: "We believe that the melody of the *Livri* will always touch music lovers." This rich-textured *tombeau** for the Comte de Livri (d. 1741) is certainly one of his most beautiful inspirations. (The first section should be repeated in between the subsequent ones and at the end.) *La Forqueray*, a real display piece, may have been a wedding present to Jean-Baptiste Forqueray, one of the foremost composers and viol players of the day, who was married in the same year. One can easily hear wedding bells in the downward scale and pealing harpsichord part of this, the longest work in the collection.

The first choice of instruments for these pieces is violin, bass viol, and harpsichord. The viol, or viola da gamba, is the lowest regular member of a family of bowed instruments that grew up not as predecessors but alongside the violin family in the sixteenth century. The two families were named (in Italian) *viole da braccia* and *viole da gamba*, i.e. arm- and leg-viols, after the way in which the smaller members were held. (Naturally one cannot hold a cello on the arm, although strictly speaking it is a "bass viola da braccio.") The viols differed from the violins as follows:

viol family	**violin family**
sloping shoulders	round shoulders
deep body	narrow body
flat back	rounded back
six strings, tuned mainly in 4ths	four strings, tuned in 5ths
C-shaped soundholes	f-shaped soundholes
bow held underarm	bow held overarm

(See plates 5 and 7)

By 1650, the greater agility and more penetrating tone of the violins had all but ousted the higher viols, but the bass viol survived for another hundred years as a useful continuo instrument. In France it also acquired a large solo literature of unprecedented virtuosity. So Rameau's pieces came to a public well prepared for their difficult viol parts.

Recordings: Tel. S-9578 (*Pièces de clavecin en concert,* Brüggen, S. & W. Kuijiken, Leonhardt); None. 71063 (same title, Veyron-Lacroix, Rampal, Neiltz).

Compare: 11, 12, 33, 53, 54; Rameau's keyboard arrangement of *La Livri*; his operas; music of Marin Marais for viol; of F. Couperin for harpsichord.

La Livri

Rondeau gracieux

La Forqueray

Bei der Wiederholung spielt man statt der letzten ganzen Note eine Viertelnote.
(Anmerkung des Komponisten)

On recommence, en faisant une noire de la derniere ronde.
(Remarque du compositeur)

On repetition the final semibreve (whole note) is to be played as a crotchet (quarter note).
(Composer's remark)

FRANZ SCHUBERT

(January 31, 1797–November 19, 1828)

Quartettsatz in C minor (December, 1820).

This isolated quartet movement never received the three companions that one would expect, perhaps because at the time of its writing Schubert was much involved in operatic projects. Many great composers have spent years trying to write successful operas which either never came to fruition (Debussy) or are soon forgotten (Berlioz, Schubert, Schumann). But despite its solitary state, this is a jewel among quartets. The sinister beginning is of course a foreshadowing of the theme which comes in eighth-notes at bar 13. Notice how the same rhythm serves as an accompaniment to S*—one of Schubert's "heaven-sent" melodies. Few Romantic composers could achieve the smoothness and continuity with which he fits this self-sufficient tune into the framework of sonata form. So often (even in Schubert), when the themes are too song-like, the duality of sonata form is never resolved, and the piece simply sounds like a collection of pleasant tunes.

Schubert was very fond of modulations to keys a third away: here he goes from C minor to E♭ to G, reached at k* where the unity of theme and rhythmic pattern still persists through a short but very memorable theme. By the end of the development, the material of P* has been used so much that Schubert does not begin the recapitulation* with it, as one would expect, but with S, reserving P for a short coda which echoes the opening of the movement. The harmonies and modulations are fascinating throughout, and the quartet writing is of crystalline clarity.

56.

Recordings: many.

Compare: 13, 24; Ch. 8, especially **60**; Schubert's (complete) *Quartet in D minor* ("Death and the Maiden"); his *Unfinished Symphony*, whose opening recalls that of this movement; string quartets of Beethoven, Mendelssohn, and Brahms.

Franz Schubert: *Quartettsatz in C minor*

Thomas Jefferson's Rotunda at the University of Virginia (1819-26).

THE CONTINUITY OF AN IDEA IN ARCHITECTURAL HISTORY

The Pantheon in Rome (circa 27 B.C.)

The sonata idea

During the later eighteenth century an idea came into being that was to change the whole principle of musical structure. Up to the mid-century it had been generally assumed that a piece of music should describe a single emotion: joy, sorrow, reverence, anger, etc. In the case of arias in ternary form (e.g. those of **33**), it was permissible for the mood to change for the middle section, but usually there was only a slight alteration of feeling and not a complete contrast. Such an assumption seems to have had its root in a belief that music, like painting, is an art of description. The meaning of a piece, according to this theory, is simply the emotion it depicts; and a good composer or performer, like a good painter, is one who can put over an emotion in so convincing a manner that the listeners experience it in their own psyches. Thus a Baroque opera, and on a smaller scale a concerto, suite, or sonata, is a tableau of many different emotional states or "affects" (i.e., particular feelings, not to be confused with "effects"), each of which can be enjoyed in an uncomplicated way.

The *sonata* idea changed all this. A movement in sonata form is not a single affect made audible, but two or more contrasting affects juxtaposed, contrasted, combined, or united. The movement no longer depicts a state: it tells a story. (I hinted at this while discussing Bach's and Beethoven's works in Chapter 6.) C.P.E. Bach, the first great exponent of the principle, frequently began a movement with a musical "problem" which he subsequently solved. In **57** this is particularly clearly illustrated: what could be more different than the noble chords of the opening bars (1–4) and the thin, almost silly passage that follows (5–10)? They seem like oil and water; yet by the end of the movement Bach has persuaded us that there can indeed be a conjunction of opposites.

This idea of a reconciliation of disparate elements is a guiding principle in most Classic and much Romantic music, at least as far as "abstract" works (sonatas, symphonies, etc.) are concerned. It is plain, from this statement, that we are dealing with something more complicated and more intellectual than a song or a dance. I would not say that the Classic period was simply intellectual: the composers were too interested in harmony, the feeling element of music, for that. But I believe that a certain intellectual preparation is necessary for full enjoyment of Mozart's, Haydn's, and Beethoven's music. When one is listening to earlier, "static" music, one can simply immerse oneself in the affect which the piece offers. But in the case of "dynamic" music, one has to understand what is going on if one is not to be confused by the changing emotions—assuming, of course, that one is really listening.

Those with even a shallow acquaintance with music of the Classic period will have noticed that there is a system that governs nearly all its instrumental music:

	SYMPHONY	CONCERTO	STRING QUARTET, ETC.	SONATA
Medium	Orchestra	Solo instrument(s) with orchestra	Various chamber ensembles	1 or 2 instruments
Movements	4	3	4	3 or 4

MOVEMENTS

	First	Second	Third (omitted in 3-movt. works)	Fourth
Speed	fast	slow	moderate-fast	fast
Form	sonata	sonata variation rondo binary ternary	ternary/binary	sonata variation rondo

The system was adhered to rather strictly by composers, and for good reason: they wished to maintain their communication with the audience by a subtle blend of fulfilling and destroying expectations. The listeners of the period, hearing nothing but the music of their own day, had developed this framework of expectations like a series of molds into which composers poured music. We should attempt to do the same; and the purpose of this chapter is to present some works that assume such preparation.

First we have to understand the meaning of these forms. One of the most immediately comprehensible is the *rondo**, named from the Italian for no deeper reason than because the main theme keeps coming "round":

A B A C A D A etc.

In the shorthand of musical analysis, different letters represent different music. So a rondo is very much like a song with choruses in which each verse has a different tune. Examples **59** IV and **60** IV are two very cheerful representatives, and both are finales (last movements): the favorite place for rondos. Others in this collection are **15, 21, 50, 55a,** and **58** III.

Ternary form, sometimes called "song form" is like one round of a rondo:

A B A

It is the form of many songs, marches and dance movements. In the latter cases the "B" section is commonly known as the *trio.** (Elsewhere in music this term usually indicates a piece for three people, but in this case a string quartet or an entire orchestra may be playing. The reason for the anachronism is to be found in French court music of the late seventeenth century, when an inexhaustible appetite for dancing was supplied by music from an orchestra of stringed instruments with two oboes and a bassoon. Dances often had a middle section in which the strings were silent and the "trio" of wind instruments played alone. Somehow the term caught on and has survived ever since, although it no longer makes sense.) Ternary and rondo forms are perhaps the most archetypal of all, referring as they do to the universal human experience of cycles and the eternal return: of the heartbeat, the breath, night and day, the seasons, life and death. Another "cyclic" form is the *theme and variations,** in which a single idea is repeated several times with alterations:

$$A^1 \ A^2 \ A^3 \ A^4 \ \text{etc.}$$

It is typical that the Classic era saw the invention of the rare "double variation" form, in which two contrasted ideas are varied alternately. I give no example of this, but include several normal variation sets: **9b, 37,** and **39.**

Binary or two-part form has a peculiarity about it: both parts are usually repeated:

A A B B

or, to use the conventional repeat signs:

‖: **A** :‖: **B** :‖

The "B" section is sometimes the same length as the "A" (e.g. the theme of **9b** and the dances of **10**), but more often it is longer. And such is the power of the ternary idea that a longer "B" section often includes a return of some or all of "A," either in its original form or somewhat altered (the latter indicated by a prime symbol):

‖: **A** :‖: **B a** :‖   or   ‖: **A** :‖: **B A'** :‖
(e.g. **11,** Minuet)   (e.g. **58** III, Trio)

A typical third movement (Minuet and Trio-**58**-or Scherzo and Trio-**60**) combines binary and ternary forms thus:

	A	B	A
HIGHER LEVEL: *(ternary form)*	Minuet or Scherzo	Trio	Minuet or Scherzo
LOWER LEVEL: *(binary form)*	‖: **A** :‖: **B** :‖	‖: **C** :‖: **D** :‖	**A B**

It is traditional to omit the repeats when the minuet returns, and to indicate the return by words such as *da capo* in order to save writing it out again. A complete performance of **58** III can be analyzed as follows:

bar nos.	1–16	1–16	17	42	17	42	56–64	56–64	65	72	65	72	1–16	17–4:
	A	A	B	A'	B	A'	C	C	D	C'	D	C'	A	B

The reader who has followed the labyrinth of forms thus far is well equipped to tackle the most interesting of all, *sonata* form. Like the Minotaur, it is a hybrid creature, again comprising both ternary and binary forms. This phenomenon demands a new but brief arsenal of terms, of which the first three are:

Exposition:* the composer's cards are placed on the table;
Development:* they are shuffled;
Recapitulation:* they come out in nearly the same order.

C.P.E. Bach's sonata (**57**) dates from the historical moment when sonata form was first emerging. The last movement can be regarded in three ways:

bar nos.	1	35	79	
BINARY FORM	‖: A :‖:	B	A′ :‖	
SONATA FORM	‖: Expo :‖:	Dev.	Recap. :‖	
TERNARY FORM	A	B	A′	(if repeats are omitted)

Here the "B" part is spun entirely out of material supplied by "A." This is the usual justification for calling it a development. The final "A" part matches the first almost exactly, and this is why it can be called a recapitulation. A movement in sonata form must satisfy both requirements.

There is, of course, much more to it. The core of the movement may be preceded by a slow introduction or followed by a *coda* or "tail," and there is some license in the matter of repeats. In addition to the model shown above, the following schemata, and more, are to be found:

Examples

60 I	‖: Expo :‖: Dev. Recap. :‖ Coda
56	‖: Expo :‖ Dev. Recap. Coda
59 I ·	Intro ‖: Expo :‖ Dev. Recap. Coda
60 II, **61, 63**	Expo. Dev. Recap. Coda
62	Expo. Dev. Recap.

Mozart, Haydn, and Beethoven frequently did not require the repeat of the second half. During the nineteenth century it became less and less usual for composers even to demand a repeat of the exposition. Consequently, modern conductors and other performers will often ignore the repeats which are specified by composers. There is some justification for believing that repetition was always optional, but in many works the balance seems to be better when one follows the composer's directions. One fears that the automatic omission of repeats is a symptom of a hurried, "get-it-over-with" attitude, antithetical to the spirit of the music. At the first performance of the *Military*

Symphony the audience actually demanded a repeat of the entire second movement! If anything had been curtailed or cut they would have felt cheated, having paid what we would consider an horrendous price for admission. But times change, and we cannot always appreciate what to them was a statement of crystalline clarity, and an exquisite pleasure.

Returning now to sonata form, it is necessary to dig deeper into what actually constitutes the element of contrast. The exposition is a basically bipartite object, containing primary and secondary themes or subjects, here called P and S. (These usually differ in mood or affect, and they always differ in key. If the piece, and hence P, is in a major key, S will usually be in the dominant* (e.g. **58** I). If in a minor key, S is usually in the relative major* (e.g. **60** I). In the development, any keys may be employed, until the home key is reached again with the recapitulation. But here P and S both reappear *with the same key center.* This may be diagrammed thus:

		EXPO.	DEV.	RECAP. AND CODA
	Home	P		P S
Keys				
	Away	S	various	

In addition to P and S, other parts of the exposition may deserve the name of "theme." A different mood, often a stormy one, may appear before S as a *transition* to the new theme and a modulation to the new key. This I call "t". After S there may be another new theme which brings the exposition to a *close*: this I call "k" (not "c," since that letter is often used elsewhere in analysis). A full exposition, such as that of No. **61,** will break down as follows:

61	**bar nos.**	1	(33)	47	(77)
	themes	P	t	S	k

The exact placing of t and k is often debatable, but S is always the point at which the new key is established.

The development often begins with a varied version of P (e.g. **57** I, **60** I, **61**) but it may start with S (**58** I), k (**59**), or something completely different. It is often the most exciting, not to say confusing, part of the movement, as the themes are varied, shattered, combined, or even forgotten altogether, and it is with a sense of homecoming after a journey that one hears the familiar sounds that mark the recapitulation.

A form that was forged over a half a century and then obsessed the best musical minds for twice that time is not to be comprehended in a moment. Long acquaintance and careful observation are needed to acquire a real feeling for the idea, to which this chapter is the merest introduction. And when all is said and done, when a piece has been analyzed and "understood" to the last degree, all will have been in vain if one cannot then forget everything one has learned, and just listen.

Suggestions for further reading: Donald Francis Tovey, *The Forms of Music* (Cleveland and New York, 1956) contains his articles for the *Encyclopaedia Brittannica* which are among the most enjoyable ever written on the subject. On the sonata, see William S. Newman, *The Sonata in the Classic Era* (Chapel Hill, 1963) and *The Sonata since Beethoven* (Chapel Hill, 1969), and Wilfred Mellers, *The Sonata Principle* (Part III of *Man and His Music,* London, 1969). The basic books in these specific fields are: Philip Barford, *The Keyboard Music of C.P.E. Bach* (London, 1965), a remarkable philosophical approach; C. M. Girdlestone, *Mozart and His Piano Concertos* (New York, 1964 and Gloucester, Mass., 1966); H. C. Robbins Landon, *The Symphonies of Joseph Haydn* (London, 1955, with *Supplement,* New York, 1961); Philip Radcliffe, *Beethoven's String Quartets* (New York, 1967), and Joseph Kerman, *The Beethoven Quartets* (New York, 1967). On Mendelssohn, see Philip Radcliffe, *Mendelssohn* (London, 1957) and Eric Werner, *Mendelssohn; A New Image of the Composer and His Age* (London, 1963). On the later composers, I. V. Nestyev, *Prokofiev* (Stanford, 1960) and Halsey Stevens, *The Life and Music of Béla Bartók* (London, 1964) are basic. Further on Bartók, see the fascinating account of Agatha Fassett, *Béla Bartók; The American Years* (New York, 1972; first published in 1958 as *The Naked Face of Genius*), and Ernö Lendvai, *Béla Bartók; An Analysis of His Music* (London, 1971).

CARL PHILIPP EMANUEL BACH

(March 8, 1714–December 14, 1788)

Württemberg Sonata No. 3 in E minor from *Sei Sonate per Cembalo* (published 1744).

57. C.P.E. Bach, the most eminent son of his father Johann Sebastian Bach, is one of those few figures of great historical importance who has never quite caught the public imagination. But the disparity between the period of J.S. Bach and Handel, and that of Mozart and Haydn, is incomprehensible without him. A composer whom all his successors, including Beethoven, revered, Emanuel was more famous than Sebastian until the "Bach Revival" of the early nineteenth century. He was securely placed from the age of 24 at the court of Frederick the Great, but found the intelligentsia of Berlin more receptive to his avant-garde tendencies than the king, who kept his salary deplorably low.

He wrote this sonata while taking a cure for the gout at Teplitz in 1743, and dedicated it to the Duke of Württemberg. Although an early work, it shows his capacity for uniting opposites, and as such his allegiance to the sonata ideal of which he, more than anyone else, is the father. The strong dynamic contrasts are written with the clavichord* rather than the harpsichord* in mind; and since the clavichord is a very quiet instrument, audible only by the performer and a few friends, this, like all of Emanuel's solo keyboard works, is music destined primarily for the player's private recreation. The style, with its frequent surprises, silences (especially in II), and sighs, is a highly subjective and emotional one. All of this explains why this music is scarcely ever played at concerts or recorded.

At this early stage of the history of sonata form, the development often takes the themes of the exposition in order, transposing and varying them (e.g. I, III). One can see here the closeness to binary movements such as those of J.S. Bach's suites (**11**). The matching endings of the two halves of the movements are also characteristic of binary form: the coda had not yet been invented.

Recordings: none.

Compare: 10, 11, 12, 54; Emanuel's other sonatas and fantasies; harpsichord sonatas of Domenico Scarlatti; piano sonatas of Haydn and Mozart.

WOLFGANG AMADEUS MOZART

(January 27, 1756–December 5, 1791)

Piano Concerto No. 23 in A major, K. 488 (1786).

58.

Mozart's piano concertos mark his emancipation from the patronage system under which virtually all composers before him had worked. Employed by a king (C.P.E. Bach), a nobleman (Haydn), a town (J.S. Bach), or an archbishop (Mozart, in Salzburg), composers had been reasonably sure of a steady income, but restricted in their movements and bound to fulfil the demands of their patrons. When Mozart left Salzburg and moved to Vienna in 1781, he had to earn his living as a freelancer by teaching piano and theory and by playing at concerts in the upper-class homes and "academies" of the city. At the busiest times he would perform as often as every other day, playing his concertos and chamber music with piano, and improvising—a necessary accomplishment for a concert pianist in the Classic era.

Mozart's achievement in his piano concertos is comparable to that of Beethoven in the symphony: by the time he had finished developing the genre, it was something quite his own, and very far removed from any of his predecessors' efforts (in Mozart's case, J. C. Bach et. al.). In these works he established the classic form for the first movement of concertos:

Exposition		**Development**
I for orchestra alone (no modulation to dominant)	II for piano with orchestra (modulates to dominant or equivalent key)	piano and orchestra, various keys
Recapitulation	**Cadenza***	**Coda**
piano and orchestra (no modulation)	Piano alone	orchestra alone

More importantly, he combined all he had learned from writing symphonies (e.g. the orchestral exposition of I), light divertimenti* for wind instruments (e.g. the winds' independent entries near the beginnings of I and III), and operatic arias (e.g. the opening of II)—not to mention his own skill as one of the finest pianists of his day. When playing his concertos he would, no doubt, have altered, embellished, and improved the written notes as the mood took him; the piano part at bars 85–92 of II may be merely a sketch, and the cadenza was traditionally extemporized on the spot. But most pianists today wisely play the cadenzas that Mozart and Beethoven wrote out.

This concerto has become a favorite, thanks to its many beautiful themes, its perfect integration of piano and orchestra, and its overall feeling of happiness. Only at moments in the slow movement does the darker side of Mozart show, in which he can be heard as the direct ancestor of Chopin.

Recordings: many.

Compare: 34, 38, 53, 58, 62; Mozart's and Beethoven's piano concertos; Mozart's symphonies.

FRANZ JOSEF HAYDN

(March 31, 1732–May 31, 1809)

Military Symphony No. 100 in G major (1794).

59.

The Military Symphony was first performed in London at the height of Haydn's career. It is worth keeping in mind that he wrote it for an audience which had shown enormous enthusiasm for his work, and which he made every effort to delight in return. They would have liked the surprise when, after a solemn Adagio, P enters in the shrillest register of the orchestra, sounding like fifes. They must have enjoyed the irrelevant key with which the development begins, and the casual way in which the recapitulation sneaks back, almost in mid-phrase. And we have the Morning Chronicle's word that they loved the absurd military music of the second movement: "Another new Symphony by Haydn, was performed for the second time; and the middle movement was again received with absolute shouts of applause. Encore! encore! encore! resounded from every seat: the Ladies themselves could not forbear . . ." What a contrast to most audiences of the present day, who sit in stony silence and glare at those who are gauche enough to begin applauding before the end of the work! When one reads of Haydn's English visits, and of the wonderful happiness he both gave and enjoyed there, one catches a glimpse of a time—perhaps the last—in which a great composer was still completely in tune with the public, and they with him.

The second movement is a rarity among Haydn's, and indeed among all, symphonic works: this is usually the place for slow and deep thoughts, not for jokes. The third movement is akin to an Austrian peasant dance, the Ländler, which Haydn (and Mahler) often used in place of the courtly minuet or the rapid scherzo. This is a good place to study his use of the woodwind section for doubling the strings with a multitude of different colors. The fourth movement is a "sonata-rondo," a favorite form for Haydn's champagne-like finales. It is, as the term suggests, a combination of the two forms, and capable of being analyzed in both ways:

RONDO

1	1	9	41	9	41	49²	86	117	217	226	265	304
A	A	B	A	B	A	C	D	E	A	F	D	A

SONATA

Exposition			Development	Recapitulation			Coda
1	49²	86	117	217	226	265	304
P	t	S		P	t	S	P
					(different)		

Recordings: many.

Compare: 56, 57, 59–62; Haydn's other symphonies, the late ones of Mozart, and Beethoven's first two.

„Militär-Sinfonie"

I

Menuetto D. C.

LUDWIG VAN BEETHOVEN

(December 16 or 17, 1770–March 26, 1827)

String Quartet in E minor, Op. 59, No. 2 (1805–6).

60.

This is the second of the three *Rasumovsky* Quartets, so named for their dedicatee. They come from Beethoven's middle period (ca. 1800–1816), during which he wrote many of his most popular works: the *Appassionata* and *Waldstein* Sonatas, the *Emperor* Concerto, the *Eroica*, Fifth, and *Pastoral* Symphonies, and the opera *Fidelio*. Do works become more famous because someone gives them a name, or are names given to works because they are famous? Nicknames are rarely ever the composer's doing, but they are wonderful for publicity, being much easier to remember than opus numbers or keys.

During his middle period, Beethoven perfected two things: the building of large musical structures from the smallest units, and the reconciliation of apparently contrary ideas into a feasible whole. In the second movement of this quartet, one can see the entire material being spun from the idea contained in the first bar: the mere interval* of a semi-tone "becomes" a whole-tone* (bar 2), becomes faster (bar 3), is extended (cello part, bars 2–3), is inverted* (bar 6), is expanded to a scale with repeated notes (bars 9–15), is prefaced by another long note to provide the S (bars 17–18, second violin part). In short, it undergoes metamorphoses almost like those of the plants which Beethoven's contemporary Goethe was studying; and this is why the piece makes such consummate sense, besides being beautiful music. (It is said to have been inspired by an evening of star-gazing.)

As for the reconciliation of contrary ideas, which was for Beethoven the heart of the sonata principle, consider the first movement. After the brusque opening chords there are two "false starts" followed by silences which are quite characteristic of Beethoven, but of no one else. He juxtaposes the keys of E minor and F major without the slightest attempt at modulation, moving to and fro as one might step on and off a table (to use Sir Donald Tovey's metaphor). If we expect the "real" start to provide a tune, we will be kept waiting a long time, because there is no tune as such—at least, there is nothing such as Mozart will always give us to hang on to (and whistle afterwards). There is melody, certainly, but only in fragments. Even with the S, traditionally the place for a more lyrical mood, the melody is only seven notes long (bars 39–40). And what do the loud staccato* chords of bars 49–50 have to do with anything? One might say, with Heraclitus, that in such a piece "All is flux"—and yet if we can make no verbal sense of it, that does not prevent it from making perfect musical sense. I know of no better proof that music is a form of intelligent discourse transcending language than the works of Beethoven (particularly the string quartets) which are so inexplicable, yet sound so inevitable. This must be the reason that no one has been able successfully to imitate his style.

When Count Rasumovsky commissioned the quartets, he hoped for some themes to remind him of his Russian homeland. Beethoven gave him short shrift here, throwing in a speeded-up Russian hymn tune at the trio of the third movement (*Maggiore*). It serves to restore the rhythm after the disturbing effect of the Scherzo which is almost inevitably heard as:

Beethoven (and, after him, Schumann) often displaced the rhythm so much as to put one into a new frame of reference, thinking the strong beat to be other than it is, the better to surprise one with a restoration of the original order (see also I, bars 58–65). This is one of many games he played with alert listeners. Another "joke" is the delightful way in which the last movement begins in, and keeps returning to, the foreign key of C major. It is very unusual for the principal subject to be in a key other than the tonic,* but here the idea seems to be to disturb the excessive equilibrium caused by the preceding movements, which are all in E major or minor. There is real humor, and joy, in the stubbornness of this rondo theme, and it takes a hefty coda (*più presto*) to kill it.

Recordings: many.

Compare: 46, 56, 58, 59, 63; Beethoven's other quartets, especially the other *Rasumovsky* Quartets, the last movement of Opus 131 (same rhythmic motives as this finale), and the third movement of Opus 132 (the apotheosis of the mood of this slow movement); Schubert's, Mendelssohn's, and Brahms's string quartets, especially the latter's A minor Quartet.

*Da capo il minore ma senza replica ed allora ancora una
volta il trio, e dopo di nuovo da capo il minore senza replica*

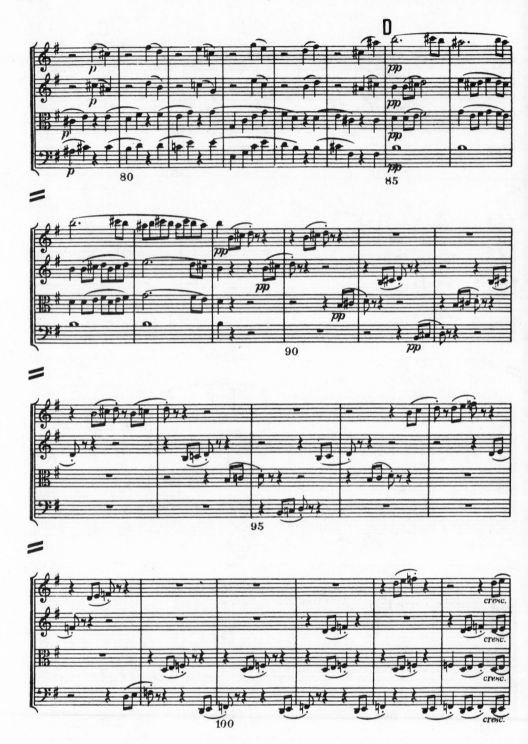

FELIX MENDELSSOHN

(February 3, 1809–November 4, 1847)

Overture: *The Hebrides* or *Fingal's Cave*, Op. 26 (1829–32).

61.

Mendelssohn is one of the few composers who from his earliest years as a child prodigy was rich, famous, happy, and productive. His music has been blamed for being comfortable, sentimental, and too popular in the Victorian era, but much of it, especially the early music, is virile and exciting. This tone poem* is one of the first of many nineteenth-century works for orchestra which sought to depict places, people, stories, and specific moods. The haunting opening occurred to him during a tour of Scotland, and he sent the theme home to his family in Berlin to illustrate "what a strange mood overcame [him] in the Hebrides"—the lonely islands off the West Coast of Scotland. Fingal's Cave, in the Hebridean isle of Staffa, is a natural archway supported on basaltic columns up to forty feet high, into which the sea rushes at high tide. In the opening theme Mendelssohn seems to have caught the very essence of the sea, as only Wagner (*The Flying Dutchman, Tristan und Isolde*) and Debussy (*La Mer*) have done since. But it took him three years, and three versions, before he was fully satisfied with the piece.

Unlike most tone poems it is in sonata form, yet the form does not seem to hinder the free flow of the music. In fact, the effect is more one of ternary form, because of the absence of repeats. As in many of his early works, Mendelssohn shows a clear debt to Beethoven. His use here of a small motive for P, rather than of a finished melody, is more typical of Beethoven than of Mendelssohn's own contemporaries Schumann, Chopin, and Liszt. But he is well within the Romantic tradition with the suave melody of S.

Recordings: many.

Compare: program music:* **12, 17, 38, 42, 71, 72;** Mendelssohn: *Scottish* and *Italian* Symphonies; Beethoven, Symphony No. 6 (*Pastoral*), the ancestor of the nineteenth century tone poem; Berlioz, *Symphonie Fantastique* (1829–30); tone poems and overtures by Berlioz, Liszt, and Smetana.

SERGE PROKOFIEV

(April 23, 1891–March 5, 1953)

First movement of *Classical* Symphony, Op. 25 (1915–17).

After Wagner, Mahler, Scriabin, Strauss, and the early Schoenberg had brought Romantic music to a climax of intensity, it became difficult for young composers to know where to go next. One could not write a more titanic opera or symphony, nor use more lush and chromatic harmonies, nor infuse music with more emotionalism. Yet the temper of the time forbade one merely to imitate: one had to go further, or do something entirely different. This symphony was the brilliant solution of the young Prokofiev. If the future looked forbidding, then why not look to the past?

62.

Prokofiev, then, returned to the forms of the Classic era, and especially to the late symphonies of Haydn (compare **59,** which has almost the same orchestration), whose wit, boisterousness, and tenderness all found their echoes in Prokofiev's own musical personality. This movement sounds like one from an eighteenth-century symphony, heard through the aural equivalent of a distorting mirror. It is in exemplary sonata form (without repeats), except that the recapitulation begins in the "wrong" key (C major), reaching the tonic (D) only with the transitional theme. There are two good reasons for this: first, P appeared in both D and C in the exposition, and this shift (one cannot call it a modulation) is now reversed; and second, there are precedents in well-known Classical works (e.g. Mozart, Piano Sonata in C major; Beethoven, Opus 10, No. 2). After this first symphony, Prokofiev concentrated more on his own, independent style. But this "Neo-classical" piece heralded an entire movement, led by Stravinsky and Hindemith and particularly strong between the two World Wars, in which composers went "back to Bach" and others for ideas to recast with twentieth-century techniques. Since the Second World War, however, it has been more usual to quote older music directly within a new framework (see **72a**).

Recordings: many.

Compare: 57–61, 63, 64, 66, 72a; Prokofiev's other symphonies, especially the Fifth; Stravinsky, Octet and *Dumbarton Oaks* Concerto; Hindemith, Chamber Concertos, Op. 36.

BÉLA BARTÓK

(March 25, 1881–September 26, 1945)

Third movement of String Quartet No. 1 (1908).

If any twentieth century composer deserves to be called a successor to
Beethoven, who used the medium of the string quartet for the profoundest thoughts of his last years, it is Bartók. In the six quartets of
this Hungarian composer we have one of the most unassailable monu-
ments of recent music; they stand alongside Stravinsky's early ballets
and Alban Berg's opera, *Wozzeck,* as modern masterpieces whose
status no one would deny. But unlike those works, they prove that the
sonata idea, even without its traditional key structure, can still serve as
the receptacle for modern ideas in a modern tonal language.

63.

Bartók united in his compositions the multiple influences of
Bach's counterpoint, Beethoven's form, Debussy's color, and folk
music with its peculiar melodic and rhythmic characteristics. (Bartók
was one of the very first collectors of folk music, and a founder of the
science now known as ethnomusicology.) But if one idea dominates all
of his works, it is that of metamorphosis. Although it dates from his
early years, this movement already shows his methods fully developed:
its substance is based upon metamorphoses of the four-note motif
heard first in bar 5, which has been searched out and defined through
the two preceding movements. This motif gives rise to almost all the
melodic material, while its prolongation in bar 8 supplies the rhythmic
motif of the S. Even the important motif in bar 20, seemingly different
on first sight, is derived by contraction through the following stages:

bar nos.

Close study reveals an astounding motivic coherence, comparable to that of Beethoven's music (see commentary to **60**). These two
composers, more than any others, exploited the profound paradox of
the sonata idea, in which the apparent contrast of disparate themes can
be transcended by their essential unity. Beethoven's most famous example, of course, is his Fifth Symphony.

A formal analysis of this movement might be worked out as follows:

	Exposition				**Development**
	P	t	S	K	
bar nos.	1	42	72	94	121 (*S,P*), 158 (fugue on *t*), 215 (*P*)

	Recapitulation			**Coda**
	P	S	k	
	250	288	320	344-end

The absence of *t* from the recapitulation must be due to the attention paid it in the development section, where it supplies the subject of a long fugal episode in which one hears echoes of Bartók's recent explorations of Hungarian folk music.

Another feature of organization found in Bartók's music is the use of the "Golden Section" (0.618:1) and the Fibonacci Series (2, 3, 5, 8, 13, 21, 34 . . .) which approaches it. Usually Bartók will place the climax of a movement 0.618 of the way through it, and this is no exception: the most triumphant affirmation, just before the recapitulation (bars 234–5), comes at precisely 0.618 of the way through the movement, the acceleration in the coda accounting for the slight disparity in bar numbers. Another important structural point, the curious G♯ minor episode that introduces the key of the fugue, comes 0.618 of the way to the climax, at bar 144. Many of Bartók's later works, notably *Music for Strings, Percussion and Celesta* and *Sonata for Two Pianos and Percussion,* obey the Golden Section down to the last detail. With these principles, Bartók found a basis for his music as natural as tonality. Like Greek temples and Gothic cathedrals, his art follows the proportions according to which plants, sea shells, and fir cones grow. The idea of metamorphosis, too, is founded in Nature, where whole organisms are evolved from tiny cells; and this must be the reason why the greatest composers have always used it in some way or another.

Recordings: 3-Col. D3S-717 and M-31196/8 (Juilliard Quartet); Con. Disc 208 (Fine Arts); 3-Vox SVBX-519 (Ramor Quartet).

Compare: 56, 60, 62, 64, 65; the remainder of this quartet and Bartók's other five quartets; string quartets of Schoenberg, Alban Berg, Anton Webern, and Stravinsky's *Concertino;* the late quartets of Beethoven.

(Budán, 1909. jan. 27-én)

ARNOLD SCHOENBERG IN 1950 with autograph
dedication to Walter Hinrischen

JOHN CAGE IN 1972

Looking forward?

Anyone leafing through this chapter will notice immediately that the music looks quite different from that in the rest of the book. The pieces seem to symbolize by their very typography the decades that separate them. Scriabin's and Schoenberg's (**64, 66**) look fairly normal, but Riley's and Cage's (**68, 69**) begin to take on the quality of a graphic design, and in *The Banshee* (**71**) and *Scratch Music* (**70**) conventional notes are abandoned altogether in the quest for new sounds. With George Crumb's pieces, (**72**), reproduced from his original manuscript, one feels that he must have enjoyed the actual process of putting the music on paper, especially in *Spiral Galaxy,* where the staff curls around itself in a visual pun. Evidently there is a revolution in musical notation as well as in music.

At the beginning of the twentieth century composers such as Richard Strauss, Schoenberg, and Scriabin were pushing tonality to its utmost bounds in their search for new means of harmonic expression. Scriabin's late *Prelude* (**64**) shows the composer at the brink of atonality, a radical step which Schoenberg and Webern had fearlessly taken a few years before. But once he had cut loose from the harmonic series and its implications, Schoenberg found himself in something of an impasse. One can already see in Scriabin's piece that dissonance is becoming more frequent than consonance: in Webern's, consonance is actually avoided in order that no vestige of tonality may remain. But if everything is dissonant, one has lost one of the most important harmonic resources: the contrast between dissonance and consonance, with all its emotional and structural im-

1003

plications. The choosing of one's notes becomes rather an arbitrary business: the man in the street might express it by saying that, if it all sounds like wrong notes, who cares which wrong ones they are? The question must have occurred, in a more sophisticated form, to Schoenberg, for he produced virtually no music between 1915 and 1923, when he emerged from silence with his brilliant solution: the Twelve-Tone System (see commentary to **66** for explanation). He used it for most of his later music, and Webern, who immediately adopted it, never abandoned it until his death in 1945.

When, after the second World War, Webern's music at last became widely known, the Twelve-Tone System saw its fullest flowering. Since Schoenberg never felt that the world valued his achievement sufficiently, it is a pity that he did not live to see the excitement with which young composers such as Milton Babbitt, Pierre Boulez, Luigi Nono, and Karlheinz Stockhausen developed the system into a "total serialism" embracing not only pitches but also rhythms, dynamics, and tone colors. Most of all, he would have enjoyed Stravinsky's *volte-face*, when this erstwhile rival and polar opposite also joined the serial club. But Stravinsky was wily enough to wait until Schoenberg was dead and there was no one who dared say "I told you so." In the 1950's and 1960's it seemed, indeed, that serialism was the way of the future. But the other pieces in this chapter show that it is only one way among many.

Satie, like Schoenberg, is the kind of composer whose ideas, despite their venerable age, can still seem "modern." His *Vexations* (**67**) is to all appearances a short piece, perhaps for piano or organ, perhaps for a trio of other instruments. The harmonies are rather strange, hovering around diminished triads, but characteristic enough of Satie's style at the time. The manuscript, however, bears the disconcerting suggestion that the piece should be played *840 times*. But that would take all day! Can he be serious?

The question of whether Satie was *ever* serious would take too long to answer here. But what if one were simply to do as he directs? At least one could be sure of an unforgettable experience. And it is often an experience, rather than a musical statement, that modern composers offer us. Terry Riley's *In C* (**68**) does not last all day, but if the players are enjoying it it can take the best part of an hour. Such an hour will be different in quality from any other hour of music in this book. One will experience no particular musical emotion, no traditional form, no variety of meter, no melody or harmony as such; what one will hear is something more fundamental still: the pure element of sound in metamorphosis.

The modern composer's concern with the element of sound began as an interest in tone color. Composers of the first half of the century such as Henry Cowell (**71**) explored new possibilities of conventional instruments. *The Banshee*, a classic work of this kind, makes the piano sound as unlike a piano as one could possibly imagine. But by now, half a century later, there is not much more left to do in this direction. I have heard violins tapped on the belly and played on the wrong side of the bridge, flutes and recorders made to play chords, trombones sung through, organs played while assistants molest the pipes, and all sorts of instruments distorted through electronic means. Composers can now relax a little and use these devices for really musical purposes, rather than simply to shock or show off (e.g. the *pizzicato** and *glissando** on the piano strings in **72**).

Nowadays nothing is forbidden in the arts. Beauty and form are still viable ideals, but ugliness, stupidity, and obscenity are also countenanced. This is a frightening situation for the artist: since he can now do anything at all, how ever is he going to choose what to do? His choice will no longer be based on custom or even on demand, but will involve his own philosophical orientation and, whether he likes it or not, constitute a statement of belief: in transcendent boredom (**67**), in the past (**72a**), in chance and choice (**68, 69**), in computers (**73**), or in anything (**70**).

Naturally there are plenty of composers who prefer not to enter this world of universal permissibility: they continue to write in modern but traditional styles, perhaps like Bartók (**63**), perhaps like Britten (**30**). But they, too, have made their choice: they believe in the continuing validity of melody, harmony, and musical organization as it has developed in full continuity with the past. This belief itself implies a rejection of some of the other trends represented here, and of the ideals that they stand for.

The last chapter dealt entirely with form—the structuring of musical sounds relative to time. All the pieces in the preceding eight chapters have form of one sort or another. But much of the music of Cage (**69**), Cardew (**70**), and others has no form as such: nothing that can be analyzed into "A's" and "B's" or even into configurations of notes such as we find in twelve-tone music. Cage allows one to use his music as one pleases; Cardew invites one to begin anywhere, do anything, and walk out when one has had enough. Both composers are concerned with a new kind of listening: not one that begins with a mental "set," expecting to hear a sonata form or a tune, but one that is like a mirror, receptive to every image that may come by. A mirror does not criticize: it only watches. Cage's ultimate statement of this aesthetic is his famous *4' 33"*, a piece which consists of four minutes and thirty-three seconds of silence, divided into three movements. The idea is that one should spend the time discovering the environmental sounds that are usually ignored and seldom heard as music.

Approached from another direction, the works in this chapter illustrate two opposite attitudes to the comparative roles of composer and performer. Over the centuries, composers have become more and more fussy about what they want performers to do. In Palestrina's day there were no tempo directions, dynamic markings, or indications of instrumentation. By Bach's time there were a few *p*'s and *f*'s, but one cannot always tell what instruments are required, or what the speed and rhythm should be. Beethoven left none of this to chance, giving more directions than any previous composer. But what a gap there is between his precision and that of Webern! And in the music of some more recent composers, the limits are reached: in Boulez's *Le Marteau sans Maître* (1954), now a hoary classic of the avant-garde, virtually every note, even in fast movements, has its own dynamic marking; and in Stockhausen's *Piano Piece II* there are chords of up to eight notes in which one is supposed to hit each note with a different velocity.

When the performer is programmed almost like a computer to play exactly the pitches, speeds, and loudnesses that the composer wants, the next logical step for a composer to take if he really knows (or thinks he knows) every last detail of a piece is to do away entirely with that unreliable creature, the human executant, and let machines do the job. It seems to work, after a fashion, with agriculture and bureaucracy, so why not with music? Hence the use of electronic synthesizers and computers. But there is a phenomenon called *enantiodromia*, the turning of a thing into its opposite, which tends to manifest when extremes are reached. In the case of music, we can experience it very vividly: when rhythms become too complicated to grasp, however rigorous their logic, they tend to sound random. And in much music of the post-Webernian avant-garde, the sounds are serially organized to the last degree, yet to any but the expert they seem totally devoid of sense.

John Cage must have realized this, for he decided quite early that the results brought about by chance and freedom were more interesting, besides encouraging a pleasanter relationship than seemed possible between the composer and performer of rigidly organized music. So he wrote pieces by random methods, invited the performers to interpret and improvise, and allowed all kinds of noises to take their place alongside the musical notes. This all went contrary to the trend of three centuries of Western music: no wonder that no composer since Wagner has had such an impact on his contemporaries in all the arts. We owe to Cage many of the impulses that move towards improvisation and chance, and towards the acceptance of any and everything as potentially a thing of beauty.

Ten years ago a composer was virtually bound to follow a school, whether that of mathematical organization, that of chance, that of continuity with the past, or others. Now it seems as if the boundaries are coming down: all the schools are beginning to recognize each others' virtues, and some fascinating mixtures are taking place. Leland Smith's piece (**73**) combines a rather free, even romantic flute solo with an accompaniment composed with the aid of a computer. George Crumb's *Dream Images* (**72a**), in a contemporary idiom, contains direct quotations from a piece of Chopin's. This is one of an increasing number of pieces that pay homage to the past by re-using it in a modern context. Another prominent American composer, George Rochberg, used to compose in a serial idiom, but has now taken the boldest of steps and writes in a style which is sometimes atonal, but more usually an unashamed re-creation of the styles of Beethoven and Mahler. In his music (e.g. *Third String Quartet*) and in quotations such as Crumb's I feel a powerful sense of nostalgia for a time when music sang in the ears and was written from the heart: when composers did not need to ask themselves what style to write in, and listeners did not question their choice. But it will be long before such a time of consensus comes again.

The world of the avant-garde is a very confusing one: so much is happening all at once, and it is difficult to see any direction in all of this frantic activity. But the term "avant-garde" seems to refer to an assumption of perpetual, directed progress, and to describe phenomena (artistic and otherwise) that are in the "vanguard," hence ahead of their time. The avant-garde composer, sociologist, or playwright is supposedly doing now what all the rest of his kind will be doing in five, ten, or fifty years' time. If we cannot understand him, it must be because we are not so "advanced" as he is. We may not like what he does, but we may as well accept that sooner or later everyone is going to be the same way unless "reactionary" forces intervene.

I find these presuppositions not only distasteful but false. Take an old avant-garde work such as Webern's *Bagatelle* (**65**), which dates from the time when the average undergraduate's grandparents were infants. There has since been plenty of musical "progress" in the same direction, but is Webern's music acceptable to the average man today—even to the average music lover? I think not. The lover of "classical" music is far more at home with Bach, Beethoven, and maybe Stravinsky; the younger generation prefers rock and folk music. And yet there have been works that were scorned at their first appearance, but have subsequently won over the general public, such as Beethoven's *Eroica* Symphony and Stravinsky's *Rite of Spring*. What is the difference between the two kinds of avant-garderies?

Perhaps the distinction lies between inevitable change and willful change. Stravinsky said of his early masterpiece: "I was the vessel through which the *Rite* passed," thus acknowledging the unconscious source of all great music. He and Beethoven did not decide one day to write epoch-making works, shattering preconceptions and paving the way to the future; they simply obeyed a compulsion and became mouthpieces for whatever forces govern human history. One suspects that when their works were completed (and do not suppose for a moment that being a mouthpiece was easy, like automatic writing) they were as overawed by what had been created through them as their listeners were to be. A mere innovator, on the other hand, would be more likely to congratulate himself for having thought up something unique, shocking, or merely clever. His "revolutionary" work will be of interest, perhaps, to other artists, but it will never enter the consciousness of the civilization as a truly inspired work will. In this sense, he is not so much ahead of his time as outside of it altogether.

Suggestions for further reading On the older twentieth-century composers, see William W. Austin, *Music in the Twentieth Century from Debussy through Stravinsky* (New York, 1966), and on some of the younger ones Peter Yates, *Twentieth-Century Music; Its Evolution from the End of the Harmonic Era to the Present Era of Sound* (New York, 1967). Anyone will enjoy browsing through Nicolas Slonimsky's fascinating "diary," *Music Since 1900* (4th ed., New York, 1971). On the Twelve-Tone System, see George Perle, *Serial Composition and Atonality* (3rd ed., Berkeley, 1971). On the composers, see Faubion Bowers, *Scriabin* (New York, 1969), Willi Reich, *Schoenberg: A Critical Biography* (New York, 1972), Rollo Myers, *Erik Satie* (New York, 1968), and Richard Kostelanetz, *John Cage* (New York, 1970). Of Cage's own writings, *Silence* (new ed., Middletown, 1973) is still the most applicable to his music. For modern notational peculiarities, see Cage's anthology *Notations* (New York, 1969) and Erhard Karkoschka, *Notation in New Music: A Critical Guide to Interpretation and Realization* (New York, 1972).

ALEXANDER SCRIABIN

(January 6, 1872–April 27, 1915).

Prelude, Op. 74, No. 4 (1915).

64.

In the early years of the twentieth century, Scriabin's style was as individualistic as Debussy's or Schoenberg's. That it did not survive as well is due to his very limited harmonic and emotional range: in his music, and especially his late music, *everything* seems to be "vague" and "indecisive," as if he is describing not the usual world of musical thought but an etheric, twilight world in which feelings and shapes waft around without definition. So in this piece, from his last opus, the harmonies wander, never settling on a real concord yet never quite abandoning tonality. The last chord, although it has both major and minor thirds, does sound like a tonic, even though it is approached from a chord based a tritone* away—a progression that took on the importance of a dominant-tonic relationship in Scriabin's harmonic system. The melody, like most of Schoenberg's (see **66**), is virtually unsingable, yet it is none the less a melody, and has direction both on a small and a large scale. Scriabin does not dwell on the harsh dissonances of major sevenths and minor ninths, as do Schoenberg and Webern, but on the ambiguous augmented triad (see bars 11–17) and tritone. From this point of harmonic impasse one can only go on to repeat oneself (which is what Scriabin seems to have done in his late works) or expand one's range in the direction of tonal resources (as did Bartók and Debussy) or completely atonal ones (as did Schoenberg).

Recording: Mon. S-2134 (Kuerti); Desto 7145 (Laredo).

Compare: 30a, 42, 62, 63, 64, 67, 72; Scriabin's early Preludes, Op. 11 (a set of 24 modelled on Chopin's); his sonatas, especially Nos. 5-10; Alban Berg, Piano Sonata.

Lent, vague, indécis

Piano

Alexander Scriabin: *Prelude*

ANTON VON WEBERN

(December 3, 1883–September 15, 1945)

No. 1 of *Six Bagatelles for String Quartet,* Op. 9 (1913).

"To see the world in a grain of sand, and Heaven in a wild flower . . ." Blake's view and Webern's are not far apart. Webern would compress on to a single page, lasting a few seconds, what most composers would take ten minutes to say. If his master, Schoenberg, was a sculptor, hewing out his works at the cost of God knows what mental suffering, then Webern was a jeweller, making miniatures that need an aural magnifying-glass to enable one to appreciate them. To play these "trifles" at a concert of string quartets, sandwiched perhaps between Mozart and Bartók, is to do Webern a disservice. To the mind attuned to half-hour pieces, they will seem to flash by and leave no impression except one of randomness. They should be studied and played over and over again until one knows every note and every nuance. Only then will their beauties be revealed, and their sounds appear as inevitable; the first violin's five notes in bars 2–3 will seem the tenderest of melodies, and the climax at bar 7 will be shattering, subsiding into an unearthly stillness at the close.

The extraordinary thing about Webern is the single-mindedness of his development. From Opus 3 onwards, he never used tonality, and never wrote a long piece. When he adopted the Twelve-Tone System in 1924, it changed his style but little, merely imposing a slightly more rigorous order on his always orderly musical thought. Even this tiny piece illustrates many features of his style: the wide-ranging melodies, often extremely short; the almost invariable harmonic language of major sevenths, minor ninths, and their inversions; the frequent use of triplet division of the beat (especially the cut-off of the second violin in bar 2: such details really mattered to Webern); the expressive use of tempo changes, and the de-emphasis of strong beats, which together serve to destroy a sense of regular meter; the constantly varying tone colors. All these things combined to make Webern the prime influence on progressive post-war composers. More than anyone else, he opened up a new world of sound—and made things very easy for imitators who lacked his intellect and taste.

65.

Recordings: Phi. 6500105 (Quartetto Italiano); RCA LSC-2531 (Juilliard Quartet); 5-DG 2720029 (LaSalle).

Compare: 17 (also written 1913), **63, 64, 66, 71, 73;** the other five *Bagatelles;* Webern, *Five Pieces for String Quartet,* Op. 5, *String Quartet,* Op. 28; other "miniatures": Schoenberg, *Six Little Piano Pieces* (1911), *Pierrot Lunaire* (1912); Berg, *Four Pieces for Clarinet and Piano* (1913).

Anton Webern: *Bagatelle*

ARNOLD SCHOENBERG

(September 13, 1874–July 13, 1951)

First movement of Violin Concerto, Op. 36 (1936).

66.

"I believe that in my new Violin Concerto I have created the necessity for a new kind of violinist." So said the composer of this remarkable exercise in virtuosity. The response of most violinists would be "Why bother?" Why go to such trouble to force the violin to make excruciating sounds when it can make beautiful ones? But one mission of the Expressionist movement in music, from Strauss' *Elektra* (1909) to Berg's *Lulu* (1934) and beyond, seems to have been the articulation of negative emotions, a process surely not unconnected with the discoveries of Sigmund Freud. Hence the "distorted melodies, discordant harmonies and disintegrated lines" (Willi Apel) of so much music by Schoenberg and his contemporaries. If one recalls the state of Germany in 1936, and the fact that Schoenberg, doubly hated by the Nazis for being a Jew and a modern composer, had already had to emigrate to the United States, one will have more understanding for this tortured music.

On a purely intellectual level, the piece exemplifies Schoenberg's mature style, and illustrates his idosyncratic use of the Twelve-Tone System, the invention with which he sought to replace tonality. According to this system, which was adopted by Alban Berg, Anton Webern, and numerous other composers, a piece is based upon a "Row," or "Series," consisting of the twelve semi-tones in a chosen order. Here is the row:

A♮ B♭ D♯ B♮ E♮ F♯ / C♮ D♭ G♮ A♭ D♮ F♮

The first three and a half bars contain a simple statement of it. The entire material of a piece, if one follows the system strictly, must be derived from the forty-eight "permutations" of the chosen row: the twelve transpositions* (starting the row on any of the twelve semi-tones), multiplied by the four possibilities of playing the row (1) forwards, (2) inverted or upside down, (3) backwards, and (4) backwards and inverted. Bars 4–7 of this movement contain a statement of the inversion, transposed up a fourth from the original position:

D♮ C♯ A♭ C♮ G♮ F♮ / B♮ B♭ E♮ D♯ A♮ F♯

Actually Schoenberg "cheats" a little here, sounding the notes of the second half in the order E♮ B♮ D♯ B♭. But this is part of his personal approach to the system, in which he tended to regard the row as a pair of six-note "hexachords" which could be treated more as bundles than as orderings of notes.

Through the use of the Twelve-Tone System, composers hoped that music could regain some of the coherence which it had lost through the abandonment of tonality. Certainly a work so tightly organized as this one should have some audible unity. But only long training, preferably in composition, will enable one to hear exactly what is going on. Most composers nowadays have used the system at some point of their careers, but the number of strict adherents seems to be on the wane.

Recordings: Col. MS-7039 (Baker, CBC Symph., Craft, cond.) 2-Col. M2-S679 (*The Music of Arnold Schoenberg,* same artists); DG 2530257 (Zeitlin, Bavarian Radio Symph., Kubelik, cond.)

Compare: 17, 38, 63; Schoenberg's *Piano Concerto* and Fourth String Quartet; violin concertos by Stravinsky (1931), Paul Hindemith (1940), and especially the beautiful one of Alban Berg (1935), whose use of the Twelve-Tone System differs from his master, Schoenberg's, to the extent that he can include a folk song and a Bach chorale without incongruity.

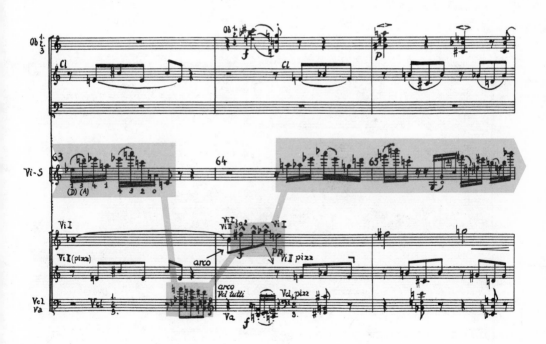

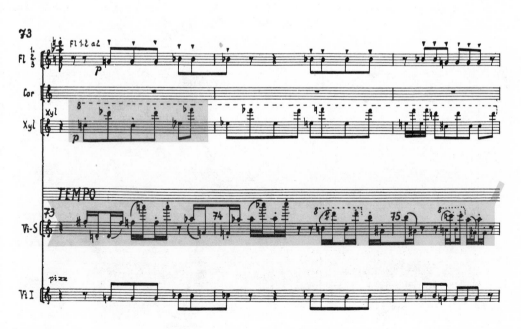

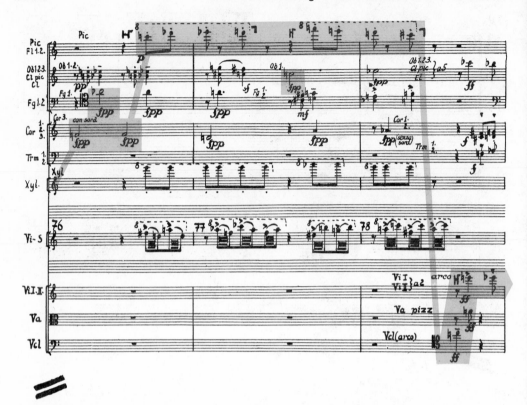

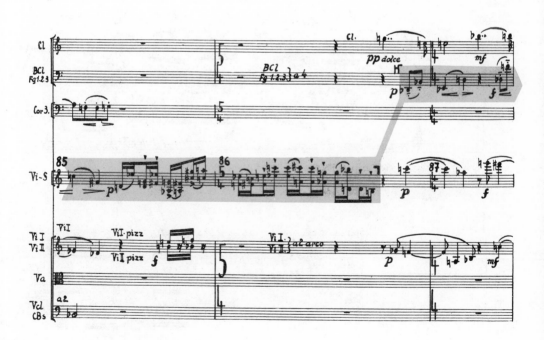

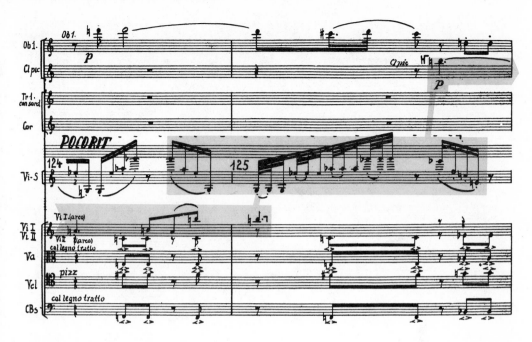

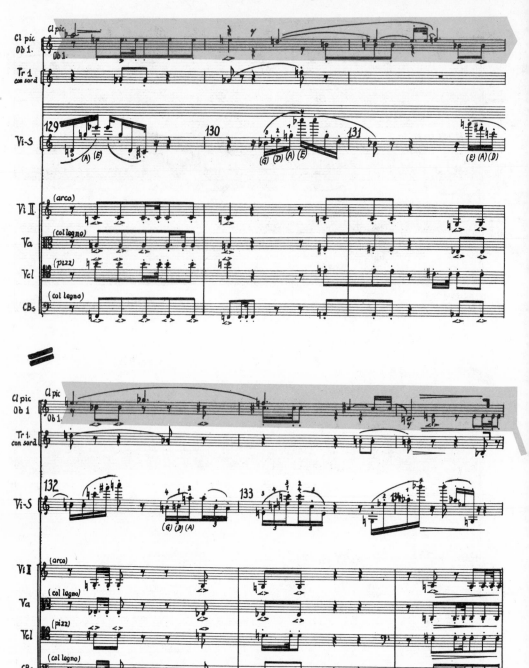

*) *Flzg = Flatterzunge*

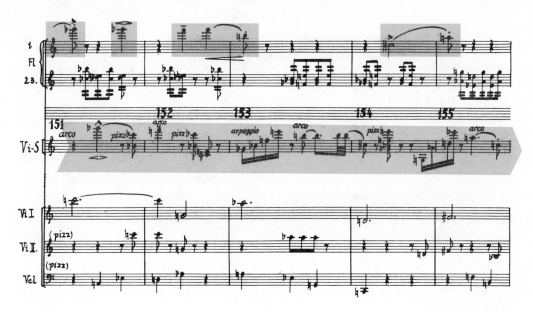

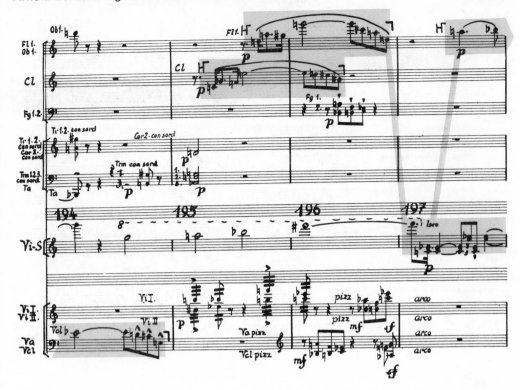

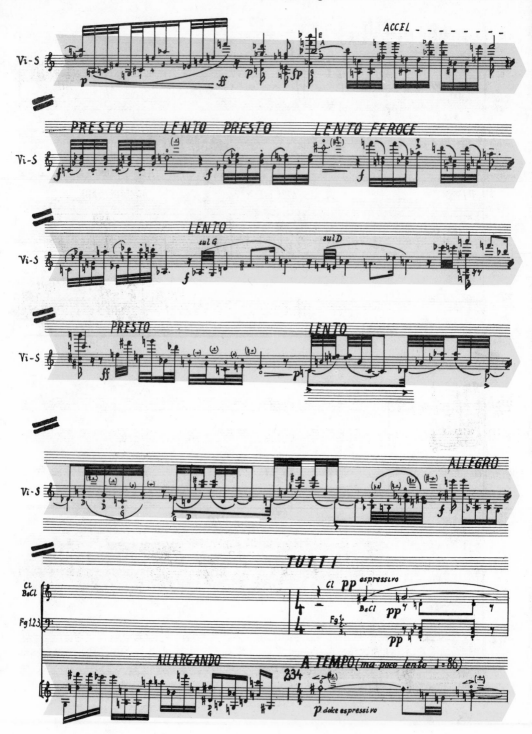

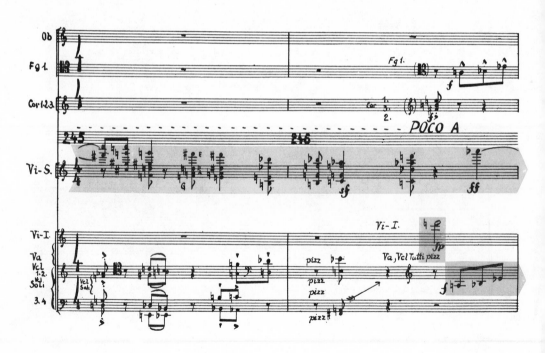

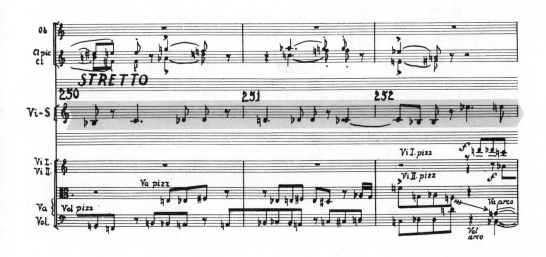

ERIK SATIE

(May 17, 1866–July 1, 1925)

Vexations (ca. 1893–95).

67.

Satie is a freak among composers, who could only have lived when he did: in the *fin de siècle* decadence of the late nineteenth century and the self-conscious modernism of the early twentieth. During the first period he was an earnest seeker, becoming involved with a Rosicrucian organization and studying seriously as he made a precarious living by teaching and night-club playing. During the second, he became a genuine eccentric and was unexpectedly lifted to fame as the figurehead of a group which included Jean Cocteau, the composers Poulenc and Milhaud, and for a time the young Picasso. These artists saw the simplicity and irony of Satie's music as an alternative to the bombast of the German school (Wagner and Strauss) and the, to them, effete "impressionism" of Debussy.

When Debussy criticized Satie's music for having no form, Satie responded to his friend by entitling his next work "Three Pieces in the Form of a Pear." Not only were his titles often humorous, but he would also add commentaries and marginal notes to the music, e.g. "Like a nightingale with a toothache." But despite these jokes, he did play an important part in the miniaturization of music early in this century. He stuck a pin in the great Romantic balloon.

The manuscript of *Vexations*, discovered after Satie's death, bears the following "Author's Notes":

> In order to play this motive to oneself 840 times in succession, one had best prepare oneself in the deepest silence by serious immobilities.

Is this a meditation exercise from his Rosicrucian days, or is it no more serious than the nightingale's toothache? John Cage and others have performed the piece, and apparently found that it becomes a more and more serious matter as one proceeds. The notation, at least, is carefully calculated to give one a hard time.

Recordings: None.

Compare: 64 (similar harmonies), **68, 69, 70;** Satie, *Messe des Pauvres* from the same period; music of LaMonte Young and Cornelius Cardew; art-work of Marcel Duchamp.

Erik Satie: *Vexations*

Très lent

TERRY RILEY

(Born June 24, 1935)

In C (1964).

68.

This piece may be performed by any number of instruments (the more the merrier), transposing into other octaves if need be, with piano. The piano's role is to play its top two C's in continuous eighth-notes, thus setting the pulse which remains the same throughout. The other instruments begin independently, on any beat, and play through these fifty-three fragments, repeating each one as many times as they wish. There must, however, be no break between repetitions; thus No. 10 for instance, becomes the pattern etc. If one breaks the continuity, one must proceed (after a pause of any length) to the next fragment.

If sufficient instruments take part, this produces a texture in which, at any given moment, about six contiguous fragments are being played in various phases. This brings about an actual chordal movement, audible through the statistical predominance of certain notes, from C–G⁷–E mi.–G⁷–G mi.(C⁷). But these are vague harmonic areas that shade into one another, not clear-cut key centers and modulations.

Ten years after In C, Terry Riley explained informally to Hugh Gardner of the East West Journal: "What I'm trying to do in my music is to fill what I see as a need. Call it a need for unity, centeredness, internal balance, whatever. I just know that I couldn't find it in the musical forms that were handed to me. It has a lot to do with how you concentrate on ideas and on how these ideas unfold. My music doesn't jump around full of contrast from one idea to the next . . . but tries to let the thread unwind in the most organic way possible. I think more of that feeling and that way of thinking is what a lot of people need today." Such ideas are worked out more fully in Riley's later, more improvisatory music, and in pieces by Steve Reich, Philip Glass, and others. They show one possible route towards the reconciliation of popular, classical, and non-Western musics.

Recordings: Col. MS-7178 (Riley, Center of the Creative & Performing Arts of NYU, Buffalo)

Compare: 67, 69, 78; Riley, *Rainbow in Curved Air* (recording); Reich, *Four Organs* (recording); Indian and Balinese music.

JOHN CAGE

(Born September 5, 1912)

Four pages from *Winter Music* (1957).

69.

The twenty pages of *Winter Music,* dedicated to the painters Robert Rauschenberg and Jasper Johns, "may be used in whole or part by a pianist or shared by two to twenty to provide a program of an agreed-upon length. The notation, in space, five systems left to right on the page, may be freely interpreted as to time. An aggregate must be played as a single ictus.* Where this is impossible, the unplayable notes shall be taken as harmonics prepared in advance. Harmonics may also be produced where they are not so required. Resonances, both of aggregates and individual notes of them, may be free in length. Overlappings, interpenetrations, are also free. The single staff is provided with two clef signs. Where these differ, ambiguity obtains in the proportion indicated by the two numbers notated above the staff. Dynamics are free. An inked-in rectangle above a pair of notes indicates a chromatic tone cluster.* The fragmentation of staves arose simply from an absence of events." (Note in the score)

Cage's music offers a curious paradox between the precision with which it is prepared (both by the composer and the performer), and the apparent indifference as to the end result. Whereas in Riley's piece (**68**) the overall form and rhythm are determined but the actual coincidences of notes left to chance, here the opposite applies: every chord is precisely notated, yet the material may be used for virtually any number of pianists for a piece of any form or length. Like the recent Stockhausen, Cage is more a philosopher than a composer. And who, considering the history of Western music in this century, can avoid philosophical questions about the very nature of music and of artistic evolution? This particular composition of Cage's seems to say simply that it is good to play chords on pianos after a little mental exercise. Is the process of deciding exactly how to apply the sometimes enigmatic instructions the equivalent of Satie's "serious immobilities"? (See **67**)

Recordings: Fin. QD-9006 (*John Cage: Winter Music, version for 4 pianos,* Flynn); DG 137009 (John Cage: *Atlas Eclipticalis/Winter Music/ Cartridge Music,* Ensemble Musica Negativa, Riehn, dir.) o.p.

Compare: 67, 68, 70, 71, 72; music of Morton Feldman, Earle Brown, and Christian Wolff.

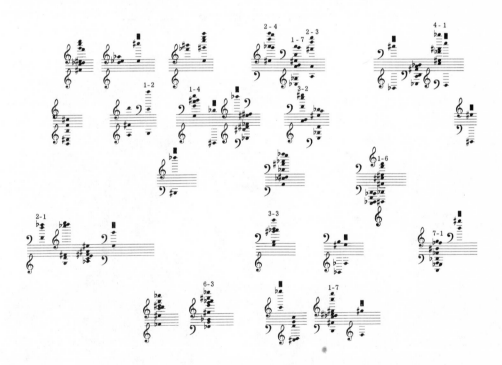

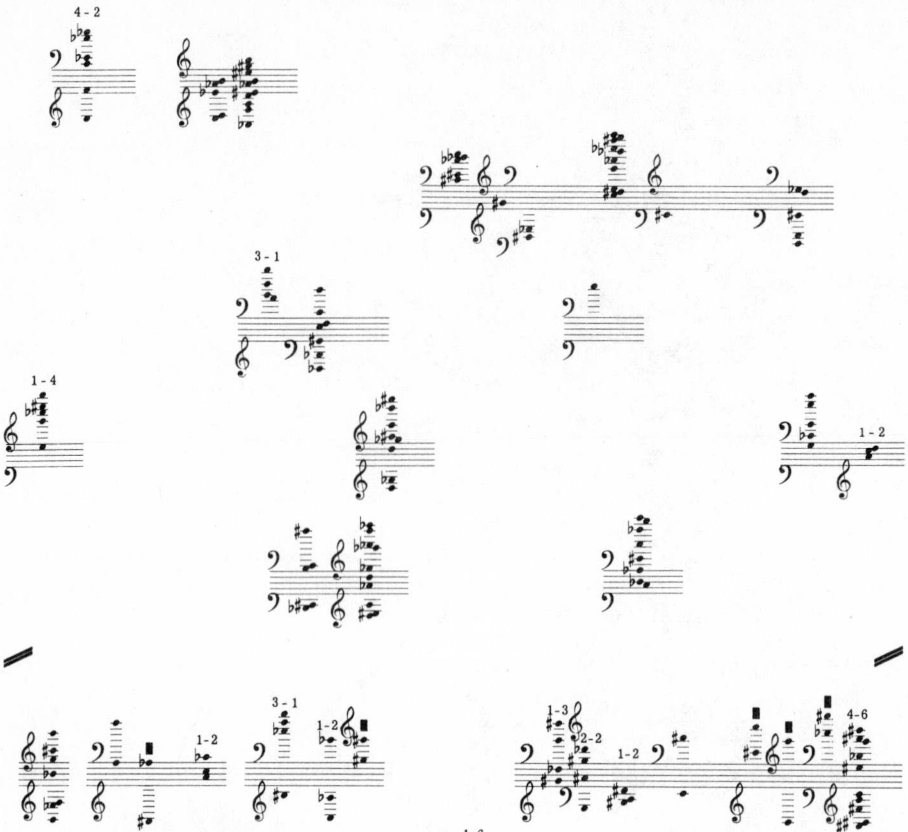
4 - 2
3 - 1
1 - 4
1 - 2
3 - 1
1-2
1-2
1-3
2-2
1-2
4-6
1-4
4-2
1-6
2-2
5-2
2-1
4-6
1-2
2-1
1-2
2-5
4-3
2-1
1-5
8-2
2-1
1-2
1-2

CORNELIUS CARDEW, editor

(Born May 7, 1935)

Some of *1001 Activities* from *Scratch Music* (ca. 1970).

70.

"Scratch Music is the basic music of the world, going on everywhere, all the time. Nothing that is not Scratch Music except regular Western musical compositions since C.P.E. Bach." (Note in *Scratch Music*)

In 1969 Cornelius Cardew and two others founded the Scratch Orchestra in London as a group for experimental performance activities. These began by being musical, or at least resulting in sounds, but they also went far beyond anything normally thought of as music, and sometimes even beyond feasible activity into the realm of "conceptual art." The *1001 Activities* are mostly of this category: here the "score" has taken over and become a literary form without any likelihood of resulting "performance." At least, one hopes not in certain cases.

Here music has expanded to embrace not only the whole world of sound but the whole of life, real and imaginary, and become so attenuated that it can scarcely be said to exist any more, except in an immaterial, ideal sense. This is the endpoint of the development initiated by John Cage. One can go no further.

Compare: 67 (is that really conceptual art, too?), **68, 69;** other *Scratch Music;* Cardew, *Treatise;* Karlheinz Stockhausen, *Aus den sieben Tagen,* a more serious approach.

554 Drop out
555 Put your foot in it
556 Be put out
557 Lose track of time
558 Lose face
559 Put your left leg in
560 Put your left leg out
561 In, out, in, out, shake it all about
562 Do as you would be done by
563 Be done by as you did
564 Eternalise
565 Dangle
566 Jangle
567 Wrangle
568 Tangle
569 Mangle
570 Spangle
571 Blow the gaff
572 Fall about laughing
573 Jump up and bang your head on the ceiling
574 Explode a hypothesis
575 Expound a theory
576 Make your blood boil
577 Imitate Che Guevara as a small badger
578 Change guard at Buckingham Palace
579 "You'll never go to heaven if you break my heart"
580 Who says?
581 Be Rife
582 Incline your head till it touches the ground
583 Break the large glass
584 Arrest a Policeman
585 Singing Balls to the Baker, arse against the wall
586 Climb every mountain
587 "Fuck my old Boots"
588 The two fingered sign of distaste in conjunction with something sweet and sugary, painted yellow, lusciously curving into the distance, taking her pants off, reaping the whirlwind and singing a twelve bar blues on the back seat of a tandem tricycle
589 Come to a pretty pass
590 Come to a pretty lass
591 Sweat like a pig
592 Burn the boats
593 Shiver me timbers
594 Splice the mainbrace
595 Drink like a fish
596 Swear like a trooper
597 Arsenic and old lace
598 Be written off
599 Wreck yourself with a rusty mattock, the handle of which is exquisitely carved, inlaid with ivory and set with precious stones
600 Translate the Hsin-Hsin Ming into Medieval Russian
601 Write a précis of the Bible in words of not more than one syllable

602 Play the whale
603 Fish for compliments
604 Fish for fivers
605 Fish for the notes
606 Land a gigantic catch
607 Make a false entry and still hold back
608 Giver her/him satisfaction
609 Take it easy, but take it
610 Demonstrate the sound of one hand
611 Fall among thieves
612 Fall into arrears
613 Fall into disfavour
614 Fall into disgrace
615 Fall into a vat of boiling dung (or oil)
616 A little of what you fancy
617 Throw the world over, the white cliffs of Dover
618 Turn a Chinese Revolution
619 Make a Venetian blind
620 Make a Maltese Cross
621 Fly in the face of danger
622 Put on a brave face
623 Fly on the face of her Majesty the Queen
624 Pollute a bowl of custard
625 Dispute a Death sentence
626 Rumble the Popish plot
627 Give a detailed exposition as to the reasons for Titus not getting his oats
628 Make peace
629 Make war
630 Make love
631 Make friends
632 Make amends
633 Rake up your past
634 Dig up your potatoes, trample on your vines
635 "Gimme that thing"
636 A cat's lick and a promise
637 Grow younger from today
638 Make-up
639 Decree a repetition, of the Spanish Inquisition
640 Keep your head in the presence of a tiger
641 Make yourself a jacket out of National Velvet
642 Invest in squirrels
643 Go on for longer than you intended
644 Go on for longer than you expected
645 Go on for ever
646 Throw fifty fits, make allowance for the proximity of spectators
647 Laugh fit to bust
648 Laugh till you cry
649 Laugh till you break your jaw
650 Lie on the bottom of a swimming pool and breathe in deeply
651 Repeat 650 wearing an atomic powered kilt and seven league boots
652 Up an' give 'em a bla' a bla' Wi' a hundred pipers an' a' an' a'
653 Moonlight and roses and parsons' noses

654 Every lassie loves his laddie, coming through the rye (misquote)
655 "Someday my prince will come", Something with a pitch fork
656 Home, home on the range, where the people are acting so strange
657 Show them who's boss, then resign your position
658 Run the gauntlet
659 Be the object of a fugue subject
660 Give a tonal answer to a rhetorically insulting question
661 Be "cut to the quick"
662 Be quick to the cut
663 Do the dirty on somebody
664 Breeze it, bugg it, easy does it
665 Lose your cool
666 Lose your virginity
667 Lose your self respect
668 Be caught with your trousers at the cleaners
669 Beat your wife with a damp squid
670 Pick your nose with a mechanical shovel
671 Feel glad all over. (How did "Glad" enjoy it?)
672 Be pipped at the post or (conversely) give somebody the pip
673 Get the pip or (conversely) give somebody the pip
674 Set the pips on a well known politician
675 Loop the loop
676 Squander your ill-gotten gains
677 Beg for mercy
678 Take yourself down a peg
679 Question your bank statement
680 Never say die
681 Do or die
682 Die the death
683 Become a dyed in the wool dogmatic
684 Unfrock a clergyman
685 Bat an eyelid
686 Turn the other cheek
687 Whippoorwill
688 Pursue a will o' the wisp
689 Make a bloomer
690 Rut
691 Split your difference
692 Turn up trumps
693 Give a light show to a heavy audience
694 Make a face at a tree
695 Give away the game
696 Let the cat out of the bag
697 Hunt the thimble
698 Make out a case for a logical bassoon
699 Syndicate every boat you row
700 Indicate every thing you see
701 Celebrate every thing you are
702 Dig a pony
703 Photograph the back of your head
704 Make a sculpture of the wind
705 Paint your anus
706 Fight the good fight, each and every night. Cor strike a light, with all thy might
707 "Know the male but keep to the role of the female"
708 Thank Lao Tzu for "707"
709 Thank D C Lau for translating "708" from the original Chinese
710 Conquer the ineluctable
711 Know the wisdom of refraining from action
712 Polish off a three-course breakfast at 3 o'clock in the afternoon
713 Leap before you look
714 Leak before you loop
715 Loop before you leak
716 Clean your teeth with a universal spanner
717 Knock your friends down with a feather
718 Swing a cat
719 Swing a Blue Whale
720 Up, up and away
721 Help an old lady across the road against her will
722 Drink a yard of ale
723 Drink a yard of whisky
724 Hold a special service in the memory of anyone attempting "723"
725 Speak now or forever hold your peace
726 Commit perjury
727 Walk around London in Indian file
728 Have a picnic on Hammersmith Bridge
729 Say the unrepeatable
730 Ball the Jack
731 Touch the moon
732 Be a bit of a bastard (which bit is up to you(?))
733 Play with your friends
734 Play with your self
735 Cycle up the steps of the Eiffel Tower, then cycle down again
736 Walk backwards for a hundred yards then run backwards for a hundred yards
737 Collapse as if exhausted, dissimulation will not be permitted
738 Brush up your Shakespeare
739 Do something for Pete's sake
740 Part your hair from ear to ear
741 Grow a moustach in the small of your back
742 Run amok
743 Make some Holy smoke without a celestial fire
744 Take off your clothes before a paying audience sitting in total darkness
745 Perform a five card trick and amaze your friends
746 Execute a lithograph of a pig in a poke
747 Count the number of hairs on the back of each hand, and take down the number of the difference, climb the same number of trees with a chamberpot and a small goat strapped to your back

748 Fiddle while Rome burns

749 Given an imitation of the Vienna Secession, blindfolded and standing in a bucket of pirana fish

750 Give a Royal Command Performance of Gavin Bryar's "Serenely beaming and leaning on a fivebar gate"

751 Turn topsy-turvy

752 Don't come that one

753 Knit your brows so that they keep your eyelids warm in winter

754 Perform "175" with your head tucked underneath your arms

755 Now for something completely different

756 Open up them Pearly Gates

757 Swim the Channel underwater

758 Fall asleep during page five of John Cage's "The Music of Changes", Book III

759 Fall awake during Group 139 of Stockhausen's "Gruppen"

760 Whistle to your hearts content

761 Take some coal to Newcastle

762 Kiss the Blarney Stone

763 Wipe your slate clean

764 Rape a canary

765 Construct a short way to Tipperary

766 Put off procrastinating till tomorrow

767 Regurgitate an eel pie

768 Put out a candle and apologise to it for so doing

769 Flush the lavatory with one almighty stroke of the pen

770 Drown one of larger types of rodent with the sweat of your brow

771 Shave the cat with a few sharp words

772 Confucian confusion

773 Be redundant

774 Learn to recognise St Peter's Square, and so is the Pope

775 Confine yourself to a wheel chair for the day and make a round tour of the bottoms of crowded staircases. (Be a nuisance!)

776 Remember something you had long since forgotten

777 Board and leave a tube train inbetween stations

778 Broadcast to the Nation

779 Paint your face in the dress tartan of the clan Macleod

780 **Satire**:– send up a balloon

781 Forfeit your right to live

782 Hold your own with one hand and someone else's with the other

783 Argue till you are black in the face (a coloured issue?)

784 Talk to a brick wall

785 Ask a ticket machine for your money back

786 Begin hesitantly, continue nervously, expound at great length and end in a blaze of glory

787 Finger pie

788 Suddenly become lop-sided

789 Grow on trees

790 Use your loaf

791 "You're no fun anymore" – illustrate with special reference to Egyptian masochism in the thirteenth century B C

792 "Let's all sing like the birdies sing, twit, twit, twit, twit-twoo"

793 "Be still and know"

794 Call the whole thing off

795 Leave your visiting card at a house of ill-repute

796 Be dishonest when writing your memoirs

797 Visit a dying race

798 Run in a dying race

799 Express the desire for a glass of half and half

800 Stain your character

801 Remove a blot from your escutcheon

802 Leap at an opportunity

803 Lift a cat from some hot bricks

804 Strangers in the night

805 Feel the urge to be pessimistic

806 Back a loser

807 Back a winner

808 Back a portrait of "La Gioconda" with an heretically obscene sonnet

809 Be pleased as punch

810 Be rotten to the core

811 Open someone else's letters

812 Walk three abreast, backwards through a hedge

813 Visit Hampton Court Palace and be amazed

814 Flashback

815 Openly dismiss your own congruity

816 Certify your own death

817 Certify your own insanity

818 "Take me back to dear old Blighty"

819 "Take me back to dear old Blighty"

820 Propose a toast

821 Drink a toast

822 Eat some toast

823 Toast the most

824 Question your own existence

825 Question your right to live

826 Feel obliged

827 Mollify a mitigation

828 Emulate an albatross

829 Remark yours faithfully

830 

831 Decipher "830"

832 Fly by night

833 Tailor a coat of arms

834 Force an entry

835 Force a reply

836 Force a window

837 Force a lock

838 (Gabriel) Fauré's a jolly good fellow

839 File a complaint

840 File a lawsuit

841 Fall down a disused well
842 Draw up your plans
843 "Bless your beautiful hide"
844 Draw up a chair
845 Cut it fine
846 Cut a fine figure
847 Dash out
848 Dash in
849 Deviate wondrously, and in bright colours and blinding flashes
850 Foam at the mouth
851 Drink a glass of water standing on your head
852 Give a damn
853 Open an old wound
854 Seal a pledge
855 Redeem a pledge
856 Pledge your support
857 Thank you for your support, I will wear it always
858 Fall into misuse
859 Issue a statement
860 Tamper with the facts
861 Sing obscene words to the tune of Annie Laurie
862 Fall over backwards
863 Even things out
864 Justify a faux pas
865 Empty the Pacific Ocean
866 Feel left out
867 Be bereft
868 Have an inkling
869 Be detached at her Majesty's Pleasure
870 Send a letter to a person of no fixed abode
871 Take a wife
872 Take a husband
873 Take five
874 Take more than you need
875 Take as many as you can carry
876 Untie the gordian knot, or not
877 Become diffuse
878 Refract
879 Reflect
880 Recumbent
881 Recalcitrant
882 Return
883 Revoke
884 Relive
885 Relieve
886 Relearn; 886a Retire
887 Retain
888 Reverberate
889 Recognise
890 Fill your glass and keep on pouring
891 Wipe the dust off your mirror, taking the mirror with it
892 Estimate your own esteem
893 Break off an engagement
894 Come in with tide and go out with the old year
895 Strike a clock for being slow

896 Catch your breath and preserve it for posterity
897 Deepen your affection
898 Deepen your understanding
899 Deepen your iniquity
900 Deepen your hatred
901 Bang like a door in a gale
902 Depress yourself
903 Repress yourself
904 Peruse
905 Covet thy neighbour's wife/husband
906 Explete at your own proclivities
907 Keck at goodness
908 Discourse raptously upon the advantage of being a vole
909 Ridicule consummately the binomial theorem
910 Adore being a stoat
911 Fall for that old trick
912 Expel all outsiders
913 Defend a fallacy
914 Feign a heart attack
915 Invent some lurid details
916 Misquote a dumb show
917 Everybody's laughing, everybody's happy
918 Overemphasise a negative aspect
919 Find a bassoonist who declined to opt for medicine
920 Brendan Behan and his funny machine
921 Not an inch of ground beneath your feet, no tile above your head
922 Fill in some bad form
923 Open a debate on violence using a crowbar and a thermic lance
924 Reveal your true identity
925 Shake hands with the wife's best friend
926 Bid your "alter ego" goodbye
927 Come across one of your ancestors while digging in a vegetable patch
928 Caricature your distress at "927"
929 Escape from a top security set of parentheses
930 Deem something worthless
931 Clap your hands and scare the clouds away
932 Divert the rain upwards by means of induction and/or static electricity
933 Feed the one thousand and make them pay through the nose
934 Circumnavigate a magnum of Bell's Blended Scotch Whisky
935 Walk the river Thames, underwater
936 Hijack a fire engine to Cuba
937 Consist of three things
938 Find a way in a manger
939 Back the first three horses, a) of the Derby, b) of the Grand National, c) of the Miss World Contest
940 Grow a beard and moustache; then shave away:—
i) the right side of the moustache and the left side of the beard. alternatively ii) the left side of the moustache and the right side of the beard. i) and ii) may be executed in any order and in any combination

HENRY COWELL

(March 11, 1897–December 10, 1965)

The Banshee (1925).

71.

With Ives and Ruggles, Cowell is one of the three great originals of American music. Virtually self-taught, he composed as he heard, assimilating many influences but never becoming bound by any one style or school. "I want to live in the whole world of music," he said, and proved it in his own works, where ideas from early American hymnody rub shoulders with Indian and Persian influence, and a bland diatonicism* is combined with the most adventurous use of dissonances such as the tone cluster.*

This is one of a number of early pieces, mostly for piano, which explore new sonic possibilities. Cowell astonished and shocked audiences at his many recitals in the 1920's with these works, in which he would pound the keyboard with fists and elbows, reach over to pluck or sweep the strings, and, in *The Banshee*, abandon the bench altogether to bury his head beneath the piano lid and produce from the instrument such sounds as one would never have thought possible. The resultant noises are appropriate to the subject, for a Banshee is an Irish spook which wails when death is approaching a family.

Recordings: CRI 109 (*Tone Cluster Pieces and Other Chamber Music*, Cowell) Folkways FM3349 (*Piano Music of Henry Cowell*, Cowell.) This album contains a recording of Cowell discussing his work.

Compare: 29, 64, 69, 72; Cowell's other piano music; Ives, *Concord Sonata;* Ruggles, *Evocations;* many recent American piano works which use the "insides."

The Banshee

Explanation of Symbols

"The Banshee" is played on the open strings of the piano, the player standing at the crook. Another person must sit at the keyboard and hold down the damper pedal throughout the composition. The whole work should be played an octave lower than written.

R. H. stands for "right hand." L. H. stands for "left hand." Different ways of playing the strings are indicated by a letter over each tone, as follows:

(A) indicates a sweep with the flesh of the finger from the lowest string up to the note given.

(B) sweep lengthwise along the string of the note given with flesh of finger.

(C) sweep up and back from lowest A to highest B-flat given in this composition.

(D) pluck string with flesh of finger, where written, instead of octave lower.

(E) sweep along three notes together, in the same manner as (B).

(F) sweep in the manner of (B) but with the back of finger-nail instead of flesh.

(G) when the finger is half way along the string in the manner of (F), start a sweep along the same string with the flesh of the other finger, thus partly damping the sound.

(H) sweep back and forth in the manner of (C), but start at the same time from both above and below, crossing the sweep in the middle.

(I) sweep along five notes, in the manner of (B).

(J) same as (I) but with back of finger-nails instead of flesh of finger.

(K) sweep along in manner of (J) with nails of both hands together, taking in all notes between the two outer limits given.

(L) sweep in manner of (C) with flat of hand instead of single finger.

GEORGE CRUMB

(Born October 24, 1929)

a. *Dream Images (Love-Death Music)*.
b. *Spiral Galaxy* from *Makrokosmos*, Volume I (1972).

The twenty-four pieces of Crumb's two-volume *Makrokosmos* are in a respectable tradition that stretches from Bach's forty-eight Preludes and Fugues through the twenty-four Preludes of Chopin, Scriabin (Op. 11), Debussy, and Messiaen to Bartók's huge teaching collection *Mikrokosmos*. The work is subtitled *Twelve Fantasy-Pieces after the Zodiac for Amplified Piano*. Each piece is associated with one of the signs, and with the initials of a person born under the sign. The richness of association is increased by the fanciful titles, and in these pieces by the quotation from Chopin (**72a**) and the symbolic notation (**72b**). Finally, Crumb prefaces the work with some of the ideas which haunted him during its composition.

72.

In contrast to the dry presentation of so many contemporary pieces, Crumb's music is unashamedly Romantic, programmatic, and enveloped in extra-musical ideas. *Makrokosmos* is a "universe" in that it includes every pianistic technique, conventional and otherwise, and every harmonic shading, from harsh noise and dissonance to consonance and even monody. In comparison to it, most of the works in this chapter seem one-sided and limited in outlook, obsessed with dissonance, chance, repetition, tone color, or subjectivity. But theirs is the ground-work without which the new generation of composers could not build in freedom.

Recordings: None. 71293 (*Makrokosmos, Vol. 1 for Piano,* Burge)

Compare: 14, 15, 64, 69, 70; the remainder of *Makrokosmos;* Crumb, *Ancient Voices of Children, Black Angels, Vox Balenae;* the older works mentioned above; George Rochberg, *Nach Bach* (for quotation); Karlheinz Stockhausen, *Refrain* (for notation).

a.

From MAKROKOSMOS VOL. I by George Crumb (Peters Edition No. 66539a)
Copyright © 1974 by C.F. Peters Corp.
373 Park Avenue South
New York, New York 10016
Reprint permission granted by the publisher.

b.

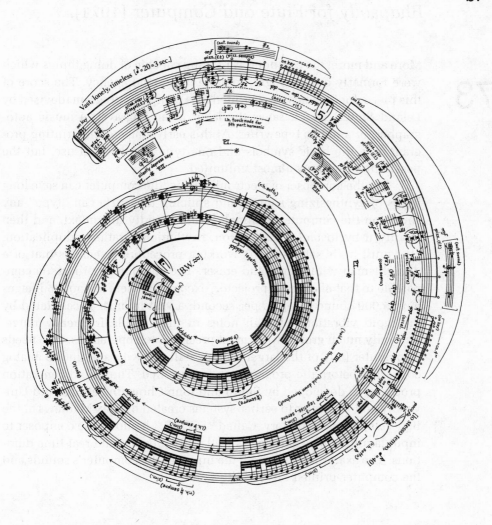

LELAND SMITH

(Born August 6, 1925)

Rhapsody for Flute and Computer (1971).

73.

More and more, the computer is proving capable of doing things which were formerly only thought possible by human agency. The score of this piece, for instance, was printed by a computer program (devised by Leland Smith) which saves the labor of an engraver, a music autographer, or a music typewriter. At this early stage of the printing program only the basic symbols and one type face were in use, but the possibilities are now almost unlimited.

For the composer of electronic music, the computer can save long hours of synthesizing sounds and splicing tapes. He can "type" any sound on the computer terminal, hear it rapidly in context, and then modify it by instant transposition, rhythmic alterations, duplication, etc., until he is satisfied. His working procedure resembles that of a draughtsman with pencil and eraser. The computer's process is comparable to that of a movie projector, except that there are not 25 images but 25,000 sound samples per second: a vast number necessitated by the rapid vibrations of high notes in the audible frequency range. Naturally much groundwork must precede such operations. One needs a computer (any of the larger models will do) with a digital to analog converter, before the program can be installed. The sound generation process was developed by Smith and John Chowning at Stanford University and is similar to earlier systems created by Max Mathews at the Bell Telephone Laboratory. Called "SCORE," it allows the composer to input familiar musical terms as well as frequencies and real-time durations. The example shows both the input for the computer's sounds and the computer-printed "live" flute score.

Recordings: None available as yet.

Compare: 72; solo flute pieces: Debussy, *Syrinx;* Varèse, *Density 21.5;* electronic music (Karlheinz Stockhausen, Morton Subotnick, Milton Babbitt, etc.); other uses of computers, e.g. Lejaren Hiller, *Computer Cantata, Iliac Suite;* Hiller and Cage, *HPSCHD.*

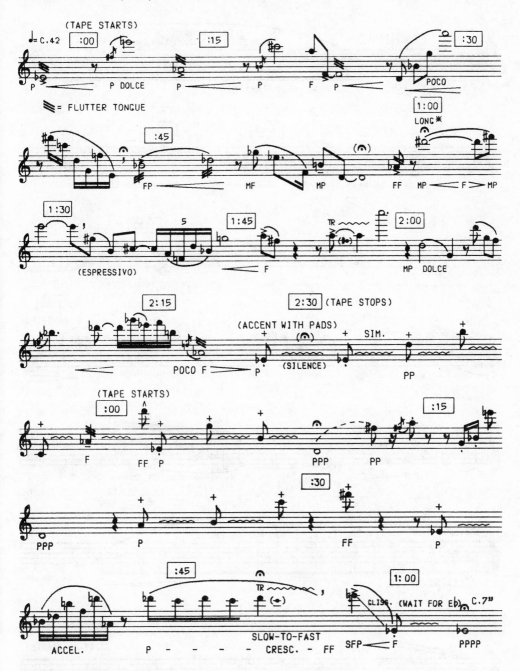

*HOLD D♯ UNTIL TAPE D♯-E STOPS.

TIME CUES ARE GIVEN BY TAPE OPERATOR (USING A STOP-WATCH.)
THE CUES ARE NOT FOR EXACT COORDINATION.

AMPLIFY THE FLUTE IN LARGE HALLS.

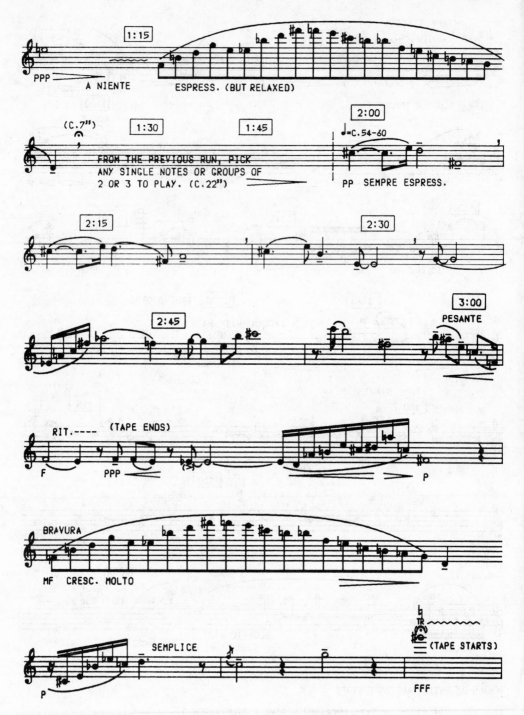

```
00100    FLTR         ;   FLUTTER TONGUE SECTION OF RHAPSODY
00200    FLUTA   0 30 ALL;   ALL WILL HAVE DUR. OF 30"
00300    P2  1  2,6  ALL;    ALL WILL HAVE RANDOM NOTE DURATIONS OF 2'-6'
00400    P4 200 ALL;   AMPLITUDES
00500    P5 F2 ALL;   ENVELOPE
00600    P6 1 11,16  ALL;   FOR FM.
00700    P3  NOTES/DS4/D5/F/D4*;
00800    P13 P3 ALL;   MODULATING FREQ. IS THE SAME AS FUND.
00900    P12  1  3,5  ALL;   RANDOM MOD. INDEX.
01000    P11 0 ALL; FOR STEREO
01100    P7 F4; SHAPE OF MODULATION
01200    P8 3 ALL; RAND. VIBRATO
01300    P9 1  0,1 ALL;   RAND. RATE OF CHANGE FOR VIB.
01400    END;
01500
01600    FLUTB   5.6/P3 NOTES/FS5/AS4/E6/AF4*/END;
01700    FLUTC   6.4/P3 NOTES/E3/G/BF5/EF3*/END;
01800    FLUTD 7.2/P3 NOTES/GS5/A3/DF6/D5*/P11 REP 12 1/P12 0/P4 1 30,300 A
01900    FLUTE 7.33/P3 NOTES/B2/FS5/FS6/B6*/END;
02000    FLUTF 8.23/P3 NOTES/CS5/C7/EF6/C4*/END;
02100    FLUTG 9.17/P3 NOTES/A2/D6/F/AF4*/END;
02200    FLUTH 9.67/P3 NOTES/BF4/G5/B6/F3*/P11 REP 11 4/P12 0/END;
02300    RUN;
```

```
FLTR .DAT              EDIT FILE NAME=RH          V ARRAY= 149/2000   TEMPO FACTOR= 1.00
   RANDOM NUMBER =       1

      FLUTA  RANDOM TF = .00          DURATION = 30.00"
      FLUTB  RANDOM TF = .00          DURATION = 30.00"
      FLUTC  RANDOM TF = .00          DURATION = 30.00"
      FLUTD  RANDOM TF = .00          DURATION = 30.00"
      FLUTE  RANDOM TF = .00          DURATION = 30.00"
      FLUTF  RANDOM TF = .00          DURATION = 30.00"
      FLUTG  RANDOM TF = .00          DURATION = 30.00"
      FLUTH  RANDOM TF = .00          DURATION = 30.00"

  <  FLTR .DAT
PLAY;
FLUTA    0.000    5.582 DS    200.000 F2     14.608 F4     3.000    0.269    0.000
         0.000    3.171 DS   ;< 1 FLUTA   1 > 0.000
<FLUTB   0.000    5.600 ****** REST < 2 FLUTB   -1
<FLUTC   0.000    6.400 ****** REST < 3 FLUTC   -1
<FLUTD   0.000    7.200 ****** REST < 4 FLUTD   -1
<FLUTE   0.000    7.330 ****** REST < 5 FLUTE   -1
<FLUTF   0.000    8.230 ****** REST < 6 FLUTF   -1
<FLUTG   0.000    9.170 ****** REST < 7 FLUTG   -1
<FLUTH   0.000    9.670 ****** REST < 8 FLUTH   -1

FLUTA    5.582    5.949 D*2   200.000 F2     15.380 F4     3.000    0.641    0.000
         0.000    3.094 D*2  ;< 1 FLUTA   2 > 5.582
FLUTB    5.600    3.998 FS*2  200.000 F2     13.257   0.000    3.000    0.855    0.000
         0.000    3.227 FS*2 ;< 2 FLUTB   1 > 5.600

FLUTC    6.400    3.940 E/2   200.000 F2     12.707   0.000    3.000    0.539    0.000
         0.000    3.553 E/2  ;< 3 FLUTC   1 > 6.400
```

```
FLUTD    7.200    3.160 GS*2   190.197 F2      13.450    0.000   3.000   0.877    0.000
         3.281    0.000 GS*2  ;< 4 FLUTD   1 >  7.200

FLUTE    7.330    4.179 B/4    163.326 F2      15.683    0.000   3.000   0.316    0.000
         0.000    3.023 B/4   ;< 5 FLUTE   1 >  7.330

FLUTF    8.230    4.874 CS*2    68.927 F2      14.570    0.000   3.000   0.998    0.000
         0.000    3.558 CS*2  ;< 6 FLUTF   1 >  8.230

FLUTG    9.170    5.358 A/4     94.655 F2      15.394    0.000   3.000   0.397    0.000
         0.000    3.625 A/4   ;< 7 FLUTG   1 >  9.170

FLUTB    9.598    4.163 AS     200.000 F2      12.548    0.000   3.000   0.388    0.000
         0.000    4.709 AS    ;< 2 FLUTB   2 >  9.598

FLUTH    9.670    2.700 AS     211.133 F2      15.188    0.000   3.000   0.842    0.000
         4.375    0.000 AS    ;< 8 FLUTH   1 >  9.670

FLUTC   10.340    2.884 G/2    200.000 F2      15.878    0.000   3.000   0.706    0.000
         0.000    3.284 G/2   ;< 3 FLUTC   2 > 10.340
FLUTD   10.360    4.879 A/2     34.634 F2      12.659    0.000   3.000   0.978    0.000
         4.206    0.000 A/2   ;< 4 FLUTD   2 > 10.360

FLUTE   11.509    5.324 FS*2   270.341 F2      15.197    0.000   3.000   0.628    0.000
         0.000    3.089 FS*2  ;< 5 FLUTE   2 > 11.509
FLUTA   11.531    4.021 F*2    200.000 F2      13.357 F4     3.000   0.909    0.000
         0.000    3.511 F*2   ;< 1 FLUTA   3 > 11.531

FLUTH   12.370    5.430 G*2    115.610 F2      11.469    0.000   3.000   0.964    0.000
         4.597    0.000 G*2   ;< 8 FLUTH   2 > 12.370

FLUTF   13.104    3.725 C*8    163.667 F2      11.270    0.000   3.000   0.667    0.000
         0.000    4.894 C*8   ;< 6 FLUTF   2 > 13.104

FLUTC   13.224    2.697 AS*2   200.000 F2      13.879    0.000   3.000   0.553    0.000
         0.000    3.166 AS*2  ;< 3 FLUTC   3 > 13.224

FLUTB   13.761    4.786 E*4    200.000 F2      11.031    0.000   3.000   0.322    0.000
         0.000    4.921 E*4   ;< 2 FLUTB   3 > 13.761

FLUTG   14.528    4.239 D*4    223.926 F2      13.976    0.000   3.000   0.067    0.000
         0.000    4.212 D*4   ;< 7 FLUTG   2 > 14.528

FLUTD   15.239    5.004 CS*4   204.800 F2      11.955    0.000   3.000   0.926    0.000
         4.173    0.000 CS*4  ;< 4 FLUTD   3 > 15.238

FLUTA   15.552    5.332 D      200.000 F2      15.565 F4     3.000   0.906    0.000
         0.000    4.608 D     ;< 1 FLUTA   4 > 15.552

FLUTC   15.921    4.027 DS/2   200.000 F2      14.581    0.000   3.000   0.642    0.000
         0.000    3.417 DS/2  ;< 3 FLUTC   4 > 15.921

FLUTF   16.829    5.938 DS*4   231.058 F2      12.248    0.000   3.000   0.004    0.000
         0.000    4.525 DS*4  ;< 6 FLUTF   3 > 16.829
FLUTE   16.833    3.131 FS*4    53.287 F2      15.880    0.000   3.000   0.841    0.000
         0.000    4.097 FS*4  ;< 5 FLUTE   3 > 16.834

FLUTH   17.800    5.217 B*4    263.263 F2      14.938    0.000   3.000   0.499    0.000
         4.419    0.000 B*4   ;< 8 FLUTH   3 > 17.800

FLUTB   18.547    4.517 GS     200.000 F2      11.891    0.000   3.000   0.905    0.000
         0.000    4.075 GS    ;< 2 FLUTB   4 > 18.546

FLUTG   18.767    4.829 F*4    187.665 F2      11.224    0.000   3.000   0.550    0.000
         0.000    4.212 F*4   ;< 7 FLUTG   3 > 18.767

FLUTC   19.948    3.069 E/2    200.000 F2      11.980    0.000   3.000   0.321    0.000
         0.000    4.532 E/2   ;< 3 FLUTC   5 > 19.948
FLUTE   19.964    5.911 B*4     75.084 F2      13.616    0.000   3.000   0.403    0.000
         0.000    4.370 B*4   ;< 5 FLUTE   4 > 19.965
```

```
FLUTD   20.243    4.608 D*2     103.187 F2      11.806    0.000   3.000    0.213    0.000
         3.953    0.000 D*2   ;< 4 FLUTD    4 > 20.243

FLUTA   20.884    2.867 DS      200.000 F2      11.868 F4        3.000   0.304    0.000
         0.000    4.477 DS    ;< 1 FLUTA    5 > 20.884

FLUTF   22.767    5.646 C       298.888 F2      11.381    0.000   3.000    0.233    0.000
         0.000    4.244 C     ;< 6 FLUTF    4 > 22.767

FLUTC   23.017    4.531 G/2     200.000 F2      12.383    0.000   3.000    0.197    0.000
         0.000    3.628 G/2   ;< 3 FLUTC    6 > 23.017
FLUTH   23.017    4.982 F/2     279.117 F2      11.112    0.000   3.000    0.144    0.000
         3.822    0.000 F/2   ;< 8 FLUTH    4 > 23.017
FLUTB   23.064    2.352 FS*2    200.000 F2      15.269    0.000   3.000    0.473    0.000
         0.000    4.131 FS*2  ;< 2 FLUTB    5 > 23.063

FLUTG   23.596    2.894 GS       58.357 F2      11.458    0.000   3.000    0.170    0.000
         0.000    3.835 GS    ;< 7 FLUTG    4 > 23.595

FLUTA   23.751    2.330 D*2     200.000 F2      15.149 F4        3.000   0.407    0.000
         0.000    3.782 D*2   ;< 1 FLUTA    6 > 23.751

FLUTD   24.851    5.067 GS*2    275.353 F2      15.797    0.000   3.000    0.970    0.000
         4.900    0.000 GS*2  ;< 4 FLUTD    5 > 24.851

FLUTB   25.416    5.519 AS      200.000 F2      14.447    0.000   3.000    0.189    0.000
         0.000    4.753 AS    ;< 2 FLUTB    6 > 25.416

FLUTE   25.875    3.761 B/4     150.060 F2      15.468    0.000   3.000    0.236    0.000
         0.000    4.631 B/4   ;< 5 FLUTE    5 > 25.876

FLUTA   26.081    2.839 F*2     200.000 F2      15.070 F4        3.000   0.232    0.000
         0.000    4.765 F*2   ;< 1 FLUTA    7 > 26.080

FLUTG   26.490    3.663 A/4     128.569 F2      14.396    0.000   3.000    0.673    0.000
         0.000    3.678 A/4   ;< 7 FLUTG    5 > 26.489

FLUTC   27.548    3.377 AS*2    200.000 F2      14.468    0.000   3.000    0.737    0.000
         0.000    4.033 AS*2  ;< 3 FLUTC    7 > 27.548

FLUTH   27.999    5.252 AS      278.979 F2      15.768    0.000   3.000    0.938    0.000
         4.724    0.000 AS    ;< 8 FLUTH    5 > 27.999

FLUTF   28.413    4.589 CS*2     51.495 F2      13.958    0.000   3.000    0.695    0.000
         0.000    3.989 CS*2  ;< 6 FLUTF    5 > 28.413

FLUTA   28.920    5.153 D       200.000 F2      15.351 F4        3.000   0.822    0.000
         0.000    4.193 D     ;< 1 FLUTA    8 > 28.919

FLUTE   29.636    5.868 FS*2    112.073 F2      15.726    0.000   3.000    0.532    0.000
         0.000    4.299 FS*2  ;< 5 FLUTE    6 > 29.637

FLUTD   29.918    3.667 A/2     192.172 F2      12.926    0.000   3.000    0.555    0.000
         3.560    0.000 A/2   ;< 4 FLUTD    6 > 29.917
FINISH; < FLTR .DAT
AMPL. FACTOR=1.00, MAX.AMP.=1730, AT TIME  26.490
TOTAL DURS: FLUTA= 34.073  FLUTB= 30.935  FLUTC= 30.925  FLUTD= 33.585  FLUTE= 35.504  FL
UTF= 33.002  FLUTG= 30.153  FLUTH= 33.251
```

Translations

No. 1a, 1b: Alleluia dulce lignum

Alleluia. Sweet wood, sweet nails, bearing a sweet weight; which alone were worthy to sustain the King of Heaven and the Lord.

No. 1c: Mout me fu grief

I am in much grief for the departure of my loved one, the beauty with a shining face, white and scarlet like a rose upon a lily—that is my opinion.
Her smile is so sweet that it makes me tremble, and her green, laughing eyes make me languish. Ah, God! how could she leave me? White like a lily flower, when will I see you? Lady most prized, scarlet like a rose in May, for you I am in great pain.
　Robin loves me, I am Robin's. Robin asked me if I might be his. Robin bought me a belt and purse of silk; why should I not love him?

No. 2a: Gregorian Chant: *Kyrie eleison*

Lord, have mercy; Christ, have mercy; Lord, have mercy.

No. 3a: Aeterna Christi munera

The eternal gifts of Christ, the Apostles' glory, giving due praise, we sing with gladsome minds.

No. 3b: *Palestrina:* Gloria
Glory be to God on high, and on earth peace, good will toward men.
We praise thee, we bless thee, we worship thee, we glorify thee, we give thanks to thee for thy great glory,
O Lord God, heavenly King, God the Father Almighty.
O Lord, the only-begotten Son, Jesus Christ;
O Lord God, Lamb of God, Son of the Father, that takest away the sins of the world, have mercy upon us.
Though that takest away the sins of the world, receive our prayer.
Thou that sittest at the right hand of God the Father, have mercy upon us.
For thou only art holy; thou only art the Lord;
Thou only, O Christ, with the Holy Ghost, art most high in the glory of God the Father.
Amen.

No. 4a, 4d: *Credo*
I believe in one God the Father Almighty, Maker of heaven and earth,
And of all things visible and invisible.
And in one Lord Jesus Christ, the only-begotten Son of God;
Begotten of his Father before all worlds, God of God, Light of Light, Very God of very God;
Begotten, not made;
Being of one substance with the Father;
By whom all things were made:
Who for us men and for our salvation came down from heaven,
And was incarnate by the Holy Ghost of the Virgin Mary,
And was made man:
And was crucified also for us under Pontius Pilate;
He suffered and was buried:
And the third day he rose again according to the Scriptures:
And ascended into heaven,
And sitteth on the right hand of the Father:
And he shall come again, with glory, to judge both the quick and the dead;
Whose kingdom shall have no end.
And I believe in the Holy Ghost, The Lord, and Giver of Life,
Who proceedeth from the Father and the Son;
Who with the Father and the Son together is worshipped and glorified;
Who spake by the Prophets;
And I believe one Catholic and Apostolic Church:
I acknowledge one Baptism for the remission of sins:

And I look for the Resurrection of the
                                  dead:
And the life of the world to come.
Amen.

No. 4b, 4c: Pange lingua

Sing, O tongue, the glorious Body's mystery, and the precious Blood which the
King of men, fruit of a noble womb, shed
for the redemption of the world.

Given to us, born for us from an inviolate
Virgin, and, turning to earth, having
sown the seed of word and dwelled for a
time, he concluded with a wondrous
order.

No. 5a, 5b: Sanctus

Holy, Holy, Holy, Lord God of Sabaoth.
Heaven and earth are full of thy glory.
Hosanna in the highest.
Blessed is he who comes in the name of
the Lord.
Hosanna in the highest.

No. 6a, 6b: Agnus Dei; Ite missa est

Lamb of God, who takest away the sins of
the world,
have mercy upon us.
Lamb of God, who takest away the sins of
the world, grant us peace.

Go, [the congregation] is dismissed.
Thanks be to God.

No. 18: *Reuenthal:* Maienzit

May-time gives joy without envy: on the
contrary, its return can help us all.
On the plain, no mistake, one can see
goodly bright brown [flowers] with the
yellow ones.
Through the grass they have already
pushed up and their manyfold untold
power is that without which there is no
singing.

No. 19: *Machaut:* Se je souspir

If I sigh deeply, and tenderly weep in secret,
by my faith it is for you, my lady, when I
cannot see your beauteous and noble
body.
Your sweet, simple, and quiet conduct,
your fine clothes, elegant and comely,
and your fearless manner,
have taken my eye.
Thus I offer you entirely and with all love
my heart, which beats far from you and
has no pleasure.
If I sigh deeply, etc.

No. 20: *Landini:* Gram piant'agli ochi

With tear-filled eyes and deeply pained
heart, my spirit flows over, but I die.
Through this bitter, cruel parting I call for
death, and it will not hear me.
Against my will, this life continues and
makes me feel a thousand deaths.
But while I live I will never follow any but
your bright star and tender love.
With tear-filled eyes, etc.

No. 21: *Binchois:* De plus en plus
More and more renews,
My sweet lady, kind and fair,
My will to see you.
This gives me the very great desire
Which I have to hear news of you.

Do not think that I hold back,
For at all times it is you
Whom I wish utterly to obey.
More and more renews,
My sweet lady, kind and fair.

Alas, if you were cruel to me,
I would have such anguish in my heart
That I would wish to die.
But even that would be without ceasing to
                                  serve
In sustaining your cause.

No. 24: *Schubert:* Du bist die Ruh'

You are repose and gentle peace; you are
longing and that which stills it. I dedicate
to you, full of joy and pain, as a dwelling
here my eye and heart.

Enter into me and close the doors quietly behind you. Drive other sorrow from this breast! Let this heart be full of your joy. Let this eye be lit by your light alone, Oh, fill it completely!

No. 27: *Gabriel Fauré:* Les Berceaux

Along the quay the great boats, which the swell silently sways, do not heed the cradles which the women's hands rock.

But the day of farewells will come, for women must weep and inquisitive men must attempt the horizons which line them!

And on that day the great boats, fleeing the vanishing port, feel their mass restrained by the soul of the distant cradles.

No. 28: *Mahler:* Um Mitternacht

At midnight I have woken and looked up at the

sky; no star in the firmament smiled at me at midnight.

At midnight I have sent out my thoughts into dark confines.

At midnight.

No shining thoughts brought me comfort at midnight.

At midnight I took notice of the beating of my heart; a single pulse of pain flamed up at midnight.

At midnight I fought the battle, O Mankind, of your sorrow; and could not decide it with my own power at midnight.

At midnight I gave the power into Thy hand; Lord!

Lord over Death and Life, Thou keepest watch at midnight!

No. 33: *George Frideric Handel:* Rodelinda

Bert. Vain pageant of death! Lies of sorrow, which preserve my face and my name, and praise the haughty spirit of my proud conqueror. You say that I am dead, but my sorrow replies that it is untrue. "Bertarido was King; he fled, vanquished by Grimoaldo; he lies close to the Huns. May his soul have repose, and his ashes peace." Peace to my ashes? O tyrannous stars, to the end of my life I will fight against want and anguish!

Where are you, dear beloved? Come to console my spirit. I am oppressed with torments and only you can turn my cruel laments into joy.

But here is Unulfo. O God! Alas! My faithful one, let these arms embrace you . . .

Un. Ah, my Lord, if the cruelty of fate has snatched the sceptre from you, it has not taken from me the respect that a faithful subject owes to his sovereign. Cease, and allow me as a pledge of my respect to imprint a humble kiss on your hand, and express in it my old faithfulness and my new bondage.

Bert. Since my fate has led me to so faithful a friend, I bless it. But tell me, how is my wife Rodelinda? How is my son?

Un. That which shameful fate could not do, the false news of your death has done: her beautiful eyes run with twin streams of sorrow.

Bert. Oh God! Did you not tell her, Unulfo, that I am alive?

Un. I want to compound our deceit; and it is better for you to remain in hiding.

Bert. Loving heart, what agony! But what do I see? Unulfo, here is my wife and my son; my friend, let me embrace them . . .

Un. Oh God! Sir, I do not want your love to betray your fate.

Bert. Ah, at least after so long an exile let me press my wife to my breast, and give a kiss to my son.

Un. By enjoying them for a moment, do you want to lose them for ever?

Bert. Ah! What torment.

Un. Come back, my king!

Bert. You want me to die.

Un. No, hide and suffer a moment longer. *(They withdraw behind the urn.)*

Rod. *(Holds Falvio by the hand, and the same, concealed.)* Shades, Laments, funeral urns! You would be my heart's delight; if I found that you held not only his (carved) face, but my beloved's ashes. Shade of my dear Sun, which still roams in his image, see the faithful mourning of your wife and son, hear their sighs . . .

Bert. (I can bear no more!)

Un. (Restrain your love!)

Rod. *(Kisses the urn and makes her son kiss it.)* Receive our kisses.

Bert. (Oh, let me go!)

Un. (No, my Lord, watch and be silent.)

No. 34: *Mozart:* Die Zauberflöte

Pam. Men who feel love do not lack a good heart.

Pap. To feel sweet desire is, then, woman's first duty.

Both. We want to enjoy love; we live through love alone.

Pam. Love sweetens every sorrow; every creature pays homage to it.

Pap. It spices the days of our lives; it works in the circle of Nature.

Both. Its high purpose shows clearly that there is nothing more noble than Man and Wife. Man and Wife, Wife and Man reach up to Divinity.

Spirits. This road leads you to your goal, and you, youth, must win through manhood. There let our teaching begin: be steadfast, patient, and silent.

Tam. Kindly ones, tell me whether I can rescue Pamina.

Spirits. We cannot tell you this. Be steadfast, patient, and silent. Keep this in mind: in short, be a man! Then, youth, you will win through manhood.

Tam. The wisdom of these boys must be ever graven in my heart. Where am I now? What will happen to me? Is this the seat of the Gods? The portals and columns show that reason, diligence, and arts dwell here. Where activity is enthroned and laziness fails depravity cannot easily be master. I will venture into this portal. My intention is honourable, open, and pure. Tremble, dastardly villain! To rescue Pamina is my vow.

Voice Back!

Tam. Back? Then I will try my luck here.

Voice Back!

Tam. Here, too, they say "back." There I see another door. Perhaps I will find the entrance here.

Priest. What do you wish, bold stranger? What do you seek in this sanctuary?

Tam. Love, and virtue's just reward.

Priest. These are high-flown words. Alone, how do you mean to find them? Love and Virtue do not lead you while death and revenge inflame you.

Tam. Only revenge on the villain!

Priest. That you will certainly not find here.

Tam. Does Sarastro rule here?

Priest. Yes, Sarastro rules here.

Tam. But not in the Temple of Wisdom?

Priest. He rules in the Temple of Wisdom.

Tam. Then everything is a mockery!

Priest. Will you leave, then?

Tam. Yes, I will go, glad and free, never again to see your temple.

Priest. Explain yourself to me better: a lie is deceiving you.

Tam. Does Sarastro dwell here? That is enough for me.

Priest. If you value your life, speak. Stay! Do you hate Sarastro?

Tam. I hate him for ever!

Priest. Then tell me your reasons.

Tam. He is a monster, a tyrant!

Priest. Is what you say proven?

Tam. An unhappy woman told me, weighed down by grief and distress.

Priest. So a woman has ensnared you. A woman does little and talks much; do you, youth, believe their tongue-wagging? Oh, may Sarastro show you the reasons for his actions!

Tam. The reasons are all too clear! Did not the robber snatch Pamina mercilessly from her mother's arms?

Priest. Yes, youth, what you say is true.

Tam. Where is she whom he stole? Perhaps they are already sacrificing her?

Priest. To tell you this, dear son, is not allowed me now.

Tam. Explain this riddle; do not deceive me.

Priest. As soon as the hand of Friendship leads you into the sanctuary of everlasting brotherhood.

Tam. O eternal night, when will you disappear? When will the light reach my eyes?

Chorus. Soon, youth, or never.

Tam. Soon, you say, or never? Invisible ones, tell me, does Pamina still live?

Chorus. Pamina still lives. *Tam.* She lives? I thank you for this. Oh, if only I could show my gratitude, Almighty, to your glory with every tone as it springs from my heart!

How strong your magic tone must be, dear flute, for in your playing even wild beasts feel joy.

But only Pamina stays away. Pamina, hear me! In vain! Where, O where shall I find you? Ah, that is

Papageno's note. Perhaps he has seen Pamina, perhaps she hurries with him to me; perhaps the note brings me to her!

No. 38: *Vivaldi:* Autumn

1. *Dance and Song of the Peasants.* The peasants celebrate with dance and song the pleasure of the happy harvest.

4. *The Drunkard.* And having been so influenced by Bacchus' liquor, their pleasure
13. ends in sleep.

15. *Sleeping Drunkards.* Thus everyone ceases from dance and song. The air is pleasing and mild, and the season invites one and all to the pleasure of sweet slumber.

18. *The Hunt.* The hunter goes forth at dawn to hunt with horns, guns, and dogs.

22. *The Beast Flees.* He puts the hart to flight and follows its trail.

23. The frightened beast, worried by the loud noise of guns and dogs, is in danger of being wounded.

29. The beast, now faint, longs to flee, but is overcome and dies.

No. 44: *Monteverdi:* Domine ad adjuvandum

God, turn to my aid. Lord, hasten to my help.
Glory be to the Father, and to the Son, and to the Holy Spirit.
As it was in the beginning, is now, and ever shall be, for ever and ever,
Amen.
Alleluia.

No. 47: *Berlioz:* Grand Messe des Morts

Day of wrath; that day when the ages shall vanish in ashes, [as foretold by David and the Sibyl!]

What trembling there will be when the Judge comes, [to pronounce sentence on all!]

The awful trumpet, sounding through the sepulchral regions, summons all before the Throne.

Death and Nature will both stand amazed, as all creatures are resurrected by the summons of the Judge.

The book is brought forward in which all is written—
from it the world shall be tried.
Then, when the Judge is seated, whatever lies hidden will be revealed;
none will remain unscathed.

What then, is so wretched a creature as I to say, when He questions me; and even the upright man is barely safe?

Remember, blessed Jesus, that I was the cause of Your life; do not lose me on that day.

I pray and beseech Thee, my heart contrite and penitent, to take care of my last hour.

No. 48: *Brahms:* A German Requiem

Denn alles Fleisch es ist wie das Gras und alle Herrlichkeit des Menschen wie des Grases Blumen.
Das Gras ist verdorret und die Blume abgefallen.
So seid nun geduldig, liebe Brüder, bis auf die Zukunft des Herrn.
Siehe ein Ackermann wartet auf die köstliche Frucht der Erde und ist geduldig darüber, bis er empfahe den Morgenregen und Abendregen.
Aber des Herrn Wort bleibet in Ewigkeit.
Die Erlöseten des Herrn werden wieder kommen, und gen Zion kommen mit Jauchzen;
Ewige Freude wird über ihrem Haupte sein;
Freude und Wonne werden sie ergreifen, und Schmerz und Seufzen wird weg müssen.

No. 49: *Josquin Des Prez:* Basiez-moy

"Kiss me, my sweet friend, for love's sake I pray you." "I won't."
"And why not?"
"If I did something foolish, my mother would die from it. So that's why."

No. 51: *Luzzasco Luzzaschi:* Quivi sospiri

There sighs, weepings, and deep lamentations resounded through the starless air,
so that I began to weep. Diverse languages, horrid tongues,
words of sorrow, angry accents, high and hoarse voices, and the sound of smiting hands.

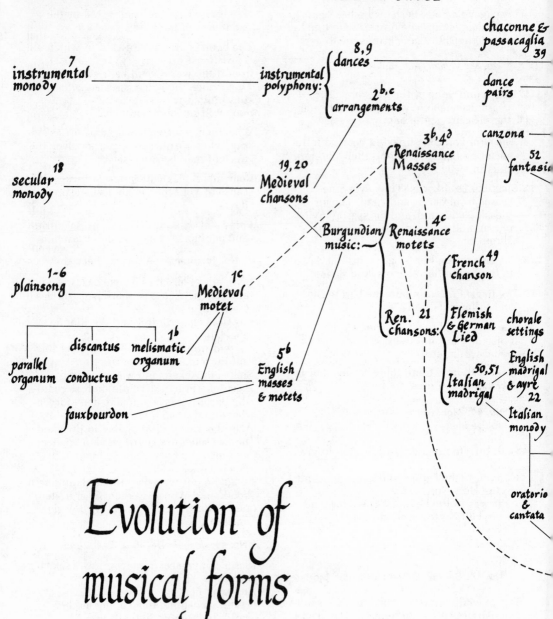

MEDIEVAL

RENAISSANCE

instrumental [7]
monody

instrumental
polyphony: { dances [8,9]

arrangements [2b,c]

chaconne &
passacaglia [39]

dance
pairs

canzona

fantasia [52]

secular [18]
monody

Medieval [19,20]
chansons

Renaissance [3b,4d]
Masses

Burgundian
music: —

Renaissance
motets [4c]

plainsong [1-6]

Medieval [1c]
motet

Ren. [21]
chansons:

French [49]
chanson

Flemish
& German
Lied

chorale
settings

discantus

melismatic [1b]
organum

parallel
organum

conductus

English [5b]
masses
& motets

Italian
madrigal [50,51]

English
madrigal
& ayre [22]

Italian
monody

fauxbourdon

oratorio
&
cantata

Evolution of
musical forms

BAROQUE　　　ROMANTIC　　　MODERN

CLASSIC

13-15, 64, 73
single pieces
(dances, preludes,
toccatas)

"character **41-2, 67, 71-2**
pieces"

10, 11
suites

sonata da camera

sonata **54**
da chiesa

38, 53
Baroque
concerto

Classic **58**
concerto

Romantic
concerto

modern **66**
concerto

chamber **55**
music
(sonatas, trios,
quartets, etc.)

Classic **57, 60**
chamber
music

Romantic **56**
chamber
music

modern **63,**
chamber **65**
music

39
fugue

Classic **59**
symphony

Romantic **46**
symphony

modern **62** chamber
symphony orchestra

French
overture

Italian
overture

Classic
overture

Romantic
overture

61
symphonic
poem

tone poem

French opera
& ballet **12**

opera
seria **33**

French
grand opera

other
national
opera

modern opera
(demise of
national
styles)

French
opéra
comique

opera
buffa

German **34**
Singspiel

German Ro-
mantic opera

36
music
drama

Italian
opera **32,37**

English
ballad opera

Italian Ro- **35**
mantic opera

16, 29,
jazz & **43**
popular
music

Romantic **47-8**
oratorio

accompanied **44-5**
masses & motets

modern
church music

various types
of songs
23-8, 30-1

1200	1300	1400	1500

School of
Nôtre Dame

Neidhart

Adam de
la Halle

Machaut

Landini

Faenza
Ms.

Dunstable

Binchois

Dufay

Josquin

Susato

Palestrina

Lasso

Byrd

Luzzaschi

Chronology of composers & works

Before 1150:

1a, 2a, 3a,
4a, b, 5a, 6a

CHAPTERS					
I	1b	1c	6b	2b 5b 4c	4d
II			7		8
III	18	19 20		21	
IV					
V					
VI					
VII				49	50 51 52
VIII					

BAROQUE	CLASSIC	ROMANTIC	MODERN
1600	1700	1800	1900

Monteverdi

C.P.E. Bach

Debussy

Frescobaldi

Gluck

Joplin

Scriabin

Cavalli

Haydn

Handy

Corelli

Mozart

Schoenberg

Purcell

Beethoven

Ives

Schubert

Vivaldi

Bartók

Donizetti

Batchelor

Rameau

Berlioz

Stravinsky

Dowland

J.S. Bach

Mendelssohn

Webern

Handel

Chopin

Satie

Schumann

Prokofiev

Liszt

Cowell

Wagner

Armstrong

Verdi

Cage

Foster

Britten

Brahms

Smith

Fauré

Crumb

Mahler

Riley

Cardew

3⁶   2ᶜ

9   10   11   12   13 14 15   16 17

22   23   24 25 26   27 28 29 30   31

32   38 39   34   35 36

37   40 41   42   43

44   45   46 47   73 72

53 54   55   56   Ch. IX 67 64 71 66 69 68 70 65

57   58 59 60   61   62 63

| 1600 | 1700 | 1800 | 1900 |

A Note on Clefs and Transposing Instruments

Some instruments use the C clef, placed on the middle line (alto clef), and some use it placed on the fourth line (tenor clef). Middle C is always the line which goes through the center of the C clef:

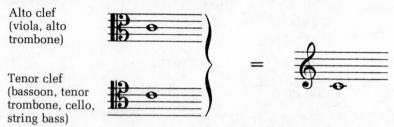

Alto clef
(viola, alto
trombone)

Tenor clef
(bassoon, tenor
trombone, cello,
string bass)

The music for some orchestral instruments is written at pitches different from the actual sounds. The following illustrates the degree of differences between the written pitch and the actual pitch of these transposing instruments:

Piccolo   reads: sounds:

Alto flute in G   reads: sounds:

English horn   reads: sounds:

Clarinet in E♭   reads: sounds:

Clarinet in B♭   reads: sounds:

Clarinet in A   reads: sounds:

Bass clarinet in B♭   reads: sounds:

Contra-bassoon	reads:		sounds:
Horn in F	reads:		sounds:
Horn in G	reads:		sounds:
Horn in A	reads:		sounds:
Horn in D	reads:		sounds:
Horn in Bb	reads:		sounds:
Trumpet in Bb	reads:		sounds:
Trumpet in D	reads:		sounds:
Trumpet in F	reads:		sounds:
Bass trumpet in Eb	reads:		sounds:
String bass	reads:		sounds:

organum early polyphonic* composition in which one or more notes are set against each one of the tenor* 1b

ornamentation the embellishment of a note or melody with extra notes, often spontaneous 54

ossia *It.*, or, alternatively

ottava, 8 va written above the staff, indicates that the music should be played an octave* higher; below the staff it indicates an octave lower

P the principle theme in sonata form*

p, piano *It.*, "plain"; soft

pp, pianissimo *It.*, very soft

PI-III refers to piano pedals: **I**, *una corda* or "soft" pedal; **II**, partial sustaining pedal; **III**, sustaining pedal

panpipes primitive and archaic wind instrument consisting of a row of pipes of different lengths, blown across the top; traditionally associated with the god Pan

part-song secular song for two or more voices, generally of equal importance, especially of the 16th century 49-51

passacaglia form based on the varied reiteration of a melodic pattern, similar to variation form (see theme and variations*) but using a shorter theme 39

passione *It.*, passion

pausa *It.*, pause

pavane dance in slow meter, 16th century 8b, 22

per *It.*, for, through, by

periods those generally accepted, with approximate dates, are: Medieval (to 1420), Renaissance (to 1600), Baroque (to 1750), Classic (to 1820), and Romantic (to 1900)

pesante *It.*, heavy

peu *Fr.*, a little

phrase a group of melodic notes heard as an entity

piacere *It.*, pleasure; *a piacere*, as you please

piú *It.*, more

pizzicato *It.*, plucked; on stringed instruments, plucking the strings with the fingers

plainsong unaccompanied religious chant 1a, 2a, 3a, 4a, 5a, 6a

plus *Fr.*, more

pochissimo *It.*, a tiny bit

poco *It.*, a little

poco a poco *It.*, little by little

polonaise *Fr.*, "Polish"; dance in moderate $\frac{3}{4}$ meter, developed into an instrumental

piece by Chopin and others 11, 14

polychoral using several choirs (of voices and/or instruments), especially in Italian music ca. 1600

polyphony virtually synonymous with counterpoint.* Adjective: "polyphonic"

postlude musical piece played after a larger work or after a play, church service, etc. 25

pressando *It.*, pressing forward

prestissimo *It.*, very fast indeed

presto *It.*, very fast

program music music with a non-musical referent, e.g. a poem, picturesque title, story, etc. 8b, 38, 42, 61, 71, 72

quasi *It.*, as if

rackett low-pitched wind instrument of squat cylindrical shape with double reed,* 16th-17th centuries

rallentando *It.*, gradually becoming slower

rebec Medieval bowed stringed instrument of a long pear shape

recapitulation the third section of a movement in sonata form* in which the original themes return in somewhat altered form

recitative setting of words in their own, free rhythm; *recitativo secco*, in opera and cantata, accompanied only by the continuo;* *recitativo accompagnato* or *stromentato*, accompanied by the strings or other instruments as well 31-34

recitativo *It.*, recitative*

reed the sounding agent in some wind instruments, made of one (single) or two (double) pieces of cane

relative major the major key three semitones higher than a minor key,* which is closely related through using the same scale*

relative minor the minor key three semitones* lower than a major key,* which is closely related through using the same scale*

reprise *Fr.*, repeat

rigeur *Fr.*, rigor, strictness

ripieno the orchestral group in a concerto grosso* 38, 53

ritardando *It.*, gradually slowing down

ritenuto *It.*, held back

ritornello (a) instrumental interlude in an aria;* (b) the recurrent *tutti** theme in a concerto* movement 32, 38, 53

rondeau *Fr.*, "rondo"; French song of the

14th-15th century in the form A B a A a b A B 21

rondo form in which a theme is stated several times between non-thematic episodes 55, 58 III, 59 IV

root the lowest note or key* note of a chord*

rubato *It.*, "robbed"; i.e., some beats are slowed down and others are speeded up for expressive effect

S the secondary theme in sonata form*

sans *Fr.*, without

sarabande dance in slow $\frac{3}{4}$ meter; part of the conventional Baroque suite*

scale a row of rising pitches. In Western music the commonest are the seven-tone "diatonic"* scales, major and minor,* and the twelve-tone "chromatic"* scale of semitones*

scherzando *It.*, playfully

scherzo *It.*, "joke"; movement in fast triple meter, usually the third in a symphony* or quartet, from 1800 on (replaced the minuet)* 60 III

secco See **recitative***

segno *It.*, "sign"; usually ※ or ℅, used to mark a place of return in a piece. See **da capo***

sehr *Ger.*, very

semitone the smallest interval used in Western music; a twelfth of an octave.* Sometimes called a "half-step"

semplice *It.*, simply

sempre *It.*, always

senza *It.*, without

sequence Medieval poetic and musical form, A A' B B' C C' etc., used extensively in the Mass before 1543 7

shawm double reed wind instrument popular up to ca. 1660; the predecessor of the oboe

simile *It.*, the same

slentando *It.*, gradually becoming slower

slide trumpet trumpet used in the 14th-18th centuries which incorporated a small slide for alteration of notes

sonata (a) 16th century: any instrumental piece; (b) 1650-1750: instrumental piece in several movements; (c) 1750 on: piece for one or two instruments in conventional forms (see Chapter VIII) 54, 57

sonata form the usual form for first movements in works of the Classic and Romantic periods, basically comprising exposition* (with at least two themes or subjects), development,* and recapitulation* (see

Chapter VIII) 56-63, 66

song-cycle a set of songs with a unifying poetic or narrative theme, 19th and 20th centuries 25

sonoro *It.*, sonorous

sopra *It.*, above

sostenuto *It.*, sustained

sotto *It.*, beneath; *sotto voce*, in an undertone

souple *Fr.*, supple

staccato *It.*, detached, shortened; indicated by dots or wedges over notes

staff, stave the five lines on which music is written

stesso *It.*, instead of

stop on an organ, the handles which operate various registers; also the registers themselves, each comprising a row of pipes of a particular tone-color

strepito *It.*, noise

stretto *It.*, pressing forward; in a fugue,* rapid successive entries of the subject

stringendo *It.*, pressing forward, accelerating

string quartet the combination of four stringed instruments: two violins, viola, and cello; also a composition for this medium, after ca. 1750 56, 60, 63, 65

subito *It.*, suddenly

suite a composition in several movements, often derived from dances and usually all in the same key 10, 11

suspension in harmony,* a note which is held over a change of chord* so as to become temporarily dissonant

symphonic poem synonymous with tone poem* 61

symphony (a) an instrumental piece, especially within a large vocal work, 1600-1740; (b) a work for orchestra, usually in four movements, after ca. 1740 46, 59, 62

syncopation the displacement of emphasis from a strong to a weak beat, common in early music and in jazz 5b, 43, 52

t the transitional theme in sonata form*

tablature method of notation in letters or numbers, especially in the 15th, 16th, and 17th centuries for lute, organ, etc. 22

tabor Medieval drum, often played together with a one-handed pipe

tanto *It.*, so much

tempo *It.*, time; **a tempo,** resume the tempo previously established

tenor (a) the high male voice (b) in Medieval

music, the part which sings or plays a pre-composed part (often from plainsong*) 1c, 5b

tenuto *It.*, held (for emphasis)

ternary form three-part form, A B A or A B A' 12, 14, 33, 58 II, 59 III

texture the quality of musical material: dense, light, contrapuntal,* chordal, etc.

theme and variations form in which a theme or tune is repeated in several varied or altered ways 9b, 31, 37, 39, 47, 52

timbre tone quality, caused by presence and distribution of notes of the harmonic series*

tombeau *Fr.*, "tomb"; a piece composed in memory of one deceased. This type of composition was particularly abundant in 17th-century French music. 55a

tonality the system of reference to a predominant tonal center or key* which is universal in music up to 1900

tone cluster a set of adjacent scale steps, diatonic* or chromatic,* played simultaneously 69, 71, 72b

tone color see **timbre***

tone poem a piece of program music,* usually for orchestra, 19th-20th centuries 61

tonic the home key* or note of a composition; the first note of the diatonic scale*

tranquillo *It.*, tranquil, peaceful

transposing instruments instruments whose music is written at a pitch other than that at which they sound (see explanation, page 1092)

transposition moving a piece or part to a different tonal center

treble (a) the highest voice in a piece, especially in early music; (b) a boy's voice

trecento *It.*, the 14th century 2b, 7, 20

tremolo *It.*, "trembling"; rapid repetition or alternation of notes

très *Fr.*, very

triad a chord comprising the first, third, and fifth degrees of the diatonic scale:* the basic chord of tonal music

trio sonata the predominant chamber music* form in the Baroque* period: a piece in 3-4 movements for two upper parts (usually violins) and continuo* 53, 55

triplum the highest part in a Medieval three-part piece; synonymous with **treble***(a) 1c

tritone the interval* of three whole tones (augmented fourth or diminished fifth), avoided in early music

tr., trill rapid alternation of the written note with the next higher tone or semitone*

trope a musical or literary insertion into an ex-isting piece or poem, common in the Medieval Mass 2a

troubadours aristocratic poet-composers of Provence (southern France), 12th-13th centuries

trouvères aristocratic poet-composers of northern France, 12th-13th centuries 1c

"Turkish music" the use of cymbals, triangle, and bass drum in the orchestra, in imitation of the Turkish Janissary bands in the 18th century 46, 59

tutti *It.*, "all"; all the instruments play together

Twelve-Tone System method of composition invented ca. 1920 by Arnold Schoenberg to replace the tonal* system (see commentary to 43), which uses all twelve tones of the chromatic* scale in a fixed order 66

una corda *It.*, "one string"; refers to the action of the pianoforte's "soft" pedal

valve device invented in 1813 which mechanically lengthens the tube of a brass instrument, thus facilitating the playing of chromatic* passages

variations see **theme and variations***

vielle *Old Fr.*, "fiddle"; the foremost bowed stringed instrument of the Middle Ages

viol bowed stringed instrument of various sizes, generally with six strings, in use during the 16th, 17th, and 18th centuries

viola da braccio *It.*, "arm viol"; bowed stringed instrument of the Renaissance era, related to the violin family

virelai French 14th-15th century song in the form A B b a A 19

vivace *It.*, lively

voce *It.*, voice

"W2" Wolfenbüttel 1099: one of the most important manuscripts of the Notre Dame school of polyphony,* now in Wolfenbüttel, Germany 1b

weich *Ger.*, soft, weak

wieder *Ger.*, again

Well-Tempered Clavier J. S. Bach's collection of 48 Preludes and Fugues, two in each of the major* and minor* keys (1722, 1744). They can only be played on an instrument tuned (tempered) in a particular way, novel in Bach's time but now universal

whole-tone scale A scale of six equal steps to the octave,* each a whole tone or major second, used especially by Debussy 42

zart *Ger.*, tender
zurückhaltend *Ger.*, holding back

Index of Composers and Pieces